Handbook
for Humans

Handbook
for
Humans

James Sloman

OCEANBLUE
PUBLISHING

This book is educational.
Before making any changes in
lifestyle, it is wisdom to consult
an experienced advisor familiar
with your personal situation.

If you would like to order this
book please call 800-852-4890

OceanBlue Publishing
98 Main, Tiburon, CA 94920

Table of Contents

Spirit

1
INNER
AWARENESS

2
OUTER
SURRENDER

Mind

3
INNER
CREATION

4
OUTER
PRODUCTION

Heart

5
INNER EQUANIMITY

6
OUTER APPRECIATION

Body

7
INNER
SIMPLICITY

8
OUTER
COMPASSION

To all of us

*W*HAT'S THE SAYING?
"Fools rush in where angels fear to tread."
Ah, yes.

When I was growing up, and even more so as an adult, I always wanted a *Handbook for Humans*. After all, we get a handbook if we buy a car; we get one if we join the Scouts; why not one for this life?

So I decided to attempt to write one for myself, and perhaps others. It would be the book that I wish someone had given to me at almost any time in my life. That book is the one you are now reading.

If I have a qualification for writing this book, it's that I've probably been more troubled and perplexed for a good deal of my life than most people I've known. Consequently, principles that many of us knew instinctively as children or adults, I've had to slowly work through in a step-by-step kind of way. Perhaps for that very reason, though, I might have a better chance to explain or clarify some of them.

In this attempt to make some sense of things, I've freely drawn on the ideas of others when it seemed that their mode of thinking explained something with unusual clarity.

In this connection I'm especially grateful to the people named in the text—who will normally be found referenced in the Book List. Their wisdom has been especially noteworthy, and I have tried to pass along their message in as clear a way as possible.

When using the ideas of other people, I've often combined them with the ideas of others or with my own personal experiences, or transformed them in some way. Thus when the text cites someone whom I admire, what follows is only my interpretation or transformation of their message.

It's truly impossible to list my debts to the many people in the past who have contributed to our human adventure towards consciousness. Any deficiency in what follows is not inherent in their work, but is due solely to me.

In this book I've clung to the notion that underneath our various tribes and differences, we're much more alike than different. We're all human beings. Even more, we're all beings. Even more, we're all part of the great fabric of existence itself. That common identity is where I've tried to speak to in this Handbook for Humans, knowing all the while that it must contain many omissions and imperfections.

It's not possible to name all the people who have contributed so much to my personal journey. I acknowledge them all here silently. I'd like to express my gratitude now to a very few—the short list—who have particularly helped in bringing this book about:

They are John Betts, Rebecca Bell, John Davis, James Elphinstone, Jackie Franklin, Richard and Florencia Gobeille, Elena Hill, Jim Jarvis, Michelle Kapuler, Kristine Kelsey., Beverly Ann Light, Daniel Marcellus, Alice Miller, Koroosh Ostowari, JT Power, Alex Romanchuck, Erica Schroeder, Jon Seskevich, Kala Tharp, Jim Tuscano, Cora Van Loon, Steve Wiegand, Gil Younger, Jeanne Vazquez, and the members of the Marin Writer's Collective.

I would like to especially thank Bill Anderson, Howard Brown, Art Cooper, Sean Hunt, Tom and Nilza Kallos, John Keiser, Peggy MacKay, Mary Poling, Carol Schroeder, Franz Wanowitz, David and Melva Waterhouse, John Weeks, Tom Zagara, Don Zordan, and the late, great Alfred Kapuler.

I'm particularly grateful to seven remarkable people: My greathearted friends Pat Raffalovich, Carroll Stephenson and Caroline Whitehead; my dear mother Ann Romanchuck; and my selfless friend Van Tharp, who assisted in a number of different ways. My irreplaceable friend and former wife Tonia. And dear Ishana for her green tea.

These are all people who, in one way or another, have given assistance during the difficulties of preparing for and creating this project. To these great hearts, and to the many others who must go unmentioned here, my appreciation and gratitude for your faith, your help, your love.

Introduction

*I*SN'T IT TRUE? In one way or another, at one time or another, we all have difficulties. None of us is immune. No matter what the external appearance may be, we all encounter suffering and pain in life. We all have to deal with it.

In this book an attempt is made to enter this dark side of our existence and come back with increased aliveness. This is done as part of a larger theme—of living and expressing our true aliveness and consciousness as much as possible.

The basic topic looked at is this: How best to use this life, this energy that we have for a short time? How best to live skillfully, in harmony, true to our truest self?

To explore this subject the book has been somewhat arbitrarily divided into *four dimensions:*

Spirit is about discovering our deepest self, and how that relates to the existence.

Mind is about our vision, our work, our contribution.

Heart is about our emotional life, our relationships.

Body is about being healthy and vital in our personal body and in our "outer body," our situation.

Each of those four dimensions is then further divided into an inner and outer chapter. *The inner chapters* (1,3,5,7) are concerned with the receptive, creative, interior aspect of that dimension. *The outer chapters* (2,4,6,8) are about the exterior, expressive aspect—taking it out into the world.

In my life I've frequently met people who displayed mastery in a particular area that I could only marvel at. They were vastly more skillful in human relations, for instance, or had a mysterious spiritual grace, or had mastered manifesting in the world, or enjoyed better health or whatever.

It was obvious that such people knew somehow things that I didn't; or perhaps had great intuitive talent in a given area. Quite often they did not actually understand how they did what they did—they were unconsciously competent.

Unfortunately, this did not describe me at all. In almost all areas of my life, I've had to grope towards a painstaking and conscious understanding of how things might work if I hoped to apply them in my own life. One of the purposes of this book, then, is to shed as much light as possible on how things are actually achieved by people who, unlike myself, are naturally gifted in a particular area.

Over 2200 years ago the Taoist master Chuang Tzu said, "When the shoe fits the foot is forgotten." When the shoe doesn't fit it's a message showing us where and how we might regain our natural harmony. And since the pain is in the present, so is the message.

Thus when we're feeling challenged by life—and who isn't at one time or another?—whatever our circumstances, whatever our situation may be—we can begin deciphering that message right here, right now, right where we are....

BOOK 1
Inner Spirit
AWARENESS

Book 1, Inner Spirit, is about discovering our true identity, our truest self, the core essence of who we are, and how to increasingly experience that truest self in the eternal present.

Awaken from Sleep

*I*MAGINE BEING ASLEEP at night and having a really interesting dream. In this dream you've gone through many adventures and now find yourself somewhere in a distant city, beset by many troubles and challenges.

You desperately want to solve these troubles and return back home, but things seem to have gotten more and more difficult of late. In fact, sometimes it seems that resolving these troubles is getting more remote, perhaps impossible.

Now if you could be a counselor to yourself in this moment, what is the best advice you could give yourself? Of course, simply to wake up. Waking up from the dream solves all the problems simultaneously and automatically. They do not need to be solved any more. They are simply *dis*solved; they are transcended by coming to consciousness.

It's hard to believe at first, but our life is very similar to this metaphor. The most radical and fundamental solution to the troubles of our life is to begin to wake up.

Now that can sound a bit silly. How can we wake up when we're already awake?

Well, there's the rub. Because those who have woken up tell us that we're still asleep. And what they mean is that our ordinary waking consciousness, the one we're using right now, is itself actually a kind of dream.

How can that be?

Let's look at our ordinary waking consciousness for a moment. Perhaps the most remarkable feature about it is that it doesn't stay the same. Our beliefs aren't the same as they were a decade or two ago. Our state of mind can change from one moment to the next. Desire followed by joy followed by boredom followed by fear, and on and on.

If we sit down and really look carefully at our state of mind for a while, we'll see constant subtle and not-so-subtle fluctuations occurring. A kind of battlefield for cross-currents of emotions, beliefs, attitudes, thoughts, desires, aversions, behavior patterns, etc. Though it seems like we're awake, these various cross-currents and fluctuations weave a kind of dream or trance, a kind of being asleep while we're awake.

An example. One time around 1977 I was attending a weekend seminar and had noticed an attractive woman. As the seminar ended, I began talking with her and asked her out. She said no. In reaction I quickly asked somebody else and they said no too. As I drove home a little bit later I was sunk in depression. Feelings of futility swept through me; thoughts of hopelessness permeated my consciousness.

At that moment, even though I was driving a car, it could be said that I was deeply asleep. I was caught up in my story, my drama, engrossed with it, identified with it. My state of mind did not seem like a feeling to me; rather, it seemed like "the truth," like "this is how it really is," like reality.

Those feelings and thoughts were like crashing waves on a stormy sea. Because of them, it was impossible to see into the still and silent depths beneath the surface.

Some moments are more extreme than others, but at all moments we're beset by fluctuations of feelings and thoughts going through our minds. Our minds are continually engaged in evaluating our environment, mulling over problems, reminiscing about the past, reacting to frustrations, deciding what we want, what we're against, and so on. These ever-changing fluctuations form our waking dream.

In this connection it's interesting to recall the Buddha's famous answer when asked what he was:

"Are you a god?"

"No."

"Are you super-human?"

"No."

"Are you an ordinary man?"

"No."

"What are you then?"

"I'm awake."

Our Truest Self

*T*HE REASON FOR becoming more awake is that it allows us access to a more spacious consciousness, a deeper clarity, one that responds to the challenges of life in a more appropriate and penetrating way. The process of awakening allows us access to our *truest self.*

Our truest self is not something separate from what we are now, or something that needs to be created. It's already here, at our core, but obscured.

Imagine that we have a lantern. The lantern is lit, the light is there. But the sides of the lantern are caked with mud, so that we can't see the light, or can't see it in its true brightness. And what is the mud which obscures this light? It's that constant parade of thoughts, emotions, beliefs, attitudes and so on across our consciousness.

At the level of inner spirit, all thoughts and emotions of whatever kind obscure the light. Beautiful, sublime, positive thoughts and feelings obscure it just as much as ugly, petty, negative ones. Surprising? Consider that the light of the sun can be blocked just as much by white clouds as by black ones. Any cloud, of any color, can block the sun.

It's really not a question of the type of thought or feeling, but rather, of movement happening within the mind. If a lake has waves on its surface, we can't see beneath that. But when the surface is still, the lake is clear and we can see down into the depths below.

Therapy and ways of working on ourselves can help us deal with some of this movement and reactivity. Conflicts and conditionings formed in childhood and currently affecting us can be greatly ameliorated by various self-processes or with a good therapist. In my life I've gone to various teachers and counselors, and done a number of different practices, and they've been invaluable. Good personal growth methods are recommended to anyone, and indeed a number of them are covered in this book.

But the fundamental tendencies of the mind towards *graspingness* and *aversion* can best be watched, in my opinion, in deep silence and solitude. This fundamental clinging nature of the mind is not born of conditioning—it precedes that— and so cannot really be reached with methods that deal with conditioning. The strong tendency to become attached comes just with having a mind.

So we all have it, this clinging to the contents of our mind, well-adjusted or not. We can be perfectly well-adjusted and still be at the mercy of our desire systems, our beliefs, our attitudes, our attachments. The deeper reality, lying beneath the movements of the mind, is still obscured.

Mindfulness

*H*ow, THEN, TO awaken to our deeper clarity, the one that responds more appropriately to situations?

A key notion is to become aware of the mind as a kind of mechanism, as something that automatically functions to produce thoughts and emotions. Notice that we don't need to do anything to cause those thoughts and feelings to be there in our mind. They come by themselves.

In this metaphor the mind can be compared to a computer. It receives input (sensations and mind states), processes it (genetic and learned programs), and then outputs the results (mind states and behavior). We can intervene to change our progression of mental states, but if we don't do so the process goes on by itself, like breathing.

Awakening begins as we begin to see the automaticity of this—the production of thoughts and emotions as a mechanism and not as our consciousness itself. This gradual process of dis-identification with the mechanism slowly begins to set us free from it.

Let's return to our example. There I was, driving home feeling depressed after the seminar. And I was totally identified with those depressed thoughts and feelings. When a thought of futility or hopelessness floated through my consciousness, for instance, it didn't seem to me that I was having a thought in my mind. No, it seemed to me that I was experiencing the very truth. That was my identification.

At that time I had practiced a little mindfulness while sitting in meditation, but hadn't been able to apply it when in the throes of a full-scale emotion in daily life. But I remembered, and resolved to try it right there. Then, for the first time in my life concerning a negative state, a strange and wonderful thing happened: I was able to jump outside of my identification. Just a shift in perspective and suddenly everything was different.

Suddenly I was outside of the feelings and thoughts, looking at them as feelings and thoughts. Suddenly it was just feelings and thoughts; it wasn't who I was any longer, it wasn't reality. It was just an end-product of the mind-mechanism, and I could see it as what it really was. The identification was broken; the spell was temporarily broken.

When that happened, I suddenly felt liberated. I was no longer the prisoner of that series of thoughts and feelings. I could have those thoughts and feelings rather than be them.

I wasn't rejecting them or embracing them or distracting myself from them. Neither was I forming opinions about them. I was simply watching them. But that subtle shift, from being them to watching them, made all the difference in the world. For that moment, I was free.

Of course the moment passed soon enough and then I was caught up again. The next series of thoughts and emotions caught me and I forgot all about awakening from my continuing dream. It's very easy to be caught up again in identification with our states of mind, because that's how we normally spend our time.

So it's very helpful to set aside some time each day, per-haps just 10 or 20 minutes to start, when we can deliberately practice this process of observation and dis-identification, and do so without the distractions of everyday life. It's been called many names by different traditions: mindfulness, witnessing, bare attention, vipassana, zazen, insight meditation, choiceless awareness, and so on. But for our purposes let's just call it *mindfulness*.

Sitting Silently

*W*HAT IS MINDFULNESS? It can be summed up by the old adage about what to do at the railroad crossing, a most profound piece of advice:

Stop, look and listen.

The single most important thing to do when we're perplexed or troubled is to stop. Just take out some time and come to a complete stop.

The temptation when we're troubled in some area is to rush around and do something. The problem must be solved, the area must be fixed, action must be taken. Indeed, action will be there at the appropriate time. But more important is for the action to come from the right place. Otherwise, it will more than likely compound the problem.

The situation can be compared to standing in a small pond filled with mud. Our efforts to clear up the pond by taking vigorous action and swirling around may only make the pond even more muddy. As tempting as it is to take action right away, clarity is the thing most needed. Only in such clarity can our actions begin to take on the rare and wonderful qualities of balance and appropriateness.

So the first thing to do is just to sit down for a little while and allow ourselves to become completely unoccupied, with no physical or mental activity. If we'll take a break and just sit on the bank of the pond it will slowly begin, in a natural process, to clear itself.

This is beautifully expressed by the awakened master who wrote in the Zenrin-kushu:

Sitting silently, doing nothing,
Spring comes, and the grass grows by itself.

In a very literal manner, this means just sitting down, relaxing, "doing nothing," and allowing a deeper clarity to emerge. Normally we think of relaxing as watching TV, reading, snacking, talking, smoking, etc. But this is different; we allow ourselves to really be without activity, to actually come completely to a stop.

Believe it or not, what's usually thought of as the act of meditation—concentrating upon something such as a mantra or a thought or an image—is still an activity also. Sitting in mindfulness, though, starts with really coming to a complete stop, just letting go completely for a moment of the impulse to do anything at all.

There is no particular posture necessary for it, but two guidelines are helpful: First, to be comfortable enough to be able to sit still for awhile, and second, to be alert enough to avoid drowsiness. For these reasons it's normally best to sit rather than stand or lie down, although a few great masters have used the posture of lying down. Sitting cross-legged on a cushion is good; so is a chair. The idea is to be both relaxed and alert at the same time.

Once we're sitting down in a quiet setting, a natural silence will begin to descend upon us. In that stillness and silence a natural interior watching of the mind's contents will gradually begin to happen. Such mindfulness is not really an activity because nothing is being done. We're not trying to change our breath or our thoughts or our feelings or anything at all. We simply watch what's there. We begin to stop, look and listen.

Look and listen at what? In a word, everything. Unlike concentration meditations, where the attention is narrowed down onto one object, mindfulness is about the opposite—an expansion of attention in order to observe everything that's moving within consciousness. It has several different aspects, to which we now turn:

Breath & Sensation

*T*HE FIRST AND most basic thing happening in our consciousness is the sensation of breathing. It's a natural process going on constantly, day and night, yet rarely do we bring our attention to it. Because it is so ever-present and basic, however, it plays a fundamental role in bringing our attention to the present.

In mindfulness practice, the breath is used as an *anchor*, as a natural foundation that we can return to when we get caught up again in our identifications. For this purpose, the breath is watched most closely at one of two places:

The first place is at what's known in the east as the *hara*, what we call the belly. The hara, or the center of the belly, is a point a couple of inches or so below the navel. Notice that as we breathe in our belly rises, and as we breathe out it falls. This rising and falling is not observed with our eyes, which are best kept closed or slightly open, but rather with our attention. It's the inner sensation of motion that's watched.

Aside from its important use as an anchor, mindfulness of breath at the belly is an amazingly powerful way to center and calm ourselves. Even 15 minutes of it has a wonderfully peaceful effect; and more so for longer periods. When we get up again, our perspective on things is calmer, wiser, more mature—just what is needed.

The other way to use our breath as an anchor is to be mindful of it at the *nostrils*. As the breath goes in and out of the nose it strikes the nostrils, and this natural sensation can be watched. With a long nose this sensation is often most noticeable near the tip; with a short nose, on the upper lip. As our attention at this point grows in sensitivity, it will come to feel almost like a slight wound, helping to further anchor our attention.

Our attention doesn't follow the breath in or out but is simply observed at the fixed point of the nostrils. It has sometimes been compared to a gatekeeper, who deals with people at the gate itself and doesn't follow them in or out once they're past the gate.

If desired, we can experiment with each of the two anchors. But then it's best to choose one and stick with it. Using the same anchor each day allows it to deepen and become stronger. Going back and forth is like digging a series of shallow holes to find a well. Only by continuing to dig at the same spot can the digger reach water. It's true for us too.

Once we're watching the breath as an anchor, the next part is to allow our attention to expand to include sensations, starting with bodily sensations.

For instance, while observing the breath we can become aware at the same time of the pressure of our body against the chair, the pressure of our feet against the floor, perhaps the sensation of a breeze. There are internal sensations as well—perhaps pain in a knee, tension in the shoulders, or an ache behind the eyes. We don't go back and forth between these things and the breath, however, but rather expand our awareness to include whatever is there.

Sounds are also part of what's happening right now. As we sit we might hear cars passing in the distance, voices from the neighborhood, perhaps rustling leaves or the sounds of birds or insects. Whatever we hear, we just include that in consciousness as well. The idea is not to habituate, but to hear each sound as if for the first time—to hear the crickets now with the same attention as ten or twenty minutes ago.

However, it's advisable to sit in as quiet a place as possible and to sit with our eyes closed, in order to minimize the sensations coming in. Particularly in the beginning, our awareness can be somewhat weak and we don't want to overwhelm it. An alternative to closed eyes is to have the eyes be half-open and resting, slightly out of focus, on one spot a few feet ahead.

Nothing is treated as a distraction; all is included. If a dog starts barking it's not an interruption of our mindfulness, but part of it. We include it in awareness, because it's part of what's happening. The knack is to include everything that's happening without becoming attached to any specific thing. In the great phrase used by Ram Dass and others, everything becomes *grist for the mill.*

Feelings/Thoughts

$\mathscr{E}$VERYTHING INCLUDES, OF course, our internal universe of thoughts and emotions. Once we've become aware with mindfulness of the various sensations going on—the breath, bodily sensations, sounds, etc.—we're ready to expand awareness to include our ongoing mental drama.

Mindfulness of thoughts and feelings is a paradoxical business, because it is simultaneously both the easiest and the most difficult thing in the world. It's the easiest because there is literally nothing to do, no activity to undertake, nothing to change. It's just a bare witnessing of what's there, a bare attention without reacting or clinging or pushing away.

On the other hand it's the most difficult thing, because the line between watching our thoughts and identifying with them can be a fine one. We can quite easily think we're being mindful when we're not. It's easy to get hooked by thoughts and emotions because it's habitual; it's what we normally do.

"Thoughts and emotions" here means the entire complex of internal ideas, beliefs, attitudes, conclusions, feelings, intentions, and so on that occur in the mind. These things are related, since certain types of thoughts, intentions, emotions, and so on occur together.

We have a feeling, say, of apathy. Associated with that feeling will be certain kinds of thoughts—that nothing matters, that everything is boring, that life is futile or whatever. That complex of feeling and thoughts will tend to occur together, and we can even recognize it like an old friend after awhile: "Ah ha, here's my old friend apathy again."

After some experience in mindfulness, we'll begin to notice that thoughts and feelings have a natural lifespan just like everything else. Each thought or feeling arises, has its moment in consciousness, and then falls away, to be followed by the next one. Of course if we identify with the thought or feeling, then we go off, lost on a "train of thought.".

Imagine sitting on the bank of a stream during autumn, watching leaves as they float downstream. Picture simply observing whatever passes at a particular point, whether the leaves are dull or bright, green or red, interesting or boring. We just note whatsoever passes by—that's mindfulness. Now let's imagine that a striking leaf comes along and our attention follows it downstream—that's being identified.

It's valuable to learn certain characteristics of identification, characteristics that can act as clues to tell us when we're identifying with our thoughts and feelings rather than being mindful of them:

The first clue, mentioned before, is seeing our feelings and thoughts as very real. If we're thinking that so-and-so is clueless, for instance, it doesn't seem to us that we're having a thought about that person. Rather, it seems that they really are that way, that that's reality. There's a feeling of, "That's really the way it is." That feeling itself is the clue, because being certain of an idea is a form of attachment to it.

Whenever we have the feeling that certain ideas or beliefs or ideologies represent the only or real truth, we are witnessing the first clue. Indeed, our particular "truths" don't seem like belief systems to us; they appear to be reality. Doubt seems absurd, impossible.

The clue comes in noticing the emotional attachment to our beliefs, as if we would sooner die than let them go. Such clinging tends to make us rigid and intolerant instead of soft and open; that's also part of the clue.

A second clue to identification is that whatever is going on right now seems like a perpetual thing. If we're having a feeling that life is futile, we feel that not only is life futile now but that it will always be futile. Of course an hour or a week from now we'll feel differently, but right now it feels like it will always be this way. That is also identification.

A third clue to identification comes when we distract ourselves to avoid a particular feeling or thought. If we weren't taking it seriously there'd be no need to distract ourselves from it. Thus suppression of a persistent feeling—by eating, drugs, shopping, watching TV, socializing, and many other ways— can be seen as another way of being attached to it, of being secretly identified with it.

Many, many times it will happen that we're mindful and then suddenly get caught up once again. We're out of the present, off on a train of thoughts, one leading to another, to another... When we notice that this is happening, that we've gone unconscious again, the best thing is to just gently return attention to the breath, our anchor.

If instead we resist the train of thoughts or put ourselves down for it or do anything at all with it, we're perpetuating the very process of being identified. If we think "Why am I doing this again?" or "Why can't I stay on track?" or "I've got to do better" or "Gee, I'm doing great" or whatever, it's all just more ways of being identified, caught up, hooked in, sucked in—all names for the same thing.

Our anchor, the breath, is so helpful precisely because it gives us some foundation to return to when we get caught up. Instead of fighting the thoughts, analyzing why they're there, feeling discouraged and so on, we can just gently return attention to the anchor. Once we're grounded in that again, we can once more let awareness expand out to include everything.

The essence of mindfulness is just completely accepting whatever comes into consciousness, just letting whatever is there be noticed, adding no opinions or judgments. And if we do add opinions or judgments, just noticing them too.

When we get better at it we don't even need to return attention to the anchor because we're grounded in it continuously. Then if judgments or boredom or agitation or discouragement or anything whatsoever arises it's just watched like any other phenomenon.

Then all thoughts and feelings are treated the same, neither clung to as reality nor pushed away. Then we just watch them all as if from a distance, watching the rise and fall of thoughts and feelings in the same way as we watch the rise and fall of our breath, the rise and fall of sounds, the rise and fall of body sensations.

In this sense thoughts and feelings are things, no different in principle from clouds passing in the sky, leaves passing down a stream, cars passing down the road. Everything is observed with the same bare attention, adding nothing, subtracting nothing.

Then, in Osho's memorable metaphor, the outer sky of external events and the inner sky of internal events become *only one sky*—all observed in the same way.

Everyday Life

*M*INDFULNESS IS A kind of knack, similar in a way to the knack of riding a bike. Nobody can really teach us how to ride one. Instead we keep getting on the bike, losing our balance and getting back on again and again until suddenly we get the knack and are riding the bike.

Mindfulness is like that, because it's a knack that we only really pick up by making the attempt to do it again and again. Suddenly, for a moment, we're witnessing instead of identifying. Gradually those moments get more frequent.

This process is actually easier than it sounds, just as the experience of riding a bike is easier than it sounds, once we have the knack. When mindfulness is there, it's a natural state of open awareness that includes everything that's going on— the totality of sensations, feelings, desires, thoughts and so on in each moment.

The practice of sitting and becoming more aware of our inner process for a time each day can then be extended into everyday life. We can expand our ability to be more mindful in the middle of our daily business—to watch the reactions and conditionings, the patterns and cravings, of our mind. This can have profoundly beneficial effects.

Mindfulness is more difficult in the midst of everyday life than while sitting in silence, because the distractions are greater. To help us, there are four tools we can use to good effect out in the world:

First, we can expand *awareness of our senses.* Primary among our sensations is, of course, the breath, which is always available as a wonderful bridge to the present moment.

For instance, while reading this paragraph we can allow our awareness to include the breath as it goes in and out at the nose, or rises and falls at the belly. Notice how we immediately came more into the moment? Awareness of our breath can become a day-long companion, helping to ground and center us throughout the day.

Other sensations can help keep us grounded too. For instance if we're out driving the car, in addition to our breath we can consciously become aware of the hum of the motor, the feel of the car on the road, the horizon in the distance, and so on. In doing that we'll suddenly come more into the present, become more aware of the thoughts and fantasies that are running through our head. We'll come awake more.

If we're doing something as simple as just walking from here to there, we can become aware of the physical sensation of walking. When we shower we can allow awareness to really feel the water. It might seem that we do this anyway, but usually while we're walking or showering we're caught up in our thoughts and feelings. Bringing awareness to our ordinary, everyday sensations can help ground us in the present.

A true story: A new monk came to a Zen master and posed a series of great metaphysical questions. Is the western idea of heaven and hell the correct one, and if so what determines where we go; or is the eastern idea of reincarnation the truth, and if so what determines our new birth?

The master listened to this series of weighty questions and then replied: "Your breakfast is getting cold." The master was not at all interested in metaphysics; he was directing the monk's attention to the here and now, to the everyday, to the truth in the present moment. We too can ground our own awareness there.

The second tool to help us be mindful in daily life is to *slow down*. As we slow down it's easier to become conscious and aware.

Try an experiment. On some occasion when you're out walking, suddenly catch yourself and bring your consciousness to your breath, to the sensations of walking itself, to the sky, to the sounds around you. Notice how you slow down? Try the same thing when you're brushing your teeth, or eating dinner, or conversing.

The interesting thing is that it also works the other way around. If we deliberately slow our physical actions down we tend to come into the present moment more. When we become more deliberate about our actions, suddenly our awareness awakens more as well.

There seems to be a correlation between speediness and unconsciousness. Have you ever had a day when you hurried on, rushing here and there? If you stopped for a moment and noticed your state of mind, it was also hurried and rushing. They tend to go together.

Conversely, slowing down physically and mentally have a tendency to go together. Just as we can most easily be mindful in silence and stillness, we can also more easily be mindful when we slow down. Then our increased wakefulness tends to make our actions more appropriate and effective.

A third tool that can help our mindfulness in daily life is called *noting*. It consists of mentally saying, once or twice, a word that represents what we're feeling or thinking. This helps us get some distance from our mind content and be less identified with it.

For instance, suppose we notice a sudden romantic or sexual attraction to someone. By mentally saying to ourselves, "attraction, attraction," we become more aware of what's happening in the mind, more able to be mindful of it. If somebody blocks our cart at the supermarket and frustration comes up, we can mentally say, "frustration, frustration." If a memory comes up, "memory, memory."

The next time we feel a desire—for sweets, for a smoke, for romance, for success—we can more easily observe it as a desire by mentally noting it: "desire, desire." As we become more aware of our patterns and desire systems in daily life, we become less controlled by them.

The point is not to suppress these things or to see them as bad; it's simply to become more aware of them, more conscious of the automatic machinery going on inside. From that greater awareness, we then do whatever we do, but from a place of greater freedom.

The device of noting, like any device, can become more of an impediment than a help after awhile. Once our awareness becomes stronger, the noting can itself become a source of unnecessary disturbance in our spaciousness. Thus once our mindfulness becomes clearer, once we become more skilled at the knack of it, we can allow a device like this to fall away.

If we hang onto a device when it's no longer needed, it becomes—in the Buddha's famous metaphor—like trying to carry a boat along with us after using it to cross a river. It was helpful at the time, but it's unnecessary baggage now.

A fourth tool for mindfulness in daily life is to become aware of our *intentions*. This is a subtle part of the mind which can be noticed just before we perform an action. We can notice an intention to look at the time just before we actually look at it; we can notice an intention to get up just before we get up, and so on.

Being mindful of intentions is valuable because intentions are the link between feelings/thoughts and action. If we see chocolate at the supermarket, say, we might first notice a desire coming up, perhaps with a subtle image of eating some. Then we may notice a sudden crystallization into an intention, followed by the action of putting it in our basket.

Another way of using intentions is to notice our intentions towards others. The next time we're with someone, we can notice how often we want something from them. We can also notice our intentions towards various situations.

The point of becoming more subtle in our mindfulness is to make the unconscious conscious. By witnessing what is there, we bring more consciousness to the nature of our mind. Then we make our choices, we purchase the chocolate or we don't, but either way we're coming from a place of more freedom, of more real choice.

Deconditioning

J. KRISHNAMURTI, AN awakened person, once was asked by an interviewer what it meant to be fully liberated. He replied that it was identical with being totally *unconditioned.* That is, his behavior was totally voluntary and was no longer driven by unconscious, automatic impulses.

It looks like our behavior is voluntary too, but it mostly isn't. The same mechanism that produces unbidden thoughts and feelings in our mind also produces automatic, mechanical behavior.

If we hypnotize someone and implant a post-hypnotic suggestion that he'll jump up and yell every time the clock strikes the hour, he'll do it—and, more importantly, he'll also believe that he's voluntarily choosing to do it. If you ask him why he's choosing to do this, he'll give you some very good reasons. And yet, though he'll believe he's choosing freely, the behavior will be purely conditioned and automatic.

It's hard to believe, but most of our behavior is also like that, driven mechanically from the unconscious part of our mind. Part of it is instinct, programmed in by the genes. Part of it is early, traumatic incidents, long ago repressed in the unconscious. Both act like post-hypnotic commands.

Any part of our unconscious that we can bring into consciousness reduces this automatic mechanicalness and helps us become more capable of true choice. A part of the immense value of gradually dis-identifying from our thought process is that it also gradually shows up as deconditioning of our behavior. Dis-identification becomes deconditioning.

When we sit silently in mindfulness for extended periods, over time we find that many past traumatic and seminal events appear in consciousness. It's as if they've been trying to be noticed, and now they finally can be. By mindful sitting, we allow them to bubble up into the light of consciousness.

As they do, any attempt to do something with them—reject them, act them out, believe them as the truth, or whatever—maintains the energy and makes them likely to act out again. Such identification gives them reality, energy, life.

But if we can just witness them then they become more flimsy each time, less real, less energetic. Their illusory, dream-like quality becomes apparent. We begin seeing the roots of our conditioned behavior, and just from that seeing we become gradually less conditioned.

Consciousness is like fire. As conditionings come from the unconscious into consciousness, they slowly burn away. The memory of those traumatic events that conditioned us remains, but their emotional charge—with its ability to unconsciously control our behavior—slowly dissipates.

It's the very detachment of mindfulness that makes this possible. It's the acceptance of each conditioned feeling and thought, without attachment or aversion, without clinging or rejection, that gradually allows its energy to merge into and rejoin consciousness.

As we take the time to mindfully sit each day, a related phenomenon occurs. We'll begin to notice certain patterns in ourselves. We notice that certain situations have arisen again and again in our life. It may be that people around us often seem selfish, or that we often get domineering bosses. It might be that we're often late, or that we often get angry, or often feel fearful, or whatever.

Of course, we have good reasons and justifications for these things, but the clue that something else is going on is the repetitiveness. When we see something in our life happening over and over, that is a clue that perhaps we ourselves are involved in creating it, that our unconscious conditioning is attracting and furthering such situations.

Just seeing and recognizing such patterns is the most powerful thing we can do about them. The very seeing of them reduces their involuntary control over us, and as we see them more clearly over time they occur less often and less forcefully in our life.

So as we grow in consciousness, our actions naturally become less robotic. We don't have to try to produce greater freedom. It happens by itself, as a by-product of our growing awakening.

Spaciousness

𝒯o say that we become less conditioned and less identified is the negative way of describing the process. But there's also a positive way of describing it, which begins with our *inner stability*, discussed in detail in chapter 5.

A reptile's chemical processes become more sluggish as the external temperature goes down. An advance of mammals, in contrast, was evolving to a constant internal temperature, enabling their bodily chemistry to proceed efficiently regardless of what was occurring outside. In effect, mammals learned to carry around their own internal weather.

Similarly, as we practice mindfulness over a period of time, we tend towards a greater *internal equilibrium*. As we witness the process of existence inside us and outside us, we slowly become more attuned to it, more harmonious and centered. We create, or rather uncover, an increasing sense of equanimity, of clarity. The mud in the pond begins to settle a bit. This deepens our enjoyment of the moment and makes it more likely that we'll respond appropriately to it. But the result goes deeper than that:

Mindfulness is like a mirror. When we stand in front of a mirror, it doesn't ask us to stay, and it doesn't ask us to go. It doesn't cling and it doesn't reject; it just faithfully reflects what is there. It doesn't try to change anything, or even inquire why it is that way. It just reflects what's there. Zenrin uses a great metaphor to describe that state of mind:

The wild geese do not intend to cast their reflection;
The water has no mind to receive their image.

When we reflect the contents of the mind in our con-sciousness—like a mirror, like a calm lake—after a while we begin to notice the lake itself, the silent, still spaciousness in which these reflections are passing.

That still silence, that calm lake where the waves have quieted down, is the truth that can't be contained in ideas. It's the deepest source of the clarity we seek when we're feeling challenged by life. Indeed, it's the source of the clarity we seek in our existence as a conscious life-form.

Stephen Levine suggests a metaphor: Imagine being on the side of a heavily-traveled road watching passing cars. At first our attention is strongly pulled by cars that look flashy or interesting; we're "caught up." Later, as our observation ripens, we can watch each car go by without being attached to it.

Even later, we start noticing the gaps between the cars more than the cars themselves. The gaps become the primary thing and the cars become less substantial, a secondary thing. And then, through the gaps between the cars, we begin to notice something else—the silent, majestic vista beyond.

In perceiving that great spaciousness no knowledge or thinking will help us, because knowledge and thoughts are all passing cars, and by their very nature cannot help us touch that emptiness. Only watching can do that for us. Trying to uncover it by thinking beautiful thoughts is like confusing a finger pointing at the moon with the moon itself.

Each of our sittings will be different, so it's valuable to let go of our expectations. Though yesterday our sitting may have been peaceful, today it may be filled with fear or restlessness or grief.

When that happens we can also be assailed by tremendous doubts about our sitting, and wonder why we're doing it at all. We may think that we haven't made any progress, that our efforts are futile. "I still can't deal with my parents" or "I still get angry" or "I'm still caught up in my thoughts."

The thing to notice is that the very awareness of these conditionings is the process of awakening. When we're unaware of them, just blindly acting them out, we are deeply asleep. Now we're more aware of them. Beginning to become aware of their existence, their persistence, their pervasiveness, is the thing itself.

If we gently persist, day after day, gradually a certain peace and equanimity begins to enter into our life. Not that we can't be caught up again; we can and will. But gradually we begin to notice the silent, majestic vista more than the parade of passing cars.

In other words, we slowly begin to notice the context, the background, more than the contents. Our thoughts, emotions, attitudes, conditionings, reactions, and so on are the contents, like cherries in a bowl. If life is a bowl of cherries, our attention imperceptibly shifts from the cherries to the container, to the space in which it all resides.

As we wake up more, as we come more into the present moment, each moment can potentially become precious and

48

beautiful even when what's going on—the cherries in the bowl—is painful or difficult.

It's a little like going to the movies. The heroine or hero may be going through numerous difficulties, yet we can still be enjoying the film. As our equanimity slowly increases, we can watch the passing panorama of our life with greater repose, with greater joy.

Paradoxically, as we tend towards greater equanimity we also become more available to life, more alive to its fragility and beauty, more open to the mystery of being alive.

No-self

$\mathcal{B}$ESIDES INCREASING OUR freedom and equanimity, there is a third way to describe this process. To explore it let's ask: What would happen if the process of mindfulness were taken to its ultimate conclusion? Where would that lead to?

The following is my hallucination about it:

Let's imagine that we began to sit in silence more often and to sit for longer periods of time. When doing so perhaps we'd get up every hour or so and take a slow walk, since it would help the body to remain calm and relaxed. And by continuing to be mindful during the walk, it could be used as an extension of our sitting.

The increased stillness from longer periods of sitting would deepen our mindfulness in daily life, which in turn would strengthen our silent sittings. And eventually these two aspects, awareness in sitting and awareness in daily life, would tend to merge, so that traces of an inner stillness would begin to show up more in our life.

As our mindfulness became more continuous and more penetrating, the smallest things of life would begin to take on tremendous significance. As Osho once said, if watched with the right eyes just a bird in flight could be the fulfillment of a lifetime. Or as the poet Goethe put it, less becomes more.

Ramana Maharshi, one of this century's great masters, when asked what the ultimate teacher was, said that it was *silence*. He said that silence teaches more deeply and more profoundly than anything else. Thus our deepening internal silence would quietly and slowly transform our life.

Our life would begin to take on a moment-to-moment fulfillment. Our cravingness inside that we try to satisfy with possessions, knowledge, power, money, achievements, food, romance and so on would slowly relax its grip, would slowly be replaced by a vast and spacious presence revealed in that eternal silence.

Taken further, this continuing awareness would begin to enter even into sleep. The sensations of dreaming and even deep sleeping can be witnessed like anything else because they are also just cherries in the bowl. So even while the body was sleeping or the mind was dreaming, the light of mindfulness would then continue.

Eventually this awareness would go on 24 hours a day, sleeping or waking, still or active. Beyond a certain point the mindfulness would become unbroken, so that there would be just one unending moment of awareness, an eternal present. Thoughts would no longer come unbidden, but would be like a saw or hammer or any other tool—available when called upon, but otherwise remaining in the tool chest.

The whole process of involuntary movement in the mind would slowly, slowly disappear. And as the process of the mind's beliefs and attitudes and reactions and cravings diminished and finally became still, a fascinating ramification would occur: The entire sense of I-ness, of being a separate entity in the universe, would also disappear. The resulting state has sometimes been described simply as *no-self*.

The reason for this strange disappearance of separate "I-ness" is because our sense of I-ness is a kind of mental dream woven by a continual stream of thoughts about our separate existence, about "who we are." Hindu yogis call this *nama-rupa*—the identification with name and form. Thus as all thoughts cease to exist, so also does our "I," our sense of ego-identity, cease to exist.

Imagine a wave on the ocean which somehow got the notion that it exists separately. Immediately problems would arise: how to make its way, how to survive. And yet its separateness would be entirely an illusion, since it would never for a single moment cease to be part of the ocean.

Fortunately, since waves don't think they also don't get burdened with the notion of being separate. But we humans do, and that is the central root of our suffering. The problem is not that we're conscious, but that we're half-conscious—our pristine consciousness is obscured by incessant movement in the mind. Often we don't think that's true until we sit down in mindful silence for the first few times. Then we begin to see how unbelievably active our mind is, constantly weaving its dream of separate existence.

Someone whose mindfulness is becoming stronger and more continuous, though, begins to experience deeper and deeper degrees of non-separation, of being the ocean instead of the wave, of being the whole sky instead of the clouds in it. It's waking up and finding out that who we are is not who we thought we were—that we're the radiant totality instead of separate little bundles trying to make our way.

There are phrases that express this, such as "All is one" or "There is nothing but God." We've all at times repeated and believed, or wanted to believe, similar expressions.

But the person entering more deeply into the *non-dual* or no-self state begins to experience the actual reality of such statements. Consciousness becomes transparent, clear, calm, empty, spacious.

In that pregnant emptiness the fruit ripens and then a moment comes when it falls from the tree, never to return. Though the individuality remains, the separateness falls away forever. Though the body is still alive, the separate person ceases to exist.

This state doesn't come about from a decision or an insight, a weekend seminar or a peak experience; there's no shortcut around the patient observation of our unconsciousness in all its variety. But when this awakening does come, it's utterly radical.

Imagine being on our deathbed. Imagine all the things we'd have to give up and let go of as we got closer and closer to death—the attachments to desires and dreams and status and possessions and beliefs and so on. In the end, everything whatsoever.

Now imagine being our current self again, but through prolonged mindfulness letting go of all these attachments well in advance of physical death. In effect, it would be like dying while still being alive. The body would still be alive, life would still be present, yet the separate individual would be gone, replaced by unfathomable spaciousness.

From the ego's point of view, absolute death. Yet also a resplendent birth. The person would be gone, and now the existence itself would live through that body, play through that hollow flute. Now the light could never be blocked, because there would be no clouds, no person, to block it.

Issues of life, death, survival, etc. would all disappear because the separate person would already be dead; so there'd be nothing left to die. The body would die someday, of course, but the separate person who was trying to survive would already be gone.

And in that absence would be *liberation*, awakening. Paradoxically, it's a liberation from ourselves, from our sense of limited self. Though our external actions might look the same, inside there would be no doer. And the death of the doer means also the death of graspingness and aversion—that is, the end of suffering.

Complete spaciousness is infinite, boundary-less, needful of nothing because it already includes everything. So for the first time we'd have no motives towards others, nothing to try to get from them, no sense of separation. What that looks like from the outside is unconditional love.

Concentration

THE PATH OF awakening has been dwelled upon in order to more clearly distinguish it from a seemingly similar but different path called *concentration meditation*.

Mindfulness and concentration seem so similar because they seem to go towards the same results—equanimity and joy and being in the present, for example. But the results actually are quite different. To see why, let's examine concentration meditation:

If mindfulness is about expanding awareness to include everything, concentration is about traveling in the opposite direction. It's about narrowing awareness down to one object and then holding it there.

That one object, the concentration object, can be almost anything. It can be the breath, a word or phrase, a musical chant, a name of the divine, an inspirational thought, a puzzling question or statement. It can also be an internal image of something, an external image such as a flame or a flower, a movement of the body such as rocking, a guru or teacher or divine object, and many other possible things.

The only requirement is that we be able to focus our attention exclusively on the object for a period of time, recycling it through consciousness over and over. This is what we do when we fall in love with someone. By constantly focusing on the beloved, we enter a mindstate of bliss. Concentration meditation does this also, but in a more deliberate way.

The effect of strongly holding attention on one thing is to temporarily force all other things out of consciousness. Depending on how well it's done, all feelings, thoughts and sensations are more or less suppressed. The whole mind-mechanism just temporarily ceases to operate. This is quite significant, because whenever thoughts and feelings are no longer parading across consciousness the natural experience is one of equanimity and rapture.

However, this is a temporary equanimity. It simulates actual awakening, but differs from it in that it's a reversible state, brought about by suppression. We're peeking through the door, so to speak, but we haven't walked through it.

Sooner or later the door closes again. We "come down," in a somewhat similar way to coming down from the high of a drug trip. When we stop concentrating upon the primary object, slowly the mind reverts to its normal state. The patterns and conditionings and mental-motion did not permanently disappear, but were only in hiding while the mind was focused upon the object.

Once we come down, once ordinary thinking-mind is restored, our patterns and conditionings return. They have to, because they're still there. No seeing into their nature was involved, no recognition or acceptance or integration of their energy was involved.

Instead of observing our thoughts and conditionings, we pushed them out of consciousness for awhile. Thus they rested underground in the unconscious, but didn't lose any energy. When we cease to concentrate upon the object, then ordinary thinking-mind and the mechanical acting-out of these conditionings is restored.

This being so, we could do a concentration meditation continuously for years, going through unimaginable states of bliss; yet within a short time of stopping be in the same mind state as before we started. It's the highest high, but still a high. It's the highest dream, but still a dream.

I remember doing a personal retreat one time 15 years ago when I did a concentration meditation continuously for three days. Intense states of bliss and equanimity and unity consciousness occurred, yet within a few hours of stopping I got into a huge argument with a close friend. In no way had I increased my consciousness.

Concentration meditation can't in and of itself lead us to awakening. What it can do, though, is give us a taste of what actual awakening would be like.

We slow our mind down temporarily and see what it would be like to be more present, more centered, more transparent, more free, more loving. Though a borrowed state, it can greatly help our motivation for the more difficult task of gradually awakening.

Concentration meditations are also very helpful in reducing stress. Many studies have confirmed that such meditations lower the breath rate, lower the heart rate and blood pressure, induce relaxing alpha and theta waves, and so on.

Of course mindfulness also tends to create these effects, but mindfulness is a more skillful knack, especially at first. In effect, it's a more difficult bike to ride. And it works more slowly. Thus concentration meditations can be very helpful when we're upset in some way and need to relax and center ourselves, but don't have the skill to just witness our state at that moment.

For instance, I can remember nights on which I woke up with deep anxiety and didn't have the courage to simply be mindful of that mind-state. Instead I wanted something very consoling and comforting, something to make the anxiety go away. Through using a concentration meditation, I was able to accomplish that result.

Mindfulness would have achieved a similar result, as well as lessening the future occurrence of that mind-state. But sometimes our ability to witness isn't developed enough to just observe something stressful, particularly if our troubles are intense. Then a concentration meditation can be invaluable in centering ourselves, in temporarily evoking a greater silence within us from which we can respond more resourcefully and appropriately.

Objects

*I*T'S A GOOD idea, then, to develop a personal concentration object for use as needed; and as mentioned earlier, almost anything can be such an object. However, the most suitable objects tend to be internal ones, such as internal sensations or sounds or images, because they're available at any time and in virtually any circumstance. Let's consider some good objects to choose from:

The breath is always an excellent and appropriate choice. The same factors that make the breath an unparalleled anchor in mindfulness also make it an excellent object of concentration. It's always there, is a natural process, is very compelling, and has no inherent conceptual content.

This last point is mentioned because it's very easy to get attached to a concentration object. When it starts producing states of equanimity and bliss, it's not unusual to believe that it's the only true way to spiritual attainment—thus increasing our intolerance and rigidity. This is most true of objects that have a "meaning." The breath, being a totally natural process, avoids this drawback and is thus an especially good object.

As a bonus, focus on the breath is unusually powerful as a natural relaxant; virtually every kind of relaxation process incorporates it. And when we want to shift to mindfulness, our anchor is already strongly developed. It's worth noting, too, that the breath is recommended by masters from more different traditions than any other concentration object.

A second possible choice might be a *mantra,* which is a Sanskrit word denoting a syllable or word or phrase that is repeated over and over. Examples might be "Om," "Ram," "Om namah shivaya," "La illaha il l'Allah hu," "Hail Mary, full of grace" and countless others.

The silent repetition of a mantra can be done almost anytime; its strong calming effect can be continued in virtually any situation. Many times, when caught up in some intense circumstance and unable to be skillful enough to be mindful or even to watch my breath, I've used a mantra to regain some composure.

The sound of a mantra can be important because certain sounds are naturally comforting or mellifluous and compel our attention more strongly than others. Many mantras involve one or more "m" sounds, associated with our natural childhood sound of humming. Many mantras invoke a name of God. Such mantras tend to hold the attention very profoundly, and as the mantra takes hold our heart can really open up in devotion.

Devotion per se, though, doesn't seem to liberate. The many religious wars, fought by people devoted to differing versions of God, are eloquent testimony to this. I also realized it in getting to know devotees of various gurus. Their devotion was touching, yet it often did not prevent them from being intolerant of others—especially of "outsiders" or the outside world. And devotion didn't seem to affect their conditioning. Once their devotion to that master ended, for whatever reason, the conditioning seemed to return in full force.

A number of mantras have been used for centuries and have stood the test of time. A widely-used one originated in Tibet: "Om mane padme hum"—"the jewel within the lotus," the inner jewel deep within us. I can testify that this mantra is extremely compelling.

Another favorite was a kind of prayer: "O gracious God, have mercy on me." This is a variation of the *hesychast's prayer*, used by many early Christian mystics of the desert, and is a call for help in seeing through the veil separating the mind from the infinite self.

If nothing else appeals, we can try using a simple word such as "love" or "peace". This was recommended by Brother Lawrence, a monk and teacher of the middle ages, and also works well.

A third possible choice would be a *koan*, a Japanese word which refers to an insoluble puzzle. The mind, which loves a good challenge, returns to this puzzle again and again in the vain attempt to solve it logically. In doing so, it recycles the koan continually through consciousness, thus making it a good concentration object.

A koan is sometimes a brief story, but more often is a question of some kind. Some classic examples are: "What was your original face before you were born?" "What is the sound of one hand clapping?" "If all returns to the One, to what does the One return?" "In winter, where are the cherry blossoms that bloom in the spring?"

The process with any koan is to hold tight to the koan at all times, disregarding any answers that come up and just returning to the question over and over. This recycles it like any other object used as a basis for concentration.

A fourth possible choice would be to combine several objects in one. For instance, the pilgrim in *Way of a Pilgrim* used a system which synchronized a mantra and an image—a *mandala*—with his breath. On the in breath he'd mentally repeat the first half of the mantra; on the out breath he'd repeat the second half; all the while maintaining an image of a loving heart in the middle of his chest. This worked better than any of these things alone.

As in other areas, it's best to pick one object (or multi-object, as above) and then stick with it. Consistent practice greatly helps. Once we've chosen an object, the way to use it is to simply focus our attention onto it and hold it there. When distracted by something, it's helpful to remember not to fight against the distraction, but just to gently refocus onto the object.

When practiced unceasingly for a while, consciousness seems to sink into the object, to unite with it, and then there is no sense of effort in keeping the attention on it. The attention stays there by itself, drowned in the object, enraptured by it, merged with it. Hence the name *absorptions* for the higher levels of concentration.

Phenomena

*W*HEN WE GO deeper into any kind of meditation, certain phenomena can occur which seem so remarkable that they can be mistaken for awakening.

These phenomena are actually impediments on the path to awakening. This is so precisely because of their compelling and awesome nature, which tends to addict us. There's a strong tendency to take them as "reality," to want to repeat them over and over, and thus to get stuck in them. It's identification at a higher and more compelling level.

The first potential impediment is the appearance of *inner lights or sounds.*

Sometimes, when concentrating or being mindful with eyes closed, images will appear before us. They may be of someone we know or once knew, or of a spiritual leader or teacher. Entire scenes may occur, with either nightmarish or heavenly qualities. They can be very impressive.

At a deeper level comes the appearance of an inner light sometimes called the *nimitta*—the sign. It seems like a light in front of our closed eyes, and can appear as a pinpoint, a star, a small disk, a wisp of smoke or other source of light.

When it appears, we're said to be in *access* concentration, because it gives access to the *first absorption.* If at that point the nimitta itself is made the object of concentration, the light gradually stabilizes and becomes steady and we're in the first absorption.

Another phenomenon that can occur is the appearance of an inner sound, sometimes called the *shabd*. It can come as the sound of bells, the sound of wind or bees, as a rustling or crackling or as other sounds. When this inner sound begins to stabilize, we are listening to the inner sound current.

When internal images, lights, sounds and tastes occur, it can be very difficult not to take them as evidence of some kind of enlightenment. While they are certainly evidence of a deepening absorption, of themselves they don't increase our insight into, or dis-identification with, the automatic mind-mechanism.

Indeed, inner manifestations are actually just a more intense product of that same mind-mechanism, and as such our intent can be to watch them with detachment like any other phenomena.

Inner images and sounds don't of themselves bring us any closer to awakening, and actually can impede our progress if we identify with them and take them as meaning something significant. In Zen, in the usual down-to-earth style, they put it this way: "Don't get hooked on going to the movies."

A second state potentially confused with liberation is the development of *siddhis*, or powers, such as the ability to read minds, to direct energy towards others, to travel out of the body and so on.

A few people have a natural talent for these powers; others develop them in the course of intense concentration. But in either case, siddhis don't liberate because they don't involve any seeing into the nature of the conditioned mind.

And like any power, they're quite seductive. They seem particularly impressive when they're seen in someone else. Such impressiveness, in ourselves or others, can trap us if we mistake it for awakening. In the last analysis, the possession of siddhis is just another power trip.

It's been said that you could pass a liberated person on the street without noticing. There's nothing "special" about them; they're not displaying any special powers or energies. Indeed, one of the extraordinary things about an awakened person is their emphasis on the ordinary, on "nothing special," on just the tomato in the garden or the drinking of tea.

The third potential impediment is the strong feeling of *ananda*—cosmic bliss. But how can that be an impediment? Isn't that what we want?

On the path of awakening, all sounds, visions, powers and bliss-states, no matter how impressive, are considered to be just more of the mind-process that's being observed mindfully in order to tune into the silent, still and vast spaciousness underneath all that.

Many times I've had peak experiences of one kind or another, and for a while I thought each one was it. "I'll feel complete and blissful and desireless like this forever." But no; sooner or later I'd find myself in everyday roller-coaster mind again, wondering where my blissful awakening had gone.

After a long while I could see the graspingness of the mind in wanting to retain these states, in wanting to possess the bliss forever. It's the same old mind-craving in a different form. Eventually I saw that even peak experiences are just one more experience, one more thing to be watched, one more step in a gradual, imperceptible unfoldment. One more lesson about attachment.

As beautiful as these three potential impediments can be, they're still a high, still part of the dream. Powers and lights and sounds, great insights and cosmic feelings are all part of the cherries in the bowl, part of the passing cars on the highway. Though fascinating and even sublime sometimes, they can't truly liberate us and are not the same as a genuine awakening, which is grounded in ordinary reality.

As many awakened masters have said, on the journey to liberation we have to go naked. No luggage. We can't bring our cherished beliefs or conditionings with us; we can't bring our cherished spiritual experiences either. If we cling to anything, it's just more identification with the cherries, with the contents, rather than consciousness itself.

The story of Buddha is very instructive in this respect. He was taught by the greatest concentration masters of his time. He mastered all the absorptions and became a great concentration master himself. He had all the great visions and powers and experiences, and went as far on this path as a being can go.

It was his great insight, perhaps the greatest any human being ever had, to see that his profound bliss was not actually liberation. That when he stopped doing what he was doing to produce these wonderful states, the ego, the conditioning, the graspingness and aversion and judgmentalness of his mind were still there waiting for him.

So he took a different path. He began watching this very mechanism of *cravingness* in his mind—and *aversion*, which is the other side of the same coin. He began watching this automatic machinery inside for grasping pleasure and rejecting pain.

He watched how his mind wanted to turn left or right as soon as it encountered any discomfort. He watched how it loved to judge other people, and how merciless its judgment could be. He watched how separate it felt deep down.

Instead of escaping from all that, he started being mindful of it all instead; just letting it all be there, accepting it—but silently watching. And it finally led him to the real thing, to true liberation.

Ordinary Moment

THE MANY NAMES given to mindfulness by various traditions all mean one thing—observing instead of escaping.

There's nothing very glamorous about being mindful of anxiety for the hundredth time. There's nothing romantic about going further into this boredom or loneliness that we want to push away. But this bare, unadorned attention can gradually lead to true freedom, to liberation from the confines of the separate-self.

Being mindful of whatever is there in consciousness sometimes feels good, sometimes feels bad, sometimes feels boring or tiring, sometimes feels wonderful. It has all the shades and hues of life, but much of the time it just feels mundane, everyday: Oh, there's the pain in my back again. There's the restlessness again. There's the doubt again, the grief again, the anger again, the judgment again.

Mindfulness seems so prosaic somehow, so pedestrian and unromantic, yet this seemingly small and unremarkable moment of being mindful—and the next, and the next—can gradually lead to our waking up from the dream, and thus resolving the challenges occurring in the dream in the most fundamental way.

It can lead to perceiving and relating to our problems differently. Remember that childhood toy that we loved so much? It probably lies unused in the closet. The toy hasn't changed, but we have. Our relationship to it has changed.

I remember the first time I caught anger as it was actually occurring. I was angry at a friend and about to pick up the phone to let him have it when I suddenly remembered myself.

It was very similar to waking up from a dream. Instead of acting out the upset, I watched it instead. As the mechanism came up, I watched all the feelings and reproaches and rationalizations run through my head, and just let them be there but without buying in. After awhile, to my amazement, it all just dissolved. The next day I was able to share my concerns in a constructive rather than destructive way.

It goes without saying that I haven't always been that lucky; yet that event did show me the possibilities that were there, and most important, made it a little bit easier to come awake the next time.

Waking up from moments of hopelessness, greed, glory, righteousness, fear, belief-clinging and all sorts of other things feels approximately the same. It feels like just an everyday, ordinary, minute-by-minute awakening out of a dream.

Perhaps the real beauty of mindfulness is that we need not become fully awakened to reap its benefits. Each little bit of conditioning that we see, each moment of mechanicalness that we observe, helps us to become a little more free.

And though it's an unromantic process, we do slowly become more attuned to life, more spontaneous and flowing. We gradually become more open, more available to life; we feel the preciousness of it more. In that sense our life does become more romantic, because it becomes more open to the flow and possibility of the universe.

Freedom doesn't exclude anything, including power and focus. But it doesn't insist upon anything either. A final metaphor can perhaps make the distinction clearer between power and freedom:

Imagine a scale of mind-states from the most negative at the bottom to the most positive at the top. At the bottom of the scale would be mind-states characterized by feelings of victimization, helplessness, anger, fear, etc. Here we feel very hopeless, powerless, cynical or apathetic. The mind is often scattered, judgmental or anxious.

As we rise in the scale we feel more positivity, more control, more power. As we go higher still on the scale the positive qualities increase, until at the very top we become what might be called a *positive power master*. At that point our mind is focused, supple, capable of powerful manifestations. We may be taken by others as being awakened, or even a bit superhuman. We may take ourselves that way.

But here's the fascinating part: True awakening isn't anywhere on this scale, but off to the side of it somewhere, unrelated to the scale altogether. There's no connection to positive or negative mind-states because it's a movement in a whole different dimension. It's waking up from a dream rather than being powerful or positive within it.

So the journey to awakening, liberation, can be started from anywhere. No matter where we are on the negative-to-positive scale, we can begin to wake up. No matter how far down we are on the scale, no matter how negative or hopeless or desperate, we can start to awaken from our dream.

Because awakening isn't a function of how positive or powerful our states of mind are, of how white or black our clouds are, but of how open and spacious and clear-sighted we can be *in relation to them*. It's not about what cherries are in the bowl, but rather, our relationship to those cherries.

Indeed, being far down on the scale can actually be a great blessing in disguise, because the suffering is so great that we can be radically moved to seek and grow. Suffering can be a most powerful impetus to start becoming mindful of the real source of that suffering.

When we're busy inside, nothing really satisfies. As we become a little more silent within, even the smallest things can bring us joy. While meeting life's challenges, we enjoy the process more. We feel the transcendent beauty of the ordinary, of "nothing special."

When we begin to glimpse the gaps between the cars and then the stillness beyond them, we begin to encounter a type of peace that passes way beyond comforting beliefs and consoling thoughts, indeed, that passes far beyond the mind's ability to comprehend. Yet in some strange way it is us.

"The kingdom of heaven is within you," Jesus said.

From that deepening silence, a very gradual but radical change can occur in the way we see and experience our life. From that growing equanimity, more appropriate actions tend to arise. That increasing inner stillness, flowing from inside to outside, becomes the foundation for everything else we do, and ultimately transforms our world.

BOOK 2
Outer Spirit
SURRENDER

Book 2, Outer Spirit, is about how the lens through which we look at life determines our experience of it, and how to radically affect that outlook.

Release the Outcome

*I*MAGINE A POWERFULLY flowing river. Imagine, also, that we're trying with all our might to walk upstream in that great river.

It's a real battle. We want to be separate, to go our own way, and the river just keeps beating and beating against us. Our effort seems endless, and the river seems so implacable, so heartless, so relentless. In fact, the river seems to be totally against us, totally opposed to everything we're trying to do. Life seems like such a struggle.

The thing to notice is that the river is not against us in any way; it's not trying to direct energy in opposition to us. It's simply flowing the way it's flowing. It is our own resistance that's creating our problem. And notice that it's *our* problem, because the river doesn't have a problem. Again, it's simply flowing the way it's flowing.

Now imagine turning around in that river, feeling its direction and then aligning ourselves with it, letting go of our resistance and just allowing ourselves to float with the river— to find its will, so to speak. Immediately then our struggle diminishes and our clarity improves.

When we're no longer struggling with the river but can let ourselves align with it, we see and function so much better. Flowing with the river, floating down it, surrendered to its vastly larger existence, we can see the banks of reality more clearly and thus make more appropriate choices.

Moreover, instead of having to cling to the bank in our struggle, we can let go of it. We can trust that life knows more than we do. We know that the outcome, whatever it is, is what it needs to be. Rather than trying to get the river of existence to adjust to us, we adjust to it.

At the deepest level we release the outcome, we let go of how it all needs to turn out. Existence will take care of that perfectly well. Our job is just to align our atom with the river's vastness, to deeply surrender to the way it is right now, in great trust and gratitude.

Our Paradigms

*T*HE PREVIOUS SECTION is an example of a *paradigm*. A paradigm can be thought of as a core idea, or a core way of looking at things. It can be thought of as the way we organize our experience, as our fundamental set of interpretations, or as a filter on our experience.

But our paradigms are not simply points of view; they're much more comprehensive than that. They're the very lens through which we look at reality. Furthermore, they're like water to a fish—so fundamental, so all-pervading that it can be difficult to become aware of them at all.

When we do catch a glimpse of our paradigms, we don't usually think of them as the lens through which we're looking, but as reality itself. In a sense that's true because they create our personal reality, the one that we live in.

Paradigms are self-reinforcing. If we fundamentally believe that the world is a terrible and bad place, we want others to believe it too; it reinforces our own sense of reality. If we believe that true love with a partner can never really happen, subconsciously we want to repeat our disappointing experiences with the next person so that we can be right again.

Does that sound dysfunctional or counter-productive to you? Probably. But does our mind work that way? Pretty much. It'll do anything whatever to be right. Our ego-mind is basically a collection of deep points of view, or paradigms, trying to perpetuate themselves.

Early traumatic incidents function like post-hypnotic commands, like scripts for a drama. The subconscious noticed that even though such experiences were hurtful, we survived them. By its dream-like logic, then, the way to survive is to keep on re-creating such experiences. Freud called this the repetition compulsion.

Thus whatever we believe at the deepest level we'll tend to experience over and over again in our life. But beyond that, we'll come to believe it more and more. We'll collect more and more evidence for it, while suppressing or minimizing evidence to the contrary. Thus each one of us goes to our death knowing that we were right about whatever it was that we were right about.

Let's take a small example to see how it works. If we feel, for instance, that men with mustaches are impolite, we'll bring that expectation to the next such man we meet. If he's impolite, it'll confirm our expectation. If he's not impolite, he'll become "the exception that proves the rule." And let him be impolite just once and we'll say, "See, I told you, men with mustaches are impolite." We're reinforcing our belief system, and at the same time shaping our personal reality.

Intensity of feeling is like the volume control in this process. Whatsoever we believe or feel strongly about we tend to create or attract. If we love bakers and hate butchers, we'll tend to attract both bakers and butchers. If we strongly fear something we'll often tend to attract that very thing, because the emotional charge we have on it lends intensity to the image of it in our primal brain.

In effect, then, the mind is like a broken record, repeating the same passages over and over. It has its "top 40 hits of the mind" that it likes to play over and over again in reality. Have you ever noticed that certain moods and thoughts, certain behaviors, certain kinds of problems or incidents come up again and again? It's something that happens to everybody.

Everything that ever happens to us conditions us to some extent. Every thought we have conditions us towards having that kind of thought again. Every action we take sets up grooves in our mind which tend to repeat the action. Every feeling, belief, intention, situation, occurrence, thought and so on has a tendency to repeat. Aristotle knew this when he said, "Excellence is not an act, but a habit."

The reason all this is important is that our paradigms have a determining influence on our attitudes and behavior. If we try to influence our attitudes and behavior directly, it's not only hard work but it's like pruning leaves from a tree. For each leaf we remove three more grow back. As every gardener knows, a plant is thickened by pruning it.

Thoreau said:

For every thousand plucking at the leaves
There is one striking at the root.

That root is our deep outlook about life and the world. Thus when we work on our paradigms—our way of looking at things—we're automatically influencing our responses and behaviors.

Suppose we encountered a stranger and he acted very preoccupied and insensitive towards us. How would we react? We might very well indicate some irritation. Now suppose we found out that he was acting that way because his wife or child had just died. Now what would our reaction be?

Notice that our attitudes and behavior would change automatically as our way of seeing the situation changed. Stephen Covey beautifully points that out.

He repeats a true story from the U.S. Naval Archives. It concerns the captain of a battleship on a dark, foggy, stormy night. A light is sighted that's on a collision course with the ship. The battleship captain directs that a signal be sent to the other ship to change course. But the other ship signals back its refusal to do so.

The captain directs that a second signal be sent: "I'm a captain, change course." The other ship refuses again. Angry now, the captain orders a third signal sent: "I'm a battleship; change your course immediately." And the answer comes back: "I'm a lighthouse."

Do you think the captain changed direction? Of course he did. Indeed, we can be certain that his whole thinking changed, his feeling changed, everything about him changed. His attitudes and behavior would change automatically as his paradigm shifted, as his way of perceiving and interpreting the situation shifted.

Trying to directly force changes in our attitudes and responses is the hard way to do things—besides which, it often just doesn't work. Because our paradigms are like maps of reality. Having a poorly-fitting paradigm is like having the wrong map to represent the territory.

If we're driving in one city but following a map of some other city, we're going to act inappropriately, to say the least. We're going to go down the wrong streets, lose our way repeatedly, be confused, etc. And no amount of working on our attitudes or behavior is going to make any difference.

Give us a correct map, however, and our driving will automatically begin correcting itself.

The Mirror

*A*s we've seen, changing our paradigms changes our responses. And that in turn changes the reality that we're living in. Why? Because existence acts as a *mirror*.

Existence is a responder; it responds to the attitudes and behavior we put out. If we put out hatred we get hatred back. If we put out love we get love back. If we put out greed or fear or anything at all the universe reflects it back to us like a giant mirror.

Imagine a day when we're feeling really good. We feel so great we're just radiating on the outside, we're really smiling. We're filled with goodwill. It's infectious, contagious. We positively beam at the people we meet, and of course for the most part they respond; who can resist?

Now the interesting thing about this is that we'll have a strong tendency to conclude on that day that the world is a really wonderful place, so friendly, so warm. And we'll be right—but we're creating it.

Now imagine feeling really bad on that day, let's say angry and bitter and upset. We scowl at the people we meet, and of course they start scowling back. We'll experience the world on that day as mean, nasty, petty. Notice that we'll experience *the world* that way.

Which is another way of saying that the world tends to reflect us. But it's only a tendency. We don't create our world; rather, we have a strong affect on it. There's a notion in some circles that we completely create our world. This can become a way of blocking out compassion. If someone has cancer: "You created your cancer, so uncreate it." Or if someone is dying: "Why aren't you choosing life?" So on. Such notions, when taken to an extreme like this, can easily be used to shield ourselves from feeling the pain of others.

We certainly have considerable influence on what happens to us, yet that influence is not perfect. There seems to be a certain amount of randomness built into things, perhaps as a kind of curry in the stew, or perhaps as a necessary ingredient of there being anything at all.

We have some influence on what happens to us. Where we seem to have vastly more influence is in our experience of what happens to us. This has been proven most conclusively by humans who have found themselves in grim circumstances.

Victor Frankl, for example, recounts his grim torture and degradation in Nazi concentration camps. Yet one day he realized that he could determine his inner response to all that was happening to him. By changing his inner response, it not only changed his experience of what was happening, but it also began to influence the outer reality as well.

This ability to change the meaning we attach to an event, and thus our experience of it, creates in effect a gap between stimulus and response. Based on its conditioning, an animal must respond in a certain way to a certain stimulus. But we semi-conscious beings have the option of being more conscious and thus changing our evaluation of the situation, so that our response changes as well.

One time I was standing in a long line and watching a young woman interact negatively with each person in line as their turn came. And when it was my turn, what came at me was so negative that I found myself caught up. I felt involuntary anger rising inside me and was about to make a caustic remark when I remembered to simply be mindful, a witness.

What I noticed was this bud of anger growing quickly inside, and externally a negative stimulus. I looked at the young woman, carefully this time, and suddenly saw someone who was extremely tired and stressed at the end of an extra long day. I re-evaluated what was happening, relaxed, and came up with a witty response. She responded to that, and we had a pleasant exchange.

By being mindful and then evaluating differently, the world had the potential to respond differently.

In terms of the personal reality that we experience, the universe seems to be a kind of clay that we can partially shape. If we know in our gut that the world is a dog-eat-dog kind of place, for instance, then we'll experience the world to be that way more and more. It becomes self-reinforcing.

If we focus on negativity and wrongness in the world and others and ourselves, we'll see more and more of that. We'll collect more and more evidence that it "really" is that way—and we'll act accordingly.

Conversely, if we focus on what's right we'll get to see more and more of that. We'll collect more and more evidence to prove that the world is really a beautiful place—and we'll act accordingly.

No matter how we choose to see things we'll be more and more convinced, as time goes on, that it really is that way.

In this sense—by continuing to create our perception of how things "really" are in this universe—we do indeed create the world that we experience.

Attention

*T*HIS NOTION—THAT our paradigms determine our experience, our behavior, and thus to a large extent the world's responses to us—is in turn part of a more general notion:

Whatever we attend to increases and becomes more real.

This notion has been formulated in many different ways by different people. A few examples are:

"With our thoughts we make the world."
"As a man thinketh, so is he."
"What we focus attention on expands."
"What we give life to, lives."

Often it seems like things happen in the world or we maneuver them around in the world and then we get to have certain desirable states of mind. And sometimes it does work that way. Sometimes by deliberately changing our external behavior we can change our self-image.

But the general principle seems to be that it's much more powerful to look in the opposite direction. That is, we direct our attention in certain ways or evaluate things in certain ways, and then these inner actions grow and expand until they bear fruit in our external experience. Inner to outer. Our inner life manifests in our outer life.

86

If we plant apple seeds we're going to create apple trees, and if we plant orange seeds we're going to create orange trees. And if we plant apple seeds, no amount of effort down the road will turn them into orange trees. So back in the beginning, on what we're planting, is a good place to focus.

The ways in which we consistently direct our attention in life largely determine the kind of life or destiny we will have.

The internal seeds that we consistently plant and water are the ones that will bloom. So when we consistently have difficulty or negativity in our life it's important to scrutinize the inner evaluations that we're creating. Ask the all-purpose question:

Where are we consistently putting our attention?

The most powerful tool we have in creating or affecting our reality is mindfulness, which allows us to slowly become dis-identified from the conditioned contents of our mind. When we are mindful we gradually dissolve our conditionings and begin to awaken, thus allowing the greater spaciousness and harmony of our true inner self to begin to naturally emerge in our life.

The second most powerful tool in affecting our reality is to begin making conscious choices in our paradigms—to begin consciously choosing the evaluations that are shaping us. The entry-point of the second tool, like the first one, is not "out there" somewhere, but way upstream—in the seeds of what we're noticing and how we're evaluating it. These seeds grow into our reality.

That gives us a clue. When we see lots of things wrong with other people, with ourselves, with our circumstances, with the world, we can recognize where this "wrongness" is fundamentally coming from. We can recognize that the world and everything in it is consistently "growing" in the way that we choose to look at it.

Thus our most effective work on the world always starts with ourselves. As we

- mindfully lessen our conditionings
- choose more useful paradigms

the world itself will seem to change for the better. Yet the real shift has been in ourselves. As James Allen said:

Man has but to right himself
to find that the universe is right.

This doesn't mean being a Pollyanna—blindly rejecting reality. It doesn't mean ignoring problems. Rather, it's a recognition that our problems are hugely influenced by how we *see*, and that the lenses through which we see can be, to a great extent, consciously chosen.

If a bottle has 50% liquid in it, that's a fact. But the evaluation of that fact, seeing the bottle as half-full or half-empty, is our own contribution. Since our evaluations expand in our consciousness, and in their effect on our world, we live more and more in a world we've played a part in choosing.

That being so, it becomes very interesting to ask:

What kind of world, personal and otherwise, would we like? What kind of world would we choose? What kind of reality would we like to notice?

Questions

QUESTIONS ARE A quite useful means of directing our attention, and thus growing and expanding the paradigm that we would like to live in. But we must ask skillful ones.

For example, instead of asking "Why does this always happen to me?" or "Why am I so stupid?" we can suspend the harsh judgmentalness of the mind and be life-affirming with ourselves instead. We can ask questions like:

"How can I use this?"
"What can I learn from this?"
"What is this trying to teach me?"
"How can I open to the pleasure in this?"

We're actually asking and answering questions all the time, though frequently at a subconscious level. An interesting aspect of the brain is that it will supply an answer to any question asked of it. Thus the nature of the questions in our internal dialogue becomes very significant.

If we ask the mind, "What's wrong with my life?" we'll get a list of answers. On the other hand, if we ask the mind "What's right with my life?" we'll get a list of answers to that. Which is true? Either. Both. Neither. It's not really a question of truth, it's a question of what we'd like to create.

If we ask ourselves the question, "How come I don't ever lose weight?" we'll get a whole list of reasons why we never can. The brain will supply us with an answer. If instead we ask, "How can I lose weight starting right now?" we'll get an answer to that.

Oftentimes, while hardly noticing it, we'll ask ourselves negative questions, which result in maladaptive feelings and states. For example:

"Why am I no good?"

"Why don't things work out for me?"

"How come I always fail in relationships?"

These questions and others like them will unfailingly get answers. But we can redirect our focus by asking ourselves more empowering questions, such as:

"What am I happy about?"

"What am I thankful for?"

"What's good about this?"

"What do I like about that person?"

"How can I get the result I want?"

"How can I make a contribution?"

It's easy to underestimate how powerful questions like this can be. For instance, if something negative has happened, the asking of the simple question "How can I use this?" or "What does this have to teach me?" can be wonderfully helpful. Just getting up in the morning and asking ourselves "What am I thankful for?" can set the tone of a whole day. If we're feeling blocked somewhere we can ask "How can I get the result I want?"

What's beautiful is that the subconscious parts of the brain automatically go to work to organize answers to any question, and continue working at it even when we turn our attention to other things. So even when we don't get a satisfactory answer right away, it will come eventually.

This was the basis for many discoveries. The theorist, experimenter, inventor, or artist would persevere in asking a particular question even though the answer seemed elusive or unobtainable, and usually, sooner or later, the answer would appear.

Because writing serves as a kind of connection between the conscious and the unconscious, it's quite helpful to focus our attention further by writing down such questions, and any answers that come.

For instance, if we're having trouble with someone we can constructively redirect our focus by putting the question "What qualities could I appreciate in this person?" at the top of a page and making a list of five or ten things, even though it may seem difficult at first.

By doing so we're planting an inner seed that will tend to bear fruit on the outside. Instead of trying to force changes in our external world or behavior, *we can begin to look through a different lens.* And as time goes on, that will automatically tend to bring about changes externally.

Opportunities

TRY AN EXPERIMENT sometime: Sit down on a hard chair and have someone from behind try to push you sideways to the left or right while you focus on resisting. Try to be pushed to the side as little as possible. Notice the effort it takes to resist.

Then instead, focus straight ahead on something on the wall and concentrate all your energy there. Now when the person tries to push you left or right, you'll be surprised. Not only will you stay more upright, but you'll do it more easily, expending much less energy. Yet the interesting phenomenon is that your inner attention isn't on resisting, but on something positive instead. Peter Drucker makes this point very well in his famous injunction to businesses of all kinds:

"Starve problems and feed opportunities."

Often we'll do just the opposite, feeding problems and starving opportunities. We'll get so caught up in focusing on our problems that they consume us, so that we see little else, have time for little else. And what we focus on expands—we have more and more problems to work with.

Feeding opportunities doesn't involve a neglect of problems, but rather, redirecting our primary focus so that time and attention are directed to related positive opportunities, expanding them instead.

For instance, in the 1962 Cuban missile crisis President Kennedy received a letter at a certain point from Chairman Khrushchev of the USSR, outlining a promising basis for a settlement. But a few hours later he received a second letter from Khrushchev, one that was threatening and aggressive. The two much different letters posed all sorts of problems. During a long meeting, nobody could figure out what to do.

Then JFK's brother Bobby joined the meeting and made the suggestion that ultimately led to a successful conclusion. What Bobby suggested was so simple that everyone had overlooked it. Here's what he proposed:

Respond to the first letter. Ignore the second.

He was starving the problem, feeding the opportunity.

Another example: A friend of mine felt she was losing management of her life. She had so many time commitments, so many obligations, so many things to get out of the way before she could start her Ph.D thesis. No matter how hard she tried, she couldn't seem to get on top of the situation. Things seemed to be spinning out of control.

After a conversation about it she decided to do the following: Even though she felt she wasn't ready, she began that very day to work on her thesis for just one hour a day—no more. Later, two hours a day, then three, then four.

Then what happened was that everything else in her life began to sort itself out. Things of lesser importance fell by the wayside, while supportive and important things got handled. A calmness and a sense of control settled on her that was quite remarkable to see.

In my case, I had to discover the great significance of this lesson the hard way. One time I was involved in a very difficult situation. My business was failing and property had been misappropriated from me in a way that affected others adversely. Threats of lawsuits were flying, my intentions were questioned, etc.

It was a terrible time. Though I tried very hard to reach a fair solution, nothing seemed to work. I felt betrayed by a former friend. I agonized over the accusations hurled at me. Everything I did to try to rectify the situation seemed to just make it worse instead.

Now in the meantime there was a book I wanted to write (not this one) which almost certainly would have remedied the situation in various ways. Yet writing the book seemed out of the question at the time because I was too upset, too consumed by my problems. In addition I travelled around a lot, trying to distract myself.

In retrospect it would have been better to stay put, get started on the book, and keep my primary focus there. That would have given a positive direction and purpose to things. It would have kept me focused on something positive, and prevented me from being immersed in the contemplation of all the problems.

Most important, for those problems which needed to be dealt with directly, it would have allowed me to see them as secondary matters in a larger, more positive context.

Circle of Influence

𝒜NOTHER WAY OF interpreting the paradigm being discussed in this chapter is to examine what Stephen Covey calls our *circle of influence.* The following discussion uses ideas based on his beautiful work:

Each of us has a large *circle of concern* and within it a smaller circle of influence. In our circle of concern are things we can be legitimately concerned about, such as the potential for ecological catastrophe, financial meltdown, or war; the existence of poverty, homelessness, starvation, tyranny; our own personal challenges and difficulties, and many, many other things.

But if we make these things our focus it does no good. It simply leads to criticism, carping, condemning, finger pointing. It leads to depression and disillusionment, to feeling like the world is a terrible place and nothing can be done. And we'll be right; we'll accumulate more and more evidence to support our point of view.

Similarly, if we repeatedly criticize other people or try to change them—our circle of concern—they'll act poorly or hostile in our presence, or they'll withdraw, and then we'll be able to say how disloyal their friendship was, or whatever. Again we'll be right; we'll pile up evidence.

But within our circle of concern is a smaller circle—our circle of influence. This inner circle of influence concerns things we can do something about. It concerns things that we can personally work on, things where we can make a difference. We can focus on that smaller circle of influence—on the things that we can do.

And once again, what we focus on expands. If we focus on our circle of concern, it will expand and grow more prominent. And since we're neglecting our circle of influence, it will grow smaller; and our ability to influence our corner of the world will diminish.

Conversely, when we focus on our circle of influence instead, *it* expands. Our circle of influence grows; we become more able to affect some of the things in our larger circle of concern. And in the meantime our life feels more positive and worthwhile, because we're making whatever difference that we can. Also, from that vantage point we can more easily see the perfection that is.

We see once again how the world mirrors us. By doing what we can, we become less conflicted and more harmonious inside; and we help the world to become less conflicted and more harmonious outside.

A more harmonious world can't result from tense, self-righteous, inharmonious people. Only by each of us becoming more harmonious and constructive, inside and in our dealings with others, can the world become more that way.

By seeking out the true, the beautiful, the worthy, the useful—both in ourselves and the world—and then expressing it and focusing on it, we create more of it. The world keeps on reflecting us. By feeding opportunities we shift attention from our circle of concern to our circle of influence.

If we ask, "What's wrong with the world?" we'll get an answer, lots of answers. If instead we ask, "What can I do starting right now to make a difference in my little corner of this world?" we'll get an answer to that.

We're feeding a different paradigm, and in so doing helping to create a different personal and shared reality.

But now let's ask: Is there some way to better access the affirming paradigm across the board? Is there some essence of it, so to speak, the adoption of which would tend to move us naturally into a more aligned and constructive direction?

Indeed there is.

The River

$\mathcal{L}$ET'S RECALL OUR metaphor of the river, and pursue it a bit further:

When we struggle against the great river, it seems so relentless in its push against us; it just won't stop. Life can seem to be a misery of endurance. Yet if we can just let go and allow ourselves to align with its flow, a miracle can occur.

Suddenly, leaving behind the endurance contest, we're free to enjoy our journey. And the surprising thing is that our goals, which we surely thought would be lost forever in letting go, often actually become more available. Because without the ceaseless battle we can see more clearly and our energy is more available. Thus we're able to respond more appropriately and creatively to our situation.

As we flow with the river we'll see things from time to time that we'll want to hang onto. Various shiny objects on the riverbank will attract our attention, and we'll be tempted to hold on somewhere. But each time we do, our resistance to the flow causes us to suffer.

The Buddha made a fascinating statement one time. His words were, "All suffering is caused by attachment." What's remarkable about that statement is that he didn't say "most" or "some" of our suffering is caused by attachment, but that *all* of it is.

When I look at my own experience, that seems to be the truth. Every time I've held on tight somewhere, saying

"This part of my life musn't change" or "I can't be happy unless I have this," I've suffered. Conversely, every time I've been able to surrender a new world has opened up for me.

It's not that the river is trying to make us suffer. It's just that it's flowing the way it's flowing, and it's our job to get in tune with it, not its job to get in tune with us. It is infinite, and we're an atom. When we can align with it, then miracles can happen. A tremendous peace can descend on our hearts. The Bhagavad Gita of the Hindus says:

Peace immediately follows surrender.

Mohammed also knew about the miracle of surrender, and transcribed many verses that talk about its wisdom.

True surrender is not resignation. Resignation is saying, "I still want this goal, but I realize I can't have it." Surrender, on the other hand, is saying, "I'm willing to go wherever the river goes. I'm willing to surrender my little mind about what should happen to the flow of Mind, to the flow of existence itself." Jesus put it this way:

Thy Will Be Done.

Surrender is an embrace with love of whatever is.

As discussed in chapter 1, the most fundamental thing we can do about our difficulties is to begin to clearly observe the contents of our inner sky, to create a little silence inside to begin to awaken from our waking sleep. But the second most fundamental thing is to let go, surrender, allow ourselves to go in the same direction as the river, to flow with it.

These are actually inner and outer forms of the same thing. When we're mindful we're totally accepting what's there. If sadness comes, we watch it; if fear comes, we watch it; if desire comes, we watch it. Acceptant observation.

Surrender is just the outer form of this acceptance. It's saying that we're completely willing to accept our lives, the universe, the situation—just as it is. Actually, this result comes about automatically and gradually through mindfulness, but we can considerably help that process along by consciously letting go, by surrendering.

At this point the mind tends to step in and say, "Now hold on. How can I solve my troubles, how can I improve my life or the world if I just accept everything the way it is?"

That's where the paradox comes in. Because a good deal of our trouble is caused by our resistance to things. When we're busy resisting something, our field of view isn't so good, and we miss a lot. But when we totally accept existence as it is, we make room for it to change, and quite often a real transformation occurs. Often it was our own resistance that was holding the problem in place.

Really letting-go brings into being, in a mysterious and spontaneous way, all the factors discussed so far about this paradigm. Automatically our attention is redirected in a way that gives our reality the potential to transform.

Let's take an example. I'd like to tell you a story:

A True Story

$\mathscr{I}$N 1973, WHILE visiting a friend at a farm commune in Massachusetts one afternoon, he and I and some others all took the hallucinogen LSD together. Perhaps a dozen people were there, and everyone had experienced the drug before except me. It was my first time. We took the sunshine acid and then went for a walk in the woods.

While walking the trip came on, and it felt so novel that I involuntarily began to slow down and fall behind the group. As the LSD reached its full strength I felt more and more strange and confused. In fact I began to feel so strange that it became clear that I was dying.

I was walking in the woods about 50 feet behind the others, and trying like crazy to control the trip, but it felt like the very life-force was just draining out of me. Everything around me felt evil, malevolent. I felt weak, unsteady, anxious; my breath came in short gasps. I felt so weak I couldn't even cry out. I was dying and surrounded by malevolence:

It was the ultimate bad trip.

And then one of the great insights of my life happened:

When it became clear that I was going to die in the next few moments, I decided to just surrender. I let go completely; there was nothing else to do. There was no point in resisting any longer.

So I just completely gave up, went into a deep let-go. I felt like a leaf flowing down a stream. And I thought to myself words to this effect: "Okay, if I'm going to die, then so be it. I'm just going to relax and let this thing show me whatever it wants to show me."

Then I got the surprise of my life.

The first thing that happened to me was that I saw that I wasn't dying. But I was in such a different and strange space that I was interpreting it as dying. When I totally let go I was suddenly able to see things more objectively, and what I saw then was that being in a very unusual space didn't mean I was dying, and didn't mean that I had to be in fear. That was just an interpretation I'd put on it.

The second thing that happened to me was that the trip turned into the most beautiful phenomenon imaginable. Everything came alive; the world became new, fresh, lovely, iridescent. And I felt united to the world, in harmony with it, in a way I hadn't felt since childhood.

It was then that I saw that the bad effects of my trip had largely been caused by my own resistance. In this instance, what had been making it horrible was me myself. The trip was just flowing in its own direction, so to speak, and there I was desperately resisting it because I wanted to be back to normal, back in control. I didn't want to be where I was.

But the journey was going to go its own way for the next 14 hours or so, and I had a choice: Either I could resist it and have a terrible time, or I could surrender to it and let it teach me whatever it wanted to teach me. And the lesson it brought, of course, was the value of surrender, of letting go into the flow of things.

Please note that I don't advocate this manner of risky experience for anyone else, nor would I likely do it myself today. It's quite possible to overdose to the point of illness or death on drugs. And there are better and less risky ways of opening up consciousness. I tell the story to give a dramatic example of how letting-go at the deepest level can sometimes radically influence a situation for the better.

Letting-go can actually be a profound way of creating. No force is being used, nobody is changing anything, and yet change occurs. When magic is discussed in chapter 8, we see that the very first principle of a magician is to deeply accept whatever the situation is right now. Not accept it so it can be made different, but truly accept it as it is.

Paradoxically, this lays the foundation for a profound change. Nothing is guaranteed in this world, but the chances for change increase dramatically. Things have the freedom to evolve to where they need to go. Perhaps most importantly, the very let-go itself is a radical alteration in our perception and experience of life.

Alignment

WHEN I TOOK the est training in the 70's, Werner Erhard or one of his trainers used to say things like, "The wall agrees with the ceiling. The ceiling agrees with the floor." And in my mind I'd be, like, "What...? What does *that* mean?" It seemed incomprehensible, deliberately obscure. In fact it took me over a decade to begin to see what he meant.

To examine agreement, let's look at our relationship to gravity. Each one of us has developed a very good relationship with gravity. We're in perfect alignment with it, because somewhere back in our formative years we learned that gravity works a certain way, that it flows in a certain direction so to speak, and that we're going to have to adjust to it just as it is, because it's not going to adjust to us.

If we trip and start falling, we can't offer any explanations to gravity on the way down. We can't say, "O gravity, I'm sorry, let me explain what happened, I won't do it again, please don't make me fall this time." We discover that gravity is going to follow through a hundred times out of a hundred. We discover that it's going to continue to work a certain way without regard to whether we like it or not.

Because of that fact, we quickly learn not to mess with gravity. We don't jump off high buildings thinking that maybe this time gravity will make one little exception. We know it won't. So we move into perfect alignment with gravity. We learn to live in accordance with gravity's unspoken rules.

And we learn not to whine or complain about gravity because it's just a given; it's just the way things are. We adjust to it just fine.

The same thing happens when we wake up in the morning. We don't go outside and say, "Damn, I wish the sun would be purple this morning. We don't waste energy saying, "Why won't it be purple just this once?" We know it's going to be yellow today and tomorrow and the next day, so we move into perfect agreement with that. It's part of the flow; the sun is yellow. We don't complain bitterly about the fact; it's just a given. We align perfectly to it.

Yet with many situations in our lives we spend energy complaining or resisting. Why can't it be different? Why does it have to be the way it is? How come she has those advantages and I don't? How come I'm not as handsome as he is? Why did I have to be in that auto accident? How come I have this disability and other people don't? Why couldn't I have grown up in a more functional way?

On and on it goes, as if our disagreement with the way things are is going to make any difference. The fact is, right now nothing can be any different than the way it is. It might change a second or a year or a billion years from now, but right now it is the way it is. By just accepting that, we move into alignment. We're no longer fighting gravity, so to speak, but learning to work with it.

We become much more effective.

We can learn a lot by studying things in their simplest cases. When we leave a room, for instance, we always go out the door. We don't try to walk out through the wall because we know that's a good way to get a bloody nose. In that sense, we're always in perfect alignment with, perfect agreement with, the structure of any room we find ourselves in.

This concept can be applied to life itself. It behooves us to observe carefully to see which way the river is flowing, what "the structure of the room is."

In essence, this is what we're doing when we're mindful, when we're being a non-reactive witness to our own inner process. We're slowly removing the dust from our eyes, the unconscious conditionings and clouds of thought that keep us from seeing the light.

And the second thing we can do is surrender, just let go. To what? To whom? To existence. To the magnificence and wisdom of existence. From that relaxed point of surrender our vision improves. Our clarity increases, and thus our responses become more appropriate and effective.

Resistance

*I*n the process of alignment, we're given a very important clue as to when we're *not* in alignment. That clue is that our nose is being bloodied a lot by running into walls.

If life is looking negative, if we're beset by difficulties that seem to have no solution, it may be well to remember the lesson of my LSD experience. That is, our experience has to stay negative so long as we're resisting something within it.

Or to use another metaphor, our experience of gravity is going to be quite negative so long as we're resisting something about the way it works.

This is equally true of our experience of life itself. Thus when we have difficulties and negativities, we can ask ourselves: Am I resisting somewhere? If so, where? What is it I'm not accepting? Am I willing to learn what this thing is trying to teach me?

Of course it will seem to our rational minds that no progress or betterment is possible if we just accept everything. But let's remember, the most profound changes are caused not by what we do but by how we see.

To see differently allows a different kind of action to arise, an action more harmonious and in-tune.

From a place of surrender our actions almost seem to arise by themselves, and they don't have a quality of force or struggle. They feel natural, appropriate. And they're much more effective.

I remember trying for years to get along better with my dad, James A. (Jim) Sloman. My dad had a horrific childhood and had many inner wounds, which he mostly took out on me. He was always criticizing me, and my constant question was: "Why won't he just accept me as I am?"

After decades it finally dawned on me that it was I who was not accepting *him,* because I was not accepting his non-acceptance of me. From then on I determined to accept him exactly as he was, including his critical opinions of me.

The result was miraculous. As time went on he noticed my increased spaciousness towards him, that I was willing to have him be exactly as he was and even appreciate that. It led to a conversation, four months before his death, when he said "I've been too hard on you, Jimmy. Please forgive me."

I burst into tears; it meant so much to me. And I realised what incredible courage and humility and growth it took to say that. I take my hat off to my dad.

But that is the power of acceptance. It can sometimes accomplish what years of resistance cannot do.

Let's remember standing in the river. If it seems to be totally against us, implacable, relentless, let's ask how our own resistance might be holding this situation in place. As an example, if we want someone to be different in some way, they're probably going to stay the same around us in order to preserve their sense of identity. If they sense that they're okay with us just as they are, they're free to change.

But does this principle mean that we never persevere in the face of difficulties? No, it doesn't mean that. Sometimes it's very appropriate to persevere even when the going is very tough. How do we know then when to persevere and when not to? The line involves our inner knowing, our inner sense of alignment.

For instance, this book. For a number of reasons, it's seemingly the wrong project at the wrong time. Logically and monetarily, I am making a mistake; I should be working on other things instead. And there are numerous obstacles.

Yet intuitively the book feels right. It feels in harmony, that in some way I'm flowing with the river instead of struggling against it. Thus when obstacles come up I do what I can about them, but don't let them become the primary focus. So great perseverance is there, and needed. But the perseverance is taking place in a context of feeling aligned inside.

If that weren't so, if I were feeling this perseverance as a negativity, then I'd be wise to stop and ask myself: Am I doing the right thing? Am I resisting somewhere? Am I aligned with the flow? Is there something else that would be more in harmony for me right now?

External resistance tends to mirror internal resistance, and vice-versa. When we're involved in something that feels in harmony, things have a tendency to fall into place. There's a subtle feeling of flowingness, even though we may be working very hard. Though there are no guarantees in life, circumstances tend to follow along when we're aligned inside.

But if the problems seem to outweigh the rewards, if there's a feeling of struggle and tension and disharmony, that can be a clue that we've somehow gotten out of alignment.

Thus it's important to pay attention to signs—how we feel internally, how things are going externally.

Paradoxically, by accepting things as they are we're then able to see if they're right for us. We're not struggling and fighting. The internal noise level goes down. We can see more clearly whatever is there.

Then if it feels right to shift our direction, we needn't criticize or condemn the river, or say that the world is for us or against us, or right or wrong. It's just that we were facing in a wrong direction; it's not a statement about the river.

In other words, we're responsible for our experience of life. We're responsible for turning around in the river, if that's needed. Existence is not going to force us to get in harmony. In effect, it respects our freedom too much to do that.

It's our job, then, to get in harmony with it, not its job to get in harmony with us. We can't ask it to change direction. It's simply going the way it's going. It's not personal; it's not pushing against us.

Acknowledging this responsibility moves us way up on the scale of positive-negative. It gives us the great power of creation. If we have the power to create our experience of the universe one way, then we also have the power to create our experience of it some other way.

Trust

*I*T'S SOMETIMES THOUGHT that letting-go means to become passive, to cease to initiate any action and just wait to see what the universe has in mind. Yet it actually means something much different, in my opinion. It simply means acting from a trust in existence.

Imagine being a musician and creating a song. Further, imagine being totally surrendered inside. Does that mean you can't create the song? No; creating the song is fine. We can create as we like, we can put high notes here instead of there, but without insisting. If the high notes don't work in this spot and need to go somewhere else—okay.

Metaphorically, existence loves for us to be creative; it loves for us to create our lives as we want. To be surrendered in the midst of this process actually helps to make it possible. Thus surrender and being responsible are not opposed, but are actually two faces of the same coin.

To be responsible means to see that we are affecting the outcome of our life and creating our experience of it, and at the same time to see that from a point of surrender we don't need to be attached to how it all turns out.

The Hindu classic *The Bhagavad Gita* tells the story of the encounter of Arjuna, the great warrior, with Krishna, the transcendent. Arjuna is concerned because he is due to fight a battle the next morning in which his friends and relatives are on the opposing side. Yet not to wage the battle would have grave consequences as well. He feels trapped, caught in an excruciating dilemma. What to do?

Krishna's advice to Arjuna was simple but profound. He told Arjuna to play the role assigned by fate, and play it well, but to leave the outcome to Him.

Such a surrender doesn't mean feeling hopeless. It has nothing to do with hopeful or hopeless because it takes place in a whole different dimension. Instead, it has to do with a softening, an allowing. When we can let go in that way the world can suddenly turn magical—as happened to me in the woods that day—though nothing outside has changed.

In effect, then, we create happiness at the level of outer spirit by an act of alchemy, by letting go of the craving that things must be, or turn out, a certain way. In a word, by letting go of the craving for happiness—or rather, our model of what happiness is supposed to look like.

Sosan, the third patriarch of Zen, said:

To live in (the Way)...
Is one with the trusting mind.

Events often have consequences that can't be foreseen from a limited viewpoint. For instance, a few million years ago a sudden cooling occurred in the earth's climate, causing a massive thinning of forests. This was a full-scale catastrophe. Yet because of it a certain primate came down from the trees and began foraging on the tall, grassy savannah on two legs—beginning a development that led to who we are today.

To live from the trusting mind is to do what we can, where we can, but from a space inside that has let go of how it all has to turn out. Suddenly we're cooperating with the flow instead of struggling to have it our way. Our external actions may even look the same, but we're experiencing them much differently inside. We're not clinging; we're not insisting.

Life takes on a sense of beatitude as the sense of struggle diminishes. Not that all obstacles vanish, but that working on them becomes somehow harmonious, part of the journey, part of the flow.

The late Ken Keyes discussed upleveling our addictions to preferences. Addictions, he said, are things we feel we have to have in order to be happy. Preferences, on the other hand, are just things that we'd prefer. When we uplevel an addiction to a preference we may prefer a certain outcome, but if it goes another way that's okay too. The sense of compulsion about things drains away.

Surrender and trust are in the middle ground between passivity and insistence, between helplessness and obsession. Right in the middle is that point where we're not apathetic, where we're willing to be creative, but where our preferences have not crossed over into craving.

To take a simple example, if we go to the ice cream store it's perfectly okay to choose a flavor—chocolate, say. But if the store is out of chocolate, it means we don't need to suffer by clinging: "Why can't they have chocolate today?" It means we're willing to be happy with vanilla, if that's what's available, if that's the way the flow is going.

When we uplevel to preferences, when we're willing to align with the river, our feeling that it's all on our shoulders begins to lift. Existence is moving the clouds, growing the trees, beating our hearts. It's a natural phenomenon, and so then is the course of our life. We cooperate with a process larger than ourselves. We cooperate with fate, so to speak.

When we surrender and let go inside, tension dissipates and then many things become possible. The world becomes right by an alchemical, internal act of allowing it to be. Then existence creates through us, and we become part of a music whose notes we may not even comprehend. Then we trust in, become part of, a phenomenon larger than ourselves.

Then the ocean itself rises in the wave.

Appreciation

APPRECIATION IS SOMETHING that arises naturally when we surrender. When we let go, we automatically begin to validate, affirm, appreciate. The world is allowed to be the beautiful place that it is.

The bird flies for all to see, but our inner eye must be open to feel it, to appreciate it. That happens when our noise level quiets down, when a little silence pervades our being, when we've let go inside enough to be trusting.

I remember the first time that what Joel Goldsmith called "the click" happened, during a meditation. The moment was ineffable; everything seemed to have come to a standstill. The sweetest, deepest silence pervaded everywhere. I opened my eyes and just watched the trees blowing in the wind—I'd never seen anything so beautiful in my life.

Such moments—and we've all had them—can happen as we allow the waves of the mind to quiet down in pure silent sitting in mindfulness; this is the most profound way. They can also happen when we let go and surrender inside. An intense perception of the world's inherent perfection can arise within us.

As we allow ourselves to perceive the world's *perfect imperfection* more, more of it becomes available to see. The world acquires more beauty, more rightness. We perceive it that way more and more, like seeing with a different lens. Surrender is a creative process. It brings things into being.

We can bring this same acceptance and affirmation to ourselves. When we allow ourselves to see the rightness in existence, we become part of that rightness. From a place of let-go, we can more easily appreciate our own worth.

This is worthiness, not an arrogant righteousness. It's not self-righteousness, the blind insistence on our own point of view, but rather, seeing the harmony and beauty and value of all of existence, including ourselves.

Self-righteousness, actually the symptom of a sense of unworthiness, involves clinging tightly to our justifications, viewpoints, defenses and beliefs. It's a futile attempt to "prove" our rightness, to force it by blocking out any other rightness except our own.

Our true rightness is part of the worthiness of all of existence. There's no feeling of force about it, no sense of exclusion, no sense that something else is wrong. It doesn't mean an effort to always think positively, to be relentlessly upbeat, or to act "spiritually." Our rightness, our splendor, our worthiness already exists; it's already in place. It's a matter of tuning into it, of seeing that it's already there.

Conversely, when we struggle to be right or positive or spiritual, it's easy to fall into the trap of denying our emotions. Many of us have an image that an evolving, awakening person would never get angry, never get frustrated, never get sad, never feel any negative emotion. But we don't deactivate and integrate our conditionings overnight.

If we carry such a notion of emotional perfection, we further suppress our emotions on top of all the repression from childhood, with consequent damage to our spontaneity, our freedom, our joy. Or we go to the other pole and express our emotions in an inappropriate way—blaming or dumping on others—which can be just as damaging.

We're often blinded and caught in our dualities. Anger must be repressed or expressed, for instance, or we feel we must dominate or be dominated. Such opposites are *horns*, Joseph Campbell says, and if we get caught on either horn we "die"—our aliveness is slowly destroyed.

The poet and humanist Robert Bly, speaking of a talk by Baker Roshi, describes a third alternative where one might feel the anger in silence and stillness, allowing the whole body to burn with anger for several hours perhaps, and yet neither repressing it nor expressing it.

And then afterwards, having the choice to express the anger or not—and if so, instead of an angry scene it might very well come out as a brief witticism that the other person remembers for years.

Such a third alternative is actually an appreciation of the anger. It's neither stuffing it away, nor projecting it onto the world from a victim stance. Rather, it is being with it, befriending it in a sense, letting it be there—yes, appreciating its beauty. Then, if and when it's expressed into the world, it tends to come out in a much different way, in a skillful and appropriate and perhaps even poetic way.

When we appreciate we see the beauty of existence, including ourselves. Then there's no need to try to be positive, no need to attain beauty or rightness, no need to suppress the negative in search of the positive. If sadness happens, good. If frustration happens, good. If indecision happens, good. If a decision comes, good. No need to force anything.

And it's all changing anyway; the energy can move somewhere else in a moment. Everything down to the smallest particle has its own beauty—it's all part of the beautiful dance.

When we're having difficulties we're often serious and heavy. We tend to focus on what's wrong, what's not going very well, what the problems are. We tend to start criticizing, complaining. Surrender short-circuits all that.

Then we do what we do but without attachment to the outcome. We appreciate whatever is there. Then we're in a spirit of playfulness, like children. When children play a game they know it really doesn't matter. They're just playing. And so are we.

Appreciation of what is allows us to open our eyes again, to become playful again, to feel great gratitude in our hearts again.

Gratitude

GRATITUDE IS THE mature fruit of letting-go. It's a great sense of benediction, of thankfulness that arises in the heart for ourselves, for all of existence—even the "negative" parts.

The Sufi mystic Bayazid and his followers were refused admittance to a town one night. They were hungry, cold and wet. Bayazid began praising God. One of his followers said, "Wait a minute, this is too much. How can you be praising God at a time like this?" Bayazid said, "Tonight I need to be cold, wet, hungry, tired. Otherwise, why would He give these great gifts to me? I must praise Him."

To the logic-chopping mind, this seems almost inconceivable. But Bayazid knew a secret; his heart was open and he was living in a different reality, even though it was just the same old "ordinary" reality.

A few years ago an article appeared about a woman who practiced gratitude as a spiritual path. Then she saw her son killed by an auto and she could feel nothing but bitterness towards the driver of that auto. Then she lived in misery.

One day, however, she allowed her heart to open in compassion towards even this driver, to feel his pain too. And she said that she didn't truly understand gratitude until that moment. Then her heart overflowed with a love that was much deeper than before, one that encompassed both the "positive" and "negative" aspects of life.

Then those aspects are seen as "not-two". Chuang Tzu, the Taoist master, said:

Pleasure and rage, sadness and joy,
Hopes and regrets, change and stability,
Weakness and decision, impatience and sloth:
All are sounds from the same flute.

A wonderful practice, especially before going to sleep, can be described as "gratitude practice" or "loving-kindness practice," and in different variations has been recommended by countless teachers. It is very powerful.

Here is one version:

We close our eyes and see ourselves as if we're a leaf floating down a stream; see ourselves stretching out our arms in total relaxation; see ourselves happy, surrendered, trusting, aligned, flowing with the infinite river of existence. Then we allow our attention to alight on something we can be grateful for. Then on a second thing we can be grateful for. Then on a third thing, and a fourth thing...

What soon becomes apparent is that the list is endless; that we're truly blessed by existence if we can only see it. We let our heart fill up with love for the blessings that have come our way, and let that love envelop our limited self, the one that has suffered so much. We let ourselves feel love for our perfect imperfection.

Then we let that love expand outward. First, to those who are close to us. We feel a loving kindness towards them, we dwell on sending love to them that they might be happy. Then we let this love expand to include friends, associates, acquaintances; and then towards anyone with whom we feel animosity or who feels animosity towards us; and finally, to the whole world, to all beings, to all of existence.

To love existence is to accept it as it is, just as it is. In that freedom and spaciousness it becomes free to change in whatever way is appropriate; we ourselves become free to change in whatever way is appropriate.

When we can accept "negativity" in ourselves and the world, we become able to see it with clear eyes for the first time. We become able to see an appropriate response to it, to awaken from the dream rather than fighting within it.

It doesn't mean ignoring reality or living in fantasy. On the contrary, in surrender, love, appreciation we see reality more clearly. When we begin to flow with the river we have more peacefulness inside with which to notice reality.

In that silence, love, gratitude we see more easily that happiness is not about accomplishing great things, but about appreciating and growing the great seed that is already there. Ordinary life becomes the source of greatest gratitude. It's so much easier to appreciate the beauty in each moment when we're not insisting that it be some other way than it is.

As always, what we pay attention to expands. Existence goes our way. As our gratitude extends to more of our life, we get more to be grateful for.

Dancing with Life

*W*HEN WE'RE TROUBLED with something it's quite tempting to go running off and immediately do all sorts of actions to rectify our situation, but if we're not yet coming from a place of trust and gratitude we may very well create more problems, enturbulence and unfulfillment.

We almost can't help but do that, because our negative lenses and conditioning, which played a major role in creating our troubles, will create more.

From a place of silence and surrender, we more easily see that the most important thing we create each moment is our state of mind. It is our cumulative state of mind that has created our current experience of life. Brother Lawrence, a great mystic of several centuries ago, used to tell novices this:

In performing any action, one-eighth of one's energy ought to go towards the action, and seven-eighths towards one's state of mind while performing it.

Focusing on our state of mind is again the principle of inside-out, of allowing changes in action to flow from changes in seeing.

When we reverse that order and try to work on problems or negativites from the outside-in, we may seem to solve them—suppress the symptoms—but long-term they often remain. This is so because we haven't really addressed their primary source, the inside. We're pruning the leaves of a tree, but the root remains.

When I entered high school I tried out for the swim team. Though I knew how to swim, I didn't understand the real principle of how to swim fast. I thought swimming fast meant a blizzard of activity.

To make the team you had to swim 40 yards in 30 seconds. On my first trial I took 33 seconds; on the second I tried harder and got it down to 31. On the third and last try I made a desperate effort and managed to do it in 29.9 seconds. My arms that day were whirling around like frantic windmills.

A few years later I was fast enough in the water to anchor our team's relays; yet because my arms were moving much more slowly it might almost seem to a spectator as if I were relaxing.

There was some truth to it, because inside I was relaxed and focused. A steady focus was being applied to my hands as they moved through the water. A focus coming from inside had replaced an emphasis on frantic activity outside.

Seeing in a different way inside, and letting that focus then emerge on the outside in a different way, is not the same as using willpower on ourselves. Trying to will ourselves to put a good face on something that we actually think is bad, is just using force on ourselves. And our true natural being cannot be revealed by force.

Instead, we can let go, surrender to life, appreciate what is there. We can allow ourselves to see and comprehend the beauty and rightness that is already in place. We can surrender to what is, "fall" in love with what is. We can let that seed of appreciation and gratitude keep growing.

Then our sense of peace and beauty grows from the inside until it becomes part of the outside too. The motions feel natural. We tend to engage in appropriate action rather than burying ourselves in a blizzard of activity.

That's just a recognition of reality. It recognizes that higher creates lower, inside creates outside, that our experience of life is fundamentally being created from inside of us. Surrender removes the sense of doingness from what we do. We no longer feel as if we have to force things around.

Then, though we may be working very hard, we're just playing with existence. Things are being done and we're participating, but we're no longer insisting on certain outcomes. A great faith and gratitude becomes part of the flavor of life. We come to see that existence is profoundly trustworthy.

Then the intent to be kind or generous or trustworthy becomes an expression coming from the inside rather than a rule being followed from outside. And having consideration for others begins to occur naturally, like breathing, like eating. Not a big deal, just ordinary life.

Consideration for ourselves occurs naturally as well. When we see the beauty that is already there in ourselves, and allow it to flourish, we become more trustworthy to ourselves, more authentic, more willing to let our truest self emerge.

As our inner surrender and gratitude grow, as we give up more and more the insistence that things must turn out a certain way, we begin to cling less. We more easily allow the natural flow of things into and out of our life without so much of the grasping or pushing away.

Our surrender, trust and appreciation allow us to take our situation less seriously, even to laugh with it. We become more authentic and effective as our actions flow from the inside, yet less concerned. We work on what we can do, and leave the outcome to the whole.

Then a kind of internal singing and dancing can arise. We're doing our part, playing our role, allowing the process to unfold. Then the natural creative majesty of existence can begin to come through us.

By allowing ourselves to see the beauty that is there and let it grow, by allowing ourselves to feel our natural surrender, trust and gratitude, we've not only deepened our alignment with life but also prepared the best palette for our canvas. Now we're ready to create in a more beautiful way.

BOOK **3**
Inner Mind
CREATION

Book 3, Inner Mind, is about
discovering our calling, our
vision, our way of making a
contribution, and how to do
the inner work of creating
that reality.

Turn on a Light

*O*sho, the late 20th century master, used a wonderful metaphor:

Imagine being in a dark room, trying to find your way and stumbling over the furniture. That furniture is a problem. We're banging into it, hurting ourselves. What to do? We could try being more careful, or rearranging the furniture, or refusing to walk around in the room. In effect, these solutions are different ways of "fighting the darkness." But they're all less than satisfactory.

What we really need is to turn on a light. When a light is turned on, the problems associated with the room being too dark clear up by themselves. We don't have to figure out ways not to stumble into the furniture. The problem of darkness is handled automatically, *as a side-effect of greater light.*

Our dragons and negativities are like that. When we try to fight them directly, we can often be trapped in polarizing solutions or no solutions. On the other hand, when we turn on a light such things tend to handle themselves.

Detached Passion

*D*ARKNESS CAN BE beautiful, but we can't see very well. Turning on a light is creating—discovering—a radiance in the darkness. But whereas in the spiritual dimension we do that through bare attention to the contents of consciousness, in the dimension of mind we do it by deliberately creating a positive focus for our lives. That is, we discover, create, and implement our *life-theme.*

The mind dimension is where we consider how to make our contribution to things. It is asking how we can put something into the pot. It concerns our manifestation in the world, the mystery of expressing our unique combination of ability and inclination and experience in a way that creates benefit for others as well as ourselves. We consciously create the song, the dance, the painting called our life.

Some of us feel that to be accepting of existence means being passive, that it means just to wait and see what comes into our life. Yet, speaking metaphorically, existence loves it when we take brush in hand and start putting something on the canvas, when we start playing with our painting and being joyfully creative just purely for the sake of making something beautiful.

Bernie Siegel has pointed out the importance for cancer patients and others of taking an active role in their own recovery. Studies have shown conclusively that cancer patients and others with a sense of self-responsibility for dealing with their illness have a much better prognosis than those who feel either helpless or that the health professionals are basically responsible for their health.

It is essential for our well-being that, in crucial matters, we make our own choices in life. Yet paradoxically, if we get too caught up or attached to our choices, our happiness and well-being also suffer. Right there in the middle—between apathy and craving, between helplessness and insistence—is where we're most effective and most happy.

When the process works, we're simultaneously making choices in our painting—red over here, blue over there—and yet inside we're surrendered to the flow of existence. We choose and create from a place of being unattached to the outcome. In effect, we serve as a creative instrument for existence to play and create through us. It's both: We act, create, choose, yet do so from a place of surrender to wherever the river will ultimately flow.

This dual level—passionate detachment—makes good sense if we see it as a process of falling into harmony about our goals, of discovering how this painting wants to turn out. Michelangelo used to speak of discovering or uncovering the sculpture frozen within the block of marble. That is what we want to do with the sculpture known as our life.

For it's our own life that's the most important work of art to uncover or create. Each of us is unique; no one has ever existed quite like us, and never will again either; existence never duplicates. Our painting is needed because there is none other quite like it.

Yet our contribution need not be some "great" undertaking. Life needs all kinds of contributions; small or large is not the point. All of every kind are equally needed. The real journey is to find something that feels right for us, that has the right fit. So existence poses a question to each of us: How can we make our unique contribution by being most truly ourselves? How can we express who we are in such a way that it's most useful to others?

We can go on piling up money or success, but it won't be fulfilling per se. It's easy to be successful and yet still feel empty-handed, as many have discovered. Thus the question posed to us is not just how to be successful, though certainly that's part of it. But life's real question is: How can we be in harmony? How can we find our unique melody, the one that allows us to both flourish and be fulfilled at the same time?

In that harmony will be found our enthusiasm, our joy in doing what we do, and a success that's satisfying. Then work can become joyous and fulfilling instead of empty and a struggle. Then the expenditure of our energy becomes its own reward. And success in worldly terms comes as a byproduct.

Flow

MIHALY CSIKSZENTMIHALYI TALKS very eloquently about the experience of *flow*. Flow is related to *enjoyment*—which is not the same as simple pleasures such as eating dessert. Enjoyment or flow occurs when we are deeply focused on some process, so that time seems almost to disappear. It occurs when we're engaged in an activity where the challenges we face, and the skills we have to meet those challenges, are evenly balanced.

If the activity we're engaged in is more challenging than our talent or skill can deal with, we feel anxiety. Conversely, if our skills are much larger than the challenges, we feel boredom. The enjoyment of flow occurs in a zone where skill and challenge are matched.

This can occur in activities that vary as widely as a tennis or chess game, listening to music, caring for children, the pursuit of a scientific theory, skiing down or climbing up a mountain, reading, writing, leading a team, working with a computer, using a machine tool, taking photographs, and so on. Any of these activities and others can create flow for us or not, depending on our individual makeup.

What activities have in common, when flow occurs, is that they engage our deep concentration, and do so in a way that combines control and satisfaction. People describe it as being "lost in the flow" or "out of time" or "totally involved," a combination of relaxation and attentive focusing.

We've all experienced this at times. Those moments when we're challenged but up to the challenge, when we're so engaged in what we're doing that only the moment exists. The moments of true enjoyment.

The key to fulfillment in the dimension of mind is to identify what kinds of activity produce this effect in us, and then to discover a life-theme related to that activity. We don't simply want a job or an occupation, but rather, something that we can learn and grow with, something we'll find satisfying if we spend a lifetime with it, something where our talents and enjoyments can be harnessed to make a contribution to ourselves and others. This is the concept of *right livelihood.*

But what about money?

Michael Phillips in 1974 published seven laws of money, and I especially like the first one. He formulated it in this way:

Do it!
Money will come when
you are doing the right thing.

That is, our proper focus is on our passion. If we find our true passion, we will find an almost unlimited number of ways to make money at it. That's been my experience. When we are doing the right thing, the way our livelihood sometimes comes through can seem to defy the laws of logic. When we're that devoted to something, it's as if the universe itself takes notice.

That doesn't mean it will necessarily be easy. It doesn't mean that we just get up in the morning and do whatever we feel like. It doesn't mean that we daydream about being something and wait for the universe to magically support us.

Everybody I know who has followed their passion has had to make extreme sacrifices at one time or another, and often frequently. Sometimes they've had to take extra jobs, or put various things off. Sometimes they've had to take two steps back in order to take three forward. Sometimes they've had to "work while others play," in Churchill's pithy phrase. Sometimes they've only been able to work at their passion ten minutes a day. But they've continued.

For that's the interesting thing about following your passion: You can't fail. Because the very following itself is your success. Even if worldly success or money doesn't come at first, even if it doesn't come for a long time or ever, even if you have to make sacrifices—and you will, count on it—the very following of your passion is success and fulfillment in itself.

Three Clues

THERE ARE SEVERAL good clues to discovering our passion, and thus by creative extension, our right livelihood.

The first clue is *past happiness*.

Let's recall an occasion or time in our life when we were performing an activity that required some skill and that made us really happy. What was it that made us so happy? What was the setting? Were we with people or alone? What were we doing? Now let's recall another time in our life when we were performing some activity that required skill and that we really enjoyed. Why were we enjoying it? What was going on at the time? What were we doing?

Let's recall several more such times or occasions in our life. What is it that makes them stand out? For each time, what were we engaged in? What was the setting? Who was there? What about each time did we particularly enjoy?

Now, most importantly, is there a common thread running through those times or occasions? Is there some quality or qualities that they share? And if so, what are those commonalities? Those common threads are an important clue, since what made us happy in the past is very likely to make us happy in the future.

These questions can be asked in more general terms: What kinds of activities or situations have tended to make me really happy, or really joyful? How could I use that knowledge in discovering my right livelihood? Realizing that what we enjoy and what we're good at tend to be the same thing, what does that tell me about my talents? What does it tell me about where I could make my best contribution?

The second clue is to examine our *present loves.*

What do I already spend time on, even if I'm not getting paid for it? How do I spend my spare time? What do I love to do so much that I already do it whenever I can?

Then, is there some way to make a little shift in that activity, and begin getting financially compensated for it? Is there some way to wobble my view of what I already do, allowing it to turn into a livelihood?

The things that we already do, just for the love of doing them, can often signal what we'd enjoy working at on a lifetime basis. It's helpful to ask ourselves if we would enjoy working at this if we were going to do it for the rest of our life. Would we still want to do it? Is it something that we'd age well with, like a good wine? Would it help us to mature, help to give us a view of the universe?

A useful question to ask ourselves is, "Will I enjoy the day-to-day process of reaching my goal?" It's not going to be all sweetness and light, of course, and we'll surely encounter many difficulties, but at some level we want to be nurtured and filled up by the very process itself, since that's where our life actually takes place.

For example, suppose we imagine we'd like to be a novelist. Do we mean that we'd like to have written a novel and enjoy the fruits of being a successful novelist, or do we mean that we'd enjoy the day-to-day writing itself? In discovering our right livelihood, it's helpful to discover what an average day would really consist of.

At one time, for instance, I wanted to be a stockbroker, and I had a pretty glamorous idea of what it would be like. But then I went and talked to a dozen or so stockbrokers about what their job really consisted of. How did they actually spend most of their time each day? What were the real activities associated with the job?

It turned out that being a stockbroker was a far different proposition than I'd thought. I still wanted to do it, but my eyes were open. I understood it now from the perspective of everyday life, which was where I would actually be experiencing that occupation.

The third clue is *future success*.

Let's imagine that we're already successful, a success beyond our wildest dreams. We've really done it, we've really made it. Imagine being tremendously successful, and then ask (and keep asking): What is it I'm so successful at? What am I engaged in? How do I spend my time? What do I especially enjoy about my successful activity?

A variation: Imagine that you're unoccupied, but have all the money and freedom you could ever want, and more. Then imagine that anything you wanted to do you could just do. All financial and other obstacles to any potential project would simply not be a problem.

To complete the picture, imagine too that you've just spent a year or two partying, playing, relaxing, traveling and vacationing to your heart's content. And it was wonderful, but you're getting bored; enough already! You want to get in the saddle and use your energies and talents somehow; you'd like to make a contribution somewhere.

If that were your situation, if money and means were no problem and anything were possible, what would you choose to do? How would you choose to use your energy? What would be important to you? How could you use that situation most wisely?

The contribution we'd choose to make if we had complete freedom of action can help us to see what we'd really like to do. If it doesn't seem possible in current circumstances, put that out of mind for the moment. Just keep asking: What would I really want to do if I could do anything?

In my experience, it's good *not* to ask questions like, "How can I make money?" or "How can I be powerful?" and so on. They tend to lead us in directions where our soul dries up because the water is too shallow. We're putting the cart before the horse, asking about taking out before pondering what to put in. Let's let money, success, and so on come as a by-product of our inner passion and devotion.

Instead, asking questions like: "What do I enjoy? What am I good at? What do I do anyway? How can I be useful? How can I best use my talents and the things I love to make a contribution in a successful way?".

Such questions tend to move us in more life-fulfilling directions. They tend to carry us towards more aliveness, towards what Carlos Castaneda's Don Juan called "a path with a heart." Isn't that a beautiful phrase?

When our right livelihood is being actualized—which almost certainly will take some patience on our part—there's no dichotomy between enjoying oneself and making a living, between "doing good" and one's livelihood. For what it's worth I'll pass along the following which, since I'm a slow learner, it took me quite a while to learn:

In the dimension of the mind, there's no greater joy than the attempt to be useful.

Two More Clues

*T*HE FOURTH CLUE is a *wisdom source.*

In discovering what we'd really like to do in life, we can imagine ourselves asking someone very wise about it. Our natural self, our wisest, deepest self that exists beyond the boundaries of our ego-persona, slowly manifests in our life as we become more silent inside; but we can partly access the wisdom of it now by simply addressing it in some symbolic form. "Ask and ye shall receive."

So we can sit or lie down, get comfortable, close our eyes, and imagine ourselves climbing a mountain or going through a deep forest and finally coming to a cave, or perhaps a temple. We go inside and encounter someone representing our truest nature—perhaps a wise person, a master, a radiant being of light, or just ourselves in a wiser form. And we can ask that person or being: "What would be best for me? How should I spend my life? How can I best use my talents to be useful and successful? What is my calling?"

An alternative to imagining a wise person is to picture an animal. We can imagine ourselves on a beach or a meadow or near a lake, just waiting. And as we wait, an animal of some kind slowly comes into the picture and comes over to us. The animal is a friend, but a magical friend; it knows many things. And we can ask it anything we like.

In doing this, we may get suggestions or answers that seem unusual or impractical. When we're pondering our right livelihood, it's a good idea to take our finger off the "suppress" button. In my experience, many of us, when asked what we'd really like, take our current situation and add about 15%. We extrapolate out a little from where we are now.

It's easy sometimes to feel quite constrained by current circumstances and have some difficulty imagining how things could be much different. But life can take radical shifts in direction when we let it, when we begin to follow our heart and our intuition. I've personally seen this in the lives of many people, including myself. It can happen to you.

Don't worry that you'll need to make scary changes overnight; it doesn't necessarily work that way at all. Often it's quite appropriate to introduce something new gradually and naturally, like growing a new plant.

For now, let's let our imaginations soar; let's ask ourselves what we'd really like to do. Let's put our circumstances off to the side for a moment, and just ask ourselves, "If I were totally free of circumstances, what would I really want to do? What would I really choose to contribute?"

Our circumstances can certainly be influential, and I don't mean to imply that they're not—but they're not decisive. What's most influential, what's really decisive, is what's going on in our heart and mind. When we open up our imagination to a passionate dream we've already begun the great process of bringing to life the reality we imagine.

The fifth clue to what we want is *death*.

Death is perhaps the greatest teacher of all, because the prospect of death puts everything in perspective. It separates the important and the trivial immediately. Because death can offer such great insight, let's pay a visit. From a tasty "recipe" by Laura Huxley in 1963, let's attend our own funeral:

Imagine that your body is lifeless and dead, no longer speaking or moving. Imagine that this lifeless body is in a funeral parlor, and that your funeral is about to begin. People are sitting down, music is playing.

First of all, how do you feel about the life you've lived? Do you have any regrets? Things you wish you'd done? What about your life do you feel really good about? What was a real joy for you? Was there something you always wanted to do but never did? Did you have a dream?

If you could have life again, if you could go back one more time, is there something you'd do differently? Is there something you'd like to do?

If you were going to give a talk now at your funeral, what would you say? How would you describe your life? What was really important to you? What did you spend your time and energy on? Where did you put your attention?

If you were suddenly given the gift of life again, what would you do with it?

Now a few people who were close to you get up to describe your life. What do they say? What would you like them to say? How do they describe you? According to them, what did you really love? What was your life about? What did you accomplish? What did you leave undone?

Now let's come back to your body, your now living body. Feel life flowing again through you. Once again you're here, alive, part of the flow of life. You have another chance. Where would you put your attention this time? What would be your passion, your livelihood?

A variation: Imagine you had only six months to live. If you had only six months and so needed to get on with it, what would you do? If you had only one more project you could do, only one more arrow in your quiver, what would you do? Perhaps it's that thing in the back of your mind that you said you wanted to get around to someday.

Because of limited time, if you focused your energy and attention on just the most important thing, what would it be? Would you have a last project? What would it be? Why not start now?

Life-theme

LOOKING AT THESE different clues and considering them together can help us discern what is really right for us, can help us become aware of our life-theme. Our life-theme is one step further up than right livelihood. It's the central theme that we'd like our life to be about, and from which our right livelihood derives. From our intuition, let's ask ourselves now what we'd like the basic theme of our life to be. Then let's write it down in a few words.

An interesting thing to know is that it doesn't really matter what we start with. All that matters is that we start with something. If it's not quite right, that's okay; it'll start evolving until it is.

Maxwell Maltz used to use the metaphor of a guided missile that's going to be fired from the ground and hit a plane in the sky. Of course the plane is a moving target, and may even be moving evasively. His point was that we must first get the missile in the air—and *then correct it on its way*.

Keeping the missile on the ground while the computer fine-tunes its calculations won't do any good, because the plane's course is constantly changing. Only if the missile gets airborne and adjusts its path along the way does it have a chance of hitting its target. The same principle applies with us. We can become aware of our main theme in life while keeping in mind that it doesn't need to be perfect or final but just something to start off with.

When I first wrote down my life-theme it must have been two hundred words or so. It included everything but the kitchen sink. Over the years it gradually simplified, and then used to sit in a little sign on my desk: "My purpose is to find true happiness and share it."

It's worth noting that it changed quite a bit over the years, from one thing to another, and will probably change again. So we don't need to get the "right" answer all at once.

If we haven't done so before, let's try taking a moment now and asking ourselves: What would I really like my life to be about? What would I like the theme or purpose of it to be? Our answers, of course, will be unique to each of us.

Our life-theme doesn't need to be about our livelihood only. Indeed, one of the surest ways to suffer is to lead an unbalanced life. Since balance is so desirable, we may want to incorporate various areas of our life, or we may want to ask ourselves about each of the following dimensions:

Spirit: What relationship would I like with the totality, with existence? How would I be if my truest self manifested in my life? How can my life best embody harmony and love and peace of mind?

Mind: What is the contribution I would like to make? What is my passion, my calling? What would be in harmony with my nature? What's something I could enjoy the process of doing each day? A path with heart?

Heart: What kind of relationships would I like with my loved ones? With friends? Associates? With my community? What would it look like to truly love? To truly be loved?

Body: How would I like to feel physically? What would I desire for my body? What kind of environment would I like to live in, relate to? How would I like to spend each day?

It would be helpful at this point to quickly write down our life-theme, and then under it a paragraph or two about each of our top four goals in life—whatever first comes to mind when we ask. Why the first things that come to mind? Because rather than our rational, edited, safe answers, we want to get our deep-seated, intuitive, gut-level ones. And if we still don't know, let's just make it up. *Let's pretend as if we do know.*

Let's let these be large, general goals, focusing on the big picture. Once more: What would we really like our life to be about? What would we really like to be and do? What can we picture ourselves being and doing?

A little time spent on these seedlings now can reap a huge harvest down the road.

The Triune Brain

$\mathcal{O}$NCE WE HAVE a life-theme and our top four goals—
at least for now—what is the most effective way to bring them
about? To answer that let's look at some interesting research
done by Paul MacLean at the National Institutes of Health.
He established that each of us has a *triune brain,* that is, that
our brain is basically divided into three parts:

The smallest, most primitive part is called the *primal
brain.* It's also called the *reptilian brain* or the *R-complex,* and
is a bit like a golf ball at the base of the brain. It's essentially
the same brain we had 150 million years ago as reptiles. Upon
further development, it appears, we didn't lose this brain, but
rather evolved other layers over it.

What is remarkable about this primal brain is that it
seems to have most of the real power, most of the psychic
energy. (After all, it was there first.) It's a basic goal-oriented
mechanism. It seems to be responsible for mobilizing the total
energies of the organism towards specific goals.

What's more, these goals are not held there as thoughts
or concepts, because the primal brain is far too primitive to
understand such niceties. Rather, its goals are held in the form
of *images.* Pictures. Images are the basic currency with which
it operates.

But these image-pictures are not simply visual. They're
primarily visual, since most of our information about reality
comes through our eyes, but they also include other senses

such as sound, touch and smell. Here's what's so intriguing about these images: The organism seems to automatically try to bring them about, to actualize them in reality.

It's an automatic mechanism, and be it noted, devoid of value judgments. The primal brain isn't concerned with the meaning of the pictures, or with whether they're good or bad, desirable or undesirable. It doesn't comprehend such things. It simply mobilizes the organism's energy towards actualizing its images, whatever they may be.

Some of these pictures were placed there in childhood by traumatic events, a time when our view of the world was not mature. We may have images of being unlovable, feeling worthless, being guilty, failing at relationships or whatever. The pictures don't need to be logical or mature or to make sense; they only need to be there to be actualized.

If we'd like to know what pictures are currently in our primal mind, all we have to do is to look around at our life. Because our current life is a good reflection of the pictures in our primal mind. The pictures being stored internally can be seen most clearly by observing the circumstances and patterns of our external life.

To put this another way, all of us are already extremely successful at actualizing goals. We're continually bringing goals to fruition, based on the images held in our primal minds. Thus the issue isn't whether we're going to actualize goals or not, since we're already doing that, but rather, is the process going to be unconscious or conscious? The question is, are we going to manifest *conscious* goals?

Visualizing can be thought of as a process of releasing outmoded images chosen for us by traumatic incidents, and replacing them with self-chosen images. It creates pictures of our own choosing in the primal brain. It helps to make the creation of our life-painting a more mindful process.

Surrounding the primal brain is a complex of structures sometimes called the *emotional brain*. It can also be called the *mammalian brain* or the *limbic system*. It's the brain that evolved over and around the primal brain as we slowly became mammals, and it concerns a kind of feedback system which we experience as our feelings and emotions.

Imagine being the pilot of a modern jetliner coming in for a landing. Our goal is to land safely, and for this purpose the jet is on what's known as *the glidepath*—the optimal path to a good landing. If we deviate too far from the glidepath, going too far left or right or up or down, we'll hear different sounds in our earphones telling us in which direction we've deviated. Our job then is to get back on the glidepath.

If we stray further from the glidepath, the appropriate "negative" signal will intensify. On the other hand, when we guide the plane back onto the glidepath, we hear a confirming or "positive" signal.

Our emotional brain seems to work like that. When we're making good progress towards the picture-goals in the primal brain, we're rewarded by the emotional brain with a decrease in tension, a positive emotion. We "feel good."

Conversely, if we seem to be deviating from our primal picture-goals this brain produces a negative emotion such as anxiety, anger, sadness and so on, depending upon how we're deviating. We don't like how we feel. It's a negative feedback system letting us know that we need to change or correct our course in some way.

Last, the *rational mind* surrounds, covers the emotional brain. It's also called the *cortex,* or the *rational brain.* This is the newest brain, trying to evaluate the world by constructing an inner symbolic representation of it (including itself, hence self-consciousness), and then mixing and matching with those symbols to gain insight into how the world works. It's quite a neat trick, very powerful.

But let's remember: It's the primal brain, the brain that was there first, that still retains the real power. It determines the basic directions in which the organism will go.

Primal Power

$\mathcal{H}$OW DOES OUR triune-mind affect the achievement of our goals and purposes? Let's see:

Let's imagine that we're overweight, for instance, and we make the decision to lose some weight. That decision is made by our thinking brain, the cortex. "I've decided to lose some weight." The primal brain, however, doesn't even know about this decision, because it doesn't understand "weight" or "lose weight" or any other concept. Instead, it has a picture of us being overweight. It feels fulfilled, because its picture is actualized.

So now a struggle begins. We study the right things to do, we go on a diet, we make an effort. And perhaps we make some progress, perhaps manage to lose some weight. But this goes against the picture held in the primal brain, so it sends a signal to the emotional brain and we feel tension, anxiety or other negative emotion. At some point we abandon the goal and start binging, sending our weight back up.

The primal brain is satisfied now, because the picture is once again actualized. But of course, the thinking brain is now dissatisfied, because being overweight goes against its decision about, "I will lose weight." So it begins a struggle to lose weight once again...

Have you ever seen someone struggle to get their weight down, losing it and regaining it over and over? Or keeping it down only by an effort of great will? Have you ever seen someone struggle to be successful, only to sabotage it again and again? The pictures almost always win in the end, because they're in an earlier, more basic part of the brain, a part with more power.

We can struggle mightily to achieve things—try one diet after another, one success course after another, try again and again in love, etc.—but unless our conscious decisions and primal pictures are aligned, our struggles won't make much difference.

This is why *affirmations,* though of great importance, are perhaps not as powerful as visualizations. Affirmations are ideas taking place in the thinking mind, while vizualizations reach a deeper, older place in the brain. In some ways, the real value of affirmations comes from the way they help us to evoke internal pictures.

In essence, this is what we do when we make a list of things to visualize. That list, in effect, is a list of affirmations. "I'm successful" or "I'm healthy and feel it" or "I finish the project." By pausing after each item on the list and allowing images of it to form, we're starting to use the communication form that can reach the deeper, older brain.

When our pictures and our decisions become congruent with each other, miraculous things can happen. We become aligned; we do what works. Things seem to fall into place. Magical events can happen, often with the appearance of coincidence or accident. We feel in harmony.

I can remember sitting in an apartment in Chicago, dead broke. The rent was paid for the next few weeks, that was it. Yet day after day I faithfully visualized a preposterous vision—living in a beautiful house on the ocean in California, being rich and in love, having free time, pursuing creative interests and so on. I hadn't the faintest idea how all of that might come about.

Do you know, every bit of that visualization came true within little more than a year. I mention it not to brag about my fleeting accomplishments but simply to show what can be possible.

Each piece of that vision, when it came true, seemed coincidental, as if it were just an accident or a lucky break. And in one sense it may have been. But when you see enough visions come true, you do begin to get a sense that there's more going on than meets the eye.

Do such visions somehow call upon forces outside of the organism in coming into reality? Or is it that our organism functions vastly better when all parts of it are aligned? I don't know. My feeling is that, as a practical matter, it's a question that doesn't need an answer.

What does matter is that, in one way or another, the pictures in the primal brain have a very strong tendency to show up in external reality—to manifest. And as they do so, the process feels harmonious and right. Things seem to have a natural feel about them.

As a teacher of mine, Monica Rix, once said to me: "We always have a choice. We can struggle about things or we can manifest them." That was a revelation to someone who had spent most of his life struggling about things.

Because of the naturalness and harmony of the process, however, a misconception sometimes arises, that manifesting means to lay back and wait for the world to knock on our door with whatever it is we need. That we don't need to work or pitch in about it.

In my experience, manifesting doesn't mean that. It's not a license to laziness. As the saying goes, "Nothing works if we don't." Manifesting doesn't mean that hard work has no place, but rather, that the sense of struggling is diminished. Whatever work is there is an appropriate, even beautiful part of the process. Even when it feels very difficult there's still an unseen harmony there as well.

The basic idea of visualizing is to turn on a light—to create something positive inside ourselves and then let it grow and mature into reality, rather than trying to push reality around externally. It's inner to outer, higher to lower. When done properly, it's going with the flow of the river in a creative way. Let's look now at the elements of effective visualization:

Begin at the End

*F*OR A PERIOD of time I experimented with the idea of visualizing almost as if it were a chemistry set. What happens if I do this? What happens if I do that? Houses, money, romance, success, cars, etc. And all those things are fine.

But after a while it began to dawn on me that I could be driving around in a Porsche and not necessarily be feeling good, that a lot of my goals didn't necessarily have much to do with real happiness. So I began to let my most fundamental visualization be to just feel myself being happy.

Sounds a little surprising, doesn't it? We hardly think of the primary component of a good image as being a feeling or state of mind. But it's the secret key to ending up with what we really want.

The real end-results we desire are not accomplishments or circumstances of one kind or another; those are actually just means to an end, and don't guarantee anything. The real outcomes we seek are states of mind. Just about everything we do is probably for the purpose of achieving desirable states of mind, or avoiding undesirable ones.

The basic principle of visualizing is that whatever we want to end up with we start out with instead. This is the first element of visualization. *We begin with the end.*

Thus the most important visualization we create is the state of mind that we want to end up with. If we begin with that in each vision we're most likely to end up with it.

Imagine the states of mind that you'd most like to have from living out your life-theme: contentment, love, aliveness, fulfillment, peace of mind? Whatever those states of mind might be, let's sum them up by the word "happiness." Take a moment now and imagine yourself feeling really happy. How do we do that? The answer is, from nothing. We can create the feeling of happiness simply by imagining what it would feel like; we don't need to have an external cause.

In our life, each moment conditions the next. It looks like we move things around in the external world and then become happy, but as far as I can tell, it actually works the other way around. The more we create the state of mind we'd like from nothing, the more external conditions rearrange themselves to give us reasons for it.

Thus in visualizing our goals, we can deliberately let ourselves feel joyful. We can feel and see ourselves as spacious, trusting, loving, at peace. We can deliberately imagine ourselves living from a centered place as part of our life-theme. In short, our most important visualization each day is simply to see ourselves as being happy and at peace.

From that first visualization can evolve a whole string of images concerning various goals in our life, yet all coming from the same feeling and pulling in the same direction. That first feeling-image helps greatly to give focus and direction to all our other images.

If we've used the five clues discussed earlier and are still not clear about our life-theme, that's fine. We can start with this. We can just begin creating from nothing, feeling without any images the basic state of happiness and peace that we'd like to have as an end-result. If we do that consistently enough, the desired life-theme images will slowly emerge from the mists within.

If we have a partial sense of what we'd like to do, we can use that. For instance, suppose we're aware of having a special love of nature, but aren't sure beyond that. It might sound simplistic, but we can see and feel ourselves just being happy in nature. If we hold that feeling-image for a little while each day, other images will gradually emerge to join it. Our unified purpose will gradually emerge.

A fascinating aspect of visualization is that our images will evolve in such a way as to tell us things about our goals. Certain goals won't feel right when we try to picture them, and we'll know that they're not right for us. Other ones will slowly change as we picture them, thus helping us to become more aligned.

This process of the evolution of our images and goals is one of the most profound things that goes on in visualization, and is a primary element of the mystery that we can be both "creating" and "flowing with the river" at the same time.

To sum up, whatever states of mind we're trying to get from the result we begin with instead. We can begin to get accustomed to experiencing the states of mind that we want to end up with. We create, or rather discover, the actual seed that we want to grow and ripen, a seed that forms the core of our pictures.

Focus on Results

Focusing on results in our visualizing means placing attention on the outcomes we want, not on the means to get us there. The means are dealt with in our day-to-day planning and action. But in visualizing we focus on the actual outcomes we'd like. We can do this by picturing what we would like as if it has already happened. We pretend that it's occurring now; we feel it, see it and hear it that way.

To visualize being a botanist, for instance, we picture ourselves actually being that botanist already, working with plants each day. Though planning will later play a part, we don't have to figure out all the steps to that goal in advance. For one thing, we know that our visions can come about in surprising ways.

As another example, if we'd like to be a modern dancer we picture ourselves actually dancing in a dance performance, working with a dance company. We picture the performance, the applause; we're right there. We picture ourselves already being what we'd like to be.

The idea is to give the primal brain a clear target to go towards. Then the means are found or created along the way. Sometimes it occurs as if by accident, sometimes as a good idea, sometimes as a good plan. But by leaving the means out of our visualization, we allow the best means to emerge.

If we want a life-partner, for instance, we picture that outcome: What would it feel like to relate to a life-partner?

What sort of things would you say to each other, how would you communicate? How would you do things together, how show affection? That kind of relating, that flow of love is the real end-result that's wanted.

On the other hand, if we make the visualization about a specific other person, we limit the energy. We short-circuit the energy because we're trying to infringe on the freedom of another. If we insist that our partnership has to come through Jane or Tom, we're limiting the power of existence to bring it to us. Then we're saying it has to come only through this one door, this one means, and we cripple ourselves. Then countless other potential doors are closed to us.

Or if we focus on the means in a different way and imagine ourselves going to a dating service or answering ads in the Personals to meet someone, we're still not visualizing optimally. The end we really want is the close relationship itself, so that's the thing to visualize.

Visualizing the end-result also means visualizing what we'd really like. If we really want to be a computer engineer then that's the thing to imagine, even if it seems like we can't afford college, or we're too old, or too disabled or whatever—even if it seems quite impossible right now. Otherwise we aren't really giving ourselves a chance.

There are no guarantees in life, but many things that seem impossible have come true. Unless we allow something to take shape in our minds it's difficult for it to happen in external reality. Thus visualizing the end-result means giving ourselves permission to visualize our true preferences.

Those preferences may or may not come true. The river may flow some other way. But one way to ensure that our preferences don't come true is never to give them a chance. And the first step to giving them that chance is to really go for them in our imagination. More often than we might imagine, we'll find ourselves painting the painting that we thought we couldn't paint.

The other side of the coin is allowing our goals to be human. This doesn't mean avoiding difficult goals, but rather, avoiding superhuman ones. We could set goals, for example, of living forever or of being the richest person in the world. Such goals, by being unbalanced, lead us away from enjoying our humanity, from being fulfilled by the possible.

To satisfy our ego, we could visualize goals such as flying to Jupiter every night, or materializing objects out of thin air, or being a foot taller, but such goals would really be ways to avoid reaching goals that are achievable and human, that can mobilize our energies in fulfilling ways.

Nothing's impossible, but there are costs. If we set a goal to levitate, or to be the richest or most powerful person in the world, who's to say it's impossible? But at a minimum, it'll probably require an unremitting concentration upon this goal to the exclusion of much else in our life, to the exclusion of any balance. In that sense, a superhuman goal becomes a form of contraction.

And in the meantime, will it help this lifetime to be beautiful? Will it help us to better appreciate this beautiful sky, this beautiful moment, this beautiful person? Will it help us paint the paintings we could have painted? Will it increase our love and wisdom? By asking for the superhuman, our life runs the risk of becoming inhuman.

Our most worthwhile goals don't involve superhuman achievements, but rather the challenge of approaching goals that are human, life-affirming, doable.

Focus the Energy

$\mathscr{V}$ISUALIZING HAS A lot in common with a laser beam. A laser beam has power because the light waves are focused and congruent. Similarly, much of the power of visualizing derives from its *focus,* from the fact that the images are clear, congruent and vivid.

In making our images more focused, it's worthwhile to first look over our list of life-goals to make sure they're compatible with each other. If they don't seem to fit together, it's valuable to examine them and work with them until they do. The five clues discussed earlier can be helpful with this.

Another facet of being focused is to have a fairly brief visualization list. Elmer Wheeler once said this:

"Many men and women fail in life, not for lack of ability, or brains, or even courage, but simply because they have never organized their energies around a central goal."

To visualize effectively, we need to channel our energy. A small set of congruent goals that fit well together is going to have tremendously more power than a long laundry list of haphazard ones.

In other words, it's quite helpful to ask ourselves what's really important to us. If we expend energy on an extended list of things that we don't really feel passion for or that don't fit together, we may indeed be able to manifest some of them but we won't be tapping into the real power and potential that's available to us.

But whether our list is long or short, the main thing is just to come up with something. Though our visions will be much more powerful if our list is congruent, the list doesn't need to be final or perfect because—in association with our images—it will evolve. That's the beautiful part of it, that a kind of automatic process begins.

When I first started visualizing I had a very long list, like a long grocery list. As I visualized each day, it contracted for a while, then expanded again, then finally stabilized on a few things, which continued to evolve but at a more gradual pace. The evolution of our goals will often be like that—quite rapid at first, then slowing down and becoming more stable as we gradually come into alignment.

Though it's our visualization itself that really propels this process, nevertheless it's also worthwhile to periodically ponder and perhaps refashion the list of our goals. Both are helpful, since the sooner we can bring our list to a few focused and congruent things that really matter to us, the more likely our results will be.

In the actual process of visualizing, focusing the energy means allowing our images to be *vivid*. It means allowing them to be bold, bright, colorful, up close. It means letting sensory details really come into our picture, including other senses besides the visual.

Let's use a simple example, say an image of having a convertible. Then we might picture ourselves driving down the road in our car, hair blowing in the breeze, hearing songs on the radio, appreciating the colors of the car, listening to the

164

engine as it downshifts. We would experience this as clearly and colorfully and vividly as possible. As we bring in more sensory details, the image becomes more vivid and real and effective.

Suppose we want to be a professional cook. We might see ourselves working enjoyably in a kitchen that we like, hear the sounds of a stew simmering on the stove, enjoy the feel of our hands working with the pots and pans and a good chef's knife, admiring the dishes as they go out to customers.

If we want to be an architect, we might see ourselves drawing up blueprints, see ourselves inspecting buildings or bridges or whatever, hear the sounds of a construction site, imagine ourselves at some sort of opening ceremony for a building, feel now the gratification we'd feel then.

If a particular image isn't detailed or concrete yet, what we can do is be as vivid as possible and let the rest come as it comes. More details will come into the picture over time if we sharpen it by continuing to visualize it each day.

For example, if we want a house but we're not sure what kind yet, or where we'd like it, we can start by just picturing a kind of generic house, deliberately letting it be a little misty. As we continue to picture the house each day, details will gradually come into the picture by themselves—and it may turn into a much different house than we thought.

But even when we're deliberately letting certain details be vague, we can make the rest of the picture vivid. We may know that we want a back deck, say. And we can play with the image, changing the house to see what feels best.

In the terminology of neuro-linguistic programming, being vivid means tuning up our *sub-modalities,* that is, the hues of our different senses. In the modality of vision, for example, the sub-modalities include bright vs dim, clear vs fuzzy, color vs grayscale, close-up vs far away, 3-dimensional vs flat, and so on. In hearing, the sub-modalities can include volume, pitch, tone, etc. The sub-modalities of touch include hot vs cold, hard vs soft, smooth vs rough, etc.

What we do is allow each sub-modality to be whatever makes the picture real and compelling to us. Usually but not always, this will be a picture that is brighter, sharper, closer, in color, 3-dimensional; where the sounds are beautifully toned and pitched and easy to hear but not too loud; and where our sensations are beautifully textured.

But we're not all alike. For example, when hearing a voice in our picture some of us might prefer a loud voice and others a medium or soft voice; some a melodious tone, others a forceful tone. Most of us will prefer a picture that's bright, but some of us will prefer a more mysterious look. What's important is to adjust our sub-modalities so that, to us, our picture is real and compelling.

The idea is to make our images as close as possible to the way it would be if we were actually there, *if it were really happening right now.*

Be Positive

*T*HE FOURTH ELEMENT in effective visualizations is to be *positive*. This applies to describing our goals as well as to visualizing them.

In writing down the things we'll visualize, it's a simple but vital matter to phrase them positively. This is so because the primal brain has no way of comprehending the concept of negation. It simply doesn't know what that means. Thus it will take the thing that's being negated as the desired thing itself, tending to bring it about.

Suppose we describe one of our goals as, "I stop being overweight." What's the basic image that starts to come to mind? Instead, it's better to describe a related, positive goal, such as: "I am thin and healthy." Now an image more in line with our true intention starts forming.

Other examples: If we say, "I don't want to work at a desk job," a picture of a desk job starts to form. Instead we can say, "I have fulfilling work outside" or "I have fulfilling work with my hands." Instead of "I have a romance where we don't argue," we can put down "My partner and I communicate wonderfully and harmoniously with each other."

It would be helpful at this point to again briefly write down our life-theme at the top of a page, and under it our goals, leaving space between goals. Then under each goal we write a few images that relate to that goal. Again, it doesn't need to be perfect because it'll evolve.

For example, suppose we have a goal of being healthy and vital. Then under it we might write down descriptions of several pictures, for instance:

—Out for a walk and feeling wonderful;

—Complimented on being trim and vibrant;

—Having good energy at work.

Or suppose one of our goals is to be a concert pianist. We might write down, under that goal, images such as:

—Playing beautifully at a concert;

—Reading a favorable review;

—Recording in a studio.

Notice that each description is positive and also brief. There's value in keeping each description concise and letting the detail be in the visualization itself. Then instead of trying to put all the detail in the description, we can read a brief line or two and key into a vivid and detailed image.

The other aspect of using positive images comes during the actual visualization itself, and has to do with being very relaxed while we visualize. This will strongly influence our images to take on a positive tone.

If we visualize while we're feeling tense, our images will become associated with tension. This can convey to the primal brain that the result is to be brought about in a tense way, since tension feels like part of the picture.

The result achieved, in that case, might be a process of achieving our outcomes but in a harried, anxious way. This would work against the sense of grace and ease and alignment that is an important part of each goal.

Further, if tension becomes associated with our goal we'll be less playful about reaching it, and thus far less likely to do so.

Watching the breath, just watching it going in and out, is an extremely reliable source of tension-reduction, one included in countless different programs of relaxation. Indeed, in my experience there is no more effective way of deeply relaxing than watching the breath. Thus a few minutes of this before visualizing will pay big dividends.

Another way of doing this is to first have a session of mindfulness—calm witnessing in which watching the breath is naturally included—and then follow that with visualizing. In my opinion, this is an ideal way to do it, since it brings these two vital forms of inner work together in a one-two combination.

Finally, this principle also means feeling relaxed, easy, and positive about visualization itself. If we approach it each day as this difficult thing that we've got to do just right, we'll lower the effectiveness of what we're doing.

Perhaps the best attitude would be that of a scientist who's just experimenting to see what happens. We visualize best when we just relax and play with the energy, like a child playing with a ball on the seashore. "Nothing special," as the saying goes.

Be Personal

*M*OST OF OUR visualizations will start out in the impersonal or third-person mode; that is, we'll see ourselves in some situation as if watching it on a screen. We'll be watching ourselves as if we were "out there," as if we were an external figure. Over time, though, we'll find the image shifting to the first-person, *personal* mode, where we inhabit our body in the visualization.

Let's take the example of the convertible again. In an impersonal or third-person visualization, we'd watch ourselves drive down the road in our new convertible, we'd see ourselves enjoying it, watch our hair blow in the breeze, and so on. In a personal, first-person visualization, we'd *be there* in the car. We'd feel the breeze, see the scenery passing by. We'd feel the seats, feel the shifting gears, feel our satisfaction.

Can you sense the power of the difference? In the first person we experience more fully what it's really like to drive that convertible. Personal-mode visualizations—that is, body-inhabited ones—are capable of being much more immediate and compelling. The sensations and feelings of the experience become more vivid.

But third-person, impersonal visualizations are easier to start with. When we're first forming an image of something, it's sometimes difficult to inhabit our body in the image. Often it's easier to establish a scene by first seeing it from a distance, or as if it's on a screen. Then, as the image becomes more stable and clear, we can sharpen our focus by shifting the image to the personal mode.

The essence of visualizing is to experience a desirable end-result as if it were happening for real right now. Experiencing an image personally, in our body, is of course much truer to how we actually experience things.

Shifting from the impersonal mode to the personal one dramatically increases our feelings concerning an image. This occurs because our emotions are part of our kinesthetic sense. It's no accident that both emotions and bodily sensations are described as "feelings," or that a big part of every emotion is its kinesthetic sensation in the body.

This being so, our feelings will be experienced fully in an image only if we're inhabiting our body within it. Shifting to the personal or first-person mode in our images thus helps tremendously in experiencing the joyful and fulfilling states of mind that we want to associate with our images, that indeed form the core of our images.

Intensity of feeling—whether it's positive or negative—rivets the primal brain's attention. That's why early childhood traumas, which are so emotionally intense, implant powerful pictures in the primal mind. But, as discussed before, we can also use this fact to our benefit.

So if we're visualizing being a concert pianist, say, an important part of the picture is to imagine, while inhabiting our body, feeling fulfilled as we play for the audience. That state of mind, being part of what we want to end up with, is made a part of the picture that we start with.

The other meaning of being personal is *visualizing for ourselves only* and not for others.

All beings desire freedom. When we visualize somebody else acting in a certain way, we're actually attempting to deny freedom to that person. We're saying, in effect, that we're willing to use coercion upon them, that their freedom and goals don't matter. If we do this, we tend to cut ourselves off from the energies available to us.

Visualization works by mobilizing the energies of our organism, and through it, perhaps other and deeper energies. The most vital part of this process is an increasing alignment with existence, with the flow of the river. To attempt to compromise another's freedom is to immediately go out of the flow, and thus to become much less effective in bringing our creative images to life.

To use a previous example, if we want a life-partner we can picture that situation without involving a specific person. If we insist that it can only happen through *this* person, we're not only using force against them but restricting ourselves as well. We're saying, in effect, that existence cannot use any of the infinite doors available, but must use only this one that we're insisting upon.

Thus visualizing about someone else's behavior usually guarantees that our visualization won't be very effective. This is true even when thoughts are added such as "for their own good" or "for the highest good." It's still manipulation.

To take another example, suppose we want a certain outcome in our job. To visualize that our boss must behave in a certain way or must perform certain actions or treat us well, etc., will only tend to short-circuit our manifestation.

It's much more effective and beautiful to just visualize ourselves in the kind of work situation we'd really like, without involving specific other people. Then that result will tend to come about, either from our current job or another, either from this boss or another. We have not limited ourselves, or others either.

If we have an existing relationship that we'd like to be more caring and loving, we can visualize *ourselves* being more caring and loving. We can visualize ourselves being a more patient father, a more understanding mate, a kinder friend. The work is always on ourselves.

As we change the world changes.

If we're having a problem with someone, we can just imagine ourselves sending love to them. We don't imagine them being different—the antithesis of love—and we don't imagine them loving us, either of which infringes on their freedom.

Rather, we can send them love. We can feel compassion for them and for ourselves. We can heal ourselves. Then the situation is free to change if it wants to. When our own heart opens, the heart of the universe opens as well.

Stay Consistent

*T*HE LAST ELEMENT of visualization is *consistency*. Manifesting results from our internal images can be compared to focusing a camera. As an image becomes more focused, suddenly the shutter snaps and with some processing the picture shows up in external reality.

But not all of our images do show up. Indeed, there's a whole class of images that usually don't make it into physical reality—our daydreams. Why? What's the difference between a daydream and a visualization?

One major factor is *image-consistency*. Visualizations are consistent, although they can evolve. Daydreams are not. On Tuesday we might daydream that we're living in Rome; on Wednesday of being a carpenter in Oregon; on Thursday of being a film star. The real message that the primal brain gets from such inconsistent images is that we don't mean it. The message is that we don't really mean business.

When we visualize inconsistently, going from this image to that one, there's no real power. The pictures don't have a chance to get deeply implanted in the primal brain, and thus tend not to show up in physical reality. Or if they do show up, they tend to do so with a lot of struggle.

The second type of consistency is *time-consistency*. It's very helpful to take some time out each day, on a regular basis, to visualize our list. The important thing is not how much time we spend on it, but how consistent we are in doing it.

It's somewhat like brushing our teeth in the morning—yesterday's brushing doesn't substitute for today's.

If we visualize in a sporadic way, or frequently skip days, the real power of our focus may never germinate. Visualizing consistently and daily is how we let our subconscious know that we mean it, that this is for real, that we've decided to paint our painting.

Yet, too, once we've finished visualizing for the day, it's also wise to let go of it, to release it. There's no need to keep coming back to it before tomorrow. That would be a bit like brushing our teeth all day long; it would actually lower our effectiveness. We "set it and forget it" until the next day.

There's a time lag involved in conscious implantation of new images—usually a few weeks or so. We know that an image is implanted in the primal mind when we find ourselves almost automatically moving in that direction in our daily life. As Werner Erhard said,

"We do what works, and what we do works."

Though a traumatic incident can implant an image in us instantly, our conscious implantations don't normally have that degree of intensity and so take longer. Yet by making our visualization a normal and daily routine, we still help to make this time lag as short as possible.

While it's sometimes possible to manifest things almost immediately, it's not helpful to expect it to always be that way. Though there are many exceptions, a good guideline is that the larger and more general the goal the longer it may take to manifest.

It's important not to become discouraged if we don't see results right away. I've seen people's worthy goals sometimes take months or years to manifest. Thus a calm, steady, patient consistency is a great asset.

Consistency is also the thing that helps us improve our skill at visualizing. Like anything else, we become more adept at it the more we practice it. This is particularly true for those of us who feel that we can't visualize.

Actually, we can all do it. If we're asked to tell the color of our shoes right now without looking at them, we'll form a quick, fleeting image of them to give the answer. If we watch carefully, we can catch this image flashing through our mind. Though some of us are naturally better at it than others, we can all learn to visualize well.

If we have difficulty forming vivid images, we can just start with what we have. If we can't do color now, for instance, we can start with black-and-white. If we can't form pictures at all, we can start with feelings or sounds; the other senses will come in later by themselves. We can always do whatever we can do.

Continued practice of visualization will sooner or later bring vivid, multi-sensory pictures into view for anyone. We can all consciously create, inner to outer; we can all picture our lives as we would like them to be.

We are all visionaries. That is a birthright from nature for each of us.

BOOK **4**
Outer Mind
PRODUCTION

Book 4, Outer Mind, is about
the outer work of manifesting
our vision, our calling, and how
to bring that contribution into
existence in the world.

Water What You Want

*C*AN YOU IMAGINE preferring tomatoes in your garden but watering the weeds instead? Which plants will grow?

We might have a creative vision, but if we water other things each day they'll grow instead.

Creative visions need a different kind of water than the kind that sprinkles out of a can—they need the water of our *attention*. Whatever we give our attention to each day is sure to grow.

It is our continued attention or lack of it that causes various things in life to expand or diminish.

To take it further now, let's start by saying that the key word in the last sentence is the word "continued." It is our repeated and continued applications of attention—in a word, our commitment to something—that makes the difference in producing it, in bringing it to life.

What we repeatedly reinforce is what we get. So let's begin by looking further into the principle of *reinforcement:*

Positive Reward

REINFORCEMENT IS A very neutral principle; that is, it does not take sides. If it's applied, it works. It's up to us to use it wisely. In other words, it works just as well in a "negative" as in a "positive" way.

When we repeatedly give negative or critical attention to certain traits, situations, etc.—when we point out again and again or with great force how wrong or mistaken or bad they are—we're actually watering those things with our attention, and thus, paradoxically, helping just what we don't want to strengthen and grow.

Let's take an example. When I was young, one of the things that became important to my father at one point was turning off the lights when you left a room. And his approach was, whenever I didn't do it he'd point that out. Makes sense, doesn't it? You point out what's wrong to someone, and then it becomes right.

Well, it didn't work that way. For a while I did try to remember to do it. But I never got any reinforcement when I did it right, even after dozens and dozens of times. However, whenever I forgot—did it wrong—it would be immediately pointed out to me.

The consequence was that I never did learn to do it very well. I would constantly forget. And the reason was that since I was only being reinforced negatively, I lost all motivation to "do it right." Rapport was lost.

WATER WHAT YOU WANT

That's not an isolated example. The same sort of thing can be seen happening in countless homes and workplaces. Continual negative reinforcement brings negative results, and it becomes a vicious circle: When the negative results keep appearing, then even more negative reinforcement is applied, which brings even more negative results, and so on.

Conversely, when we reward positive things then we get more of *them*. And the primary way we reward something, of course, is with our attention. We literally create our reality with what we repeatedly and continually choose to notice. The plant that gets watered is the one that grows. To really understand this is to save much suffering in our world.

This principle is talked about by Michael LeBoeuf as the Greatest Management Principle, and he puts it this way:

"The things that get rewarded get done."

He tells the story of a sister in a parochial school who holds up a silver dollar and asks who can name the greatest man who ever lived. A little Jewish boy says, "Jesus was," and gets the dollar. The sister is somewhat surprised, and later approaches the boy and asks him if he really believed what he said about Jesus. "Of course not, sister," the little boy replies. "Everybody knows Moses was the greatest. (I love that line.) But business is business."

If we're ever puzzled by a behavior that seems illogical or unproductive or ridiculously persistent, in ourselves or in others, in families or business or wherever, we can ask what LeBoeuf calls the magic question:

"What's being rewarded?"

It is remarkable how asking this question can unravel things that otherwise seem quite mysterious, and more importantly, help us see how to intervene in a positive way.

I'll tell the following story because it illustrates that, if I can make a little progress in this area, anyone can. They say our pets reflect our personalities, and it's certainly been true for me. I got my first cat shortly after college, and it soon turned out to be highly neurotic, so much so that I had to give it away. And so did the next one, and the next one. I couldn't understand why I was getting so many neurotic cats!

Gradually I began to understand that, because of my own shortcomings, I was creating what I saw in these little animals. And as I gradually got a little bit less reactive and robotic and more understanding of my own role in creating things, my cats became less neurotic and more joyful.

My latest cat was a good test. He showed up at my door on Christmas Eve, 1990. He was very hungry, but also very untrusting, and would hiss and spit if you got anywhere near him. Whenever he did that I would ignore him, but when he showed the slightest sign of affection, no matter how minor, I would give him a little snack at once. And most important, I gave him lots of affection.

In a few months Nicky became just a delightful animal, very loving and self-confidant and himself. To put it another way, Nicky turned into the beautiful creature that he really was, that was naturally inside of him. And that's true of each of us. Our greatest challenge is to release into life the very beautiful creatures that we truly are.

To help in doing that, we can create a *kind climate* for ourselves. We can recognize and reward our strengths and beauties, and be tender with our shortcomings.

A useful image is to imagine pushing a swing. We wait until the swing comes back to us before we push it again. We ignore the swing when it's going the other way, against us; we wait until it comes back; then we push it. That is—

We push the swing in the direction it's already going.
We reinforce the positive and ignore the negative.

How does this apply to people? We apply it by being a *right-finder*. We notice and reinforce when people are doing things well or effectively, or they're making progress, or they're putting out a good effort at something that's important to them. In doing so, we help others have greater self-esteem. They become more motivated, competent and natural.

We create success, most fundamentally, by noticing it.

We see how it's already there, perhaps only in a small way right now. Then small successes breed larger ones.

In working with others, sometimes great patience is necessary. Sometimes we have to be mature enough to simply wait until we see a small success of some kind, or a step in a positive direction. Then we reinforce it.

Some of us are in positions of authority over others, such as parents or bosses, and then this principle is even more vital. William Van der Kloot, summarizing a mountain of behavioral research, puts it this way: "It's better to reward a child for cleaning his plate by giving dessert than it is to spank him for not eating the spinach."

With our attention, we're watering the plant that we do want instead of the one that we don't.

People are starved for positive reinforcement. Most people are never noticed for the hard work they do, for their attempts to better themselves, their attempts to do the right thing or to do a good job. Instead, most people get noticed only when they make a mistake or do something wrong.

We can change that. We can be the person who helps to build people up, who notices their small victories, who makes a big deal out of their successes, who encourages them. Often you may find that you're the only person in someone's life who is doing this. And sometimes, especially with young people, we can literally change the course of a person's life by what we choose to notice.

But isn't there a legitimate place then for correction, for pointing out what's wrong? Yes. After all, every teacher has to show his or her students when and how they're making mistakes. So when do we use correction, and how can we do so in a skillful way?

Practical Reward

$\mathcal{A}$ FASCINATING STUDY was done by psychologists with students of various ages. What they did was try different mixes of praise and criticism with the students, and then see what happened. And here's what they found: That the mix between praise and criticism needed to be at least 3 to 1. That is, the students had to be praised at least three-quarters of the time, and corrected no more than one-quarter of the time.

What happened when the amount of correction rose over 25% was that the students lost interest, lost motivation, and started doing very poorly. When the amount of praise stayed over 75%, however, students retained their self-esteem and their motivation and did well.

The implications of that are vast. Student or not, we human beings are all the same underneath. We all seek to be validated, in our work, in our being, in our actions, and to avoid being invalidated.

And we can do that for others. In all our relationships, we can use the principle of reinforcement by creating a basic climate of acceptance of the other. We can continually let them know that they're okay with us, even if occasionally we have to correct them. Sound basic? It is, yes. But oh, what a difference it makes.

The U.S. military intuitively follows this finding in their guidelines for correction. If you have to correct someone, they say, you first praise them, then you correct them, then you praise them again. Otherwise the person feels discouraged or you lose rapport with them, or both. From long experience they have found that correction must be used in a climate of acceptance.

It's futile to keep harping on the same undesirable act or trait, however, even if we're otherwise positive. If something continues to go wrong, then the thing to do is to ignore the problem directly, but find a related positive and focus on that instead.

Ken Keyes gives a simple example, which I adapt here: Suppose the cook is putting too much salt in the soup. We can certainly indicate a preference for less salt. At that point the cook will either respond positively—"I didn't realize it had too much salt"—or not. But if not, it's not productive to keep mentioning it against increasing resistance.

Vastly more effective, though requiring more patience and skillfulness, is to wait until the soup is a little bit less salty, —for whatever reason, maybe accidentally—and then praise the flavor with the reduced salt. "You know, the soup seemed less salty today, and it tasted really good."

Then we're reinforcing the positive. We are watering, with our attention, the plant that we do want instead of the one we don't.

Another factor of practical reinforcement is variability. As discussed in the fine work of Tony Robbins, psychologists have determined that reinforcement is far more effective if it is variable in time and amount and quality.

What do they mean?

Suppose tonight you give your wife roses, just to say you love her. She's surprised and delighted. Tomorrow night you give her roses again. She's surprised and delighted again—but just a little less so. The next night, and the next and the next, you give her roses again. What will happen? Because of the automatic habituation of our nervous systems, pretty soon she'll expect those roses every night and they'll have less and less effect. They'll no longer give the joy and thrill that they once did.

So let's say you decide to alternate your gift each night between roses and violets. The first night she gets violets she'll be surprised and pleased, but soon it will have the same effect. Her nervous system will have concluded that, "I get either roses or violets every night," and though it will still be a positive event it won't have the same impact it once did.

In other words, anything that becomes too predictable our nervous systems habituate to, and we no longer get the same feeling of reward from it. Worse, we'll come to expect it. And then if we don't get it we'll be mad or disappointed!

The way to avoid that is to vary things. Believe it or not, it's more effective to give roses on a random schedule than it is to give them every night. It's even more effective to vary the kind or number of flowers you give. And it's even more so to give flowers sometimes and other things other times. Don't underestimate the power of positive surprise!

This applies to every area imaginable. For example, at work a salary or wage is provided. It's a reward of course. But because it comes at the same time each week or month, and is the same amount or in the same range, it ceases to provide quite the same thrill that it once did.

That's why we see companies giving bonuses—it varies the financial reward. That's why we see award trips to Hawaii, perks, praise in the company newsletter, or whatever. These are examples of a varying positive reinforcement. In being a right-finder, in noticing the good in the world—and thus increasing it—we can use this principle of variability.

The final subject that needs to be addressed in terms of practical reinforcement is that rewards have much greater effect if they are given immediately. The longer we wait before reinforcing something, whether in ourselves or in others, the less effect it will have.

If somebody does a good job, our words of praise now mean much more than if we let a long delay occur. When we're trying to form a new habit, our immediate words of encouragement to ourselves when we get it right make those words much more effective.

When I was trying to form the habit of working on this book, for instance, I established two rewards right off the bat: I would drink my favorite beverage—chai with soy milk—and listen to certain types of music only when I was writing. Thus every time I sit down and write on this book I receive two rewards immediately, right while I'm in the process of it. Such seemingly little things can work incredibly well.

It's useful to use these aspects of positive reinforcement in the ways that we talk to ourselves. Say we make a mistake of some kind. If we berate ourselves, "God, that was stupid, how could I be so dumb?" we're creating the very climate of non-acceptance that will lower our self-esteem and actually make us less competent.

If on the other hand we say something like, "Well, I made a mistake here, but overall I'm pleased with my progress and I give myself credit for that," will it make a difference? Yes. We're creating for ourselves a climate of acceptance and positive regard that we'd like to get from others, and it helps greatly in whatever we're trying to do.

We've talked about the principle of reinforcement as it applies in general to every area of life. But now, let's apply it specifically to the subject of bringing our creative vision into being on a day-to-day basis.

Commitment is a name for the application of consistent reinforcement to our vision, and it's the engine that causes production to actually happen. It's appreciation of our vision on a practical and daily basis.

There are two fundamental elements of commitment— *planning* and *perseverence.*

Let's now turn to the first of those.

Golden Goose

To BEGIN OUR look into the subject of planning, let's now examine what Stephen Covey calls the balance between *production* and *production capability*. In explaining this great concept, Covey invokes Aesop's fable of the goose and the golden egg. Let's begin there:

One day a farmer finds that his goose has laid a golden egg. At first he's sceptical, but he takes the egg to market and finds that it really is gold, that he can sell it for a princely sum. The next day the same thing happens, and the next, and soon the farmer grows wealthy.

However, he also becomes greedy, and one day has an inspiration: Why not kill the goose and get all the golden eggs at once? He does so and loses everything. Not only are there no golden eggs inside, but most important, he loses the goose that produced them.

An interesting parable, because in the farmer's race to get production—golden eggs—he forgot about production capability, that is, the asset that was producing the golden eggs. We often do the same thing.

The temptation is to go straight for production, and to forget about the asset that makes production possible. This often seems to work in the short-term, but in the long-term it's disastrous. The producing asset gradually deteriorates, and over time becomes unable to generate the product on which we depend.

An example is the way in which we humans are using the resources of the planet, including water, air, soil, minerals, etc. We go about our business each day, doing whatever we do. That's production, the thing we're directly going for.

But in the process, we're too often neglecting the earth, the producing asset. Our air and water are becoming fouled, our soils and minerals depleted, greenhouse gases increasing. If this situation goes far enough, we could lose the precious asset that makes everything possible.

Another example might be the U.S. So far it's still the richest nation on earth, and we its citizens are blessed in many ways—and prodigiously conducting business. Meanwhile, the underlying asset is often forgotten. The educational system is in decline. Politicians are increasingly selling their influence. Almost a quarter of our national income is being drained off by high-tech medicine and the legal system. Debt levels are at all-time highs for individuals, businesses and government. If these trends persist, the nation will go bankrupt.

On a more personal level, if we neglect to change the oil in our car, for instance, it will eventually break down and need expensive repairs.

If two romantic partners each focus on getting selfish benefits they can become inconsiderate, take each other for granted, focus on their own needs, manipulate each other to get what they want, and so on. But in doing so, they ignore the asset, the relationship itself, that allows the other person to be loving and giving. Eventually the love, tenderness and spontaneity of the relationship break down.

This process of forgetting the asset occurs most often in failing to distinguish between *the urgent* and *the important.*

That is Stephen Covey's marvelous distinction, and let's see what the difference is between the two ideas:

The Important

CRISIS MANAGEMENT IS concerned with the urgent. Its emphasis is on the short-term, on immediate problem-solving. It's the ringing telephone, the mail that has to be answered, the financial crisis, tomorrow's deadline.

In contrast, the important is concerned with things that contribute to our long-term fulfillment, such as mindfulness, better nutrition, visualizing, planning, exercise, building our relationships and so on. Almost always these are things that don't need to be given attention right away. They can be put off until tomorrow or next month or next decade.

And the urgent seems so compelling. It acts upon us. It forces us to pay attention to it. But whatsoever we focus our attention on grows. The more attention we pay to the urgent, the more attention we need to pay to it. Then we're fighting with darkness instead of turning on a light.

We can get to the point where we're spending most of our time putting out fires, dealing with immediate crises. We can get beat up by them, like standing on a shore and being battered by an ocean wave and then standing up again only to be battered by the next, and the next...

Where the important is concerned, in contrast, we must act upon it. The important doesn't call attention to itself the way the urgent does. The important is not an urgent e-mail, not a deadline. Yet we only become truly effective by taking the initiative to pay attention to it.

An incalculable producing asset in our lives is ourselves, of course, and the things that can truly make a difference there can be neglected forever. There's never a deadline to become more spacious inside, or to learn to let go and appreciate the flow of the river. Existence will never force us to create our own internal vision, or to water what is truly important to us each day—existence respects our freedom.

Yet if we don't give some attention to how we're using our attention, we may wake up someday and say, "Where did my life go? What happened to me?"

We always have the option of putting our attention on the merry-go-round of crisis-management and staying busy, of running around to solve our troubles, of putting titillation over fulfillment. We can be selfish in our relationships, for instance, or eat any diet we choose and worry about the health problems later.

Perhaps nothing is intrinsically wrong in life, but there are costs. If we want to jump off a building it's not wrong, but there will be a cost for violating gravity's laws. Similarly, there can be a cost for violating life's principles.

Of course our immediate problems and crises do need to be taken care of. But this approach can easily perpetuate itself. Attending primarily to the urgent, the immediate, the distracting, to those things that call attention to themselves, can become self-justifying. They grow and grow, and then we feel that we have no time for anything else.

The antidote is to slowly and deliberately shift our attention to the important.

When we focus on the important, *it* expands and our crises slowly diminish. Of course, there are always challenges to handle. But instead of putting out fires all day, our life can begin to take on a balance and beauty, a softness in which we're effective rather than efficient, in which we're engaged in action rather than activity.

Balance is key. If we neglect the important long enough we'll either become ineffective, or make great progress but in a direction that's not right for us. On the other hand, if we focus exclusively on the important and don't engage the urgent at all, then we're ignoring present-time reality and thus being ineffective that way.

It's the balance between the two—taking care of the urgent but emphasizing the important—that's really effective, that really allows us to paint our painting well.

The Primary

WE ATTEND TO the important through *prioritizing*, through establishing what is primary and carrying it out on a daily basis. What this often means in practice is scheduling the important things first each day, so that they get first call on our time, energy and attention.

A great story is told about Charles Schwab, the 19th-century steel magnate. He was once approached by a man who told him he could dramatically increase his effectiveness. He asked the industrialist to try out his idea and then send him a check for whatever it was worth.

The man asked Schwab to do just one thing: To make a daily list of the six most important things he needed to do that day, prioritize them, and then start at the top of the list and work down, paying little or no attention to anything else. After trying it for awhile Schwab sent the man $25,000—equivalent to perhaps half a million today. That's how valuable he found that one idea.

A person named E. M. Gray made a life study of the common denominator of success. His purpose in this was to discover if there is some common factor that all or almost all successful people share. He found that indeed there is, though it wasn't what he expected.

Curiously, this common denominator was neither hard work nor good human relations, though they are important. The one thing that was indispensible and invariably present was the habit of putting the primary things first. Successful people always did what most needed to be done, even when it wasn't easy.

It's often valuable to put special focus for awhile on one project that's considered particularly important in fulfilling our life-theme. In existential literature this is called *the project*. The project may not get the most attention each day, but it gets first and primary attention. Our other goals and projects get attention too, but secondary to the primary one. This focusing of attention has tremendous power.

We've all heard about people performing extraordinary feats in emergencies, of such things as suddenly picking up the front end of a car to save a loved one. How can people sometimes perform seeming miracles when disaster strikes? Perhaps because for that moment in time they concentrate all their energy on one thing only. Other things are put aside for the moment.

One time in the early 70's I was holding down a full-time job at an insurance company and also trying to write a novel after work at night and on weekends. I would come home exhausted from work each night and be unable to work on the novel, and on the weekends I wanted to play. So I was making no progress and getting depressed about the situation.

The solution was to do something that seemed radical at the time. I got up at 3 o'clock each morning and gave the novel first and primary attention for three hours. After about six months of this, once I got some momentum going, other solutions presented themselves.

The method most able to help us identify a primary project is the same thing that helps us identify a life-theme—remembrance of death. When we really imagine having just six months to live, things often come into perspective very quickly. The most important thing can emerge. So let's ask ourselves a variation of that six-month question:

If we only had six months to live, only had time to accomplish one more thing—what would that one thing be? The assumption is made that we'd still continue to work; that instead of vacationing or partying for six months we'd put our energy towards one last project. What would it be?

This is the thing that perhaps we've been putting off in one way or another all our lives. Perhaps we've been caught in "the thick of thin things," but now is our chance. Imagine that we have one more chance to make a contribution, one more chance to express ourselves in the truest, most useful way. What would we do?

In January of 1990 I had been researching this book for some time, but felt I wouldn't actually be writing it for at least a year or so. I needed money, and so prepared to work instead on a theoretical book about financial markets.

But the evening I was about to begin on the market book, I asked myself the six-month question above. Suddenly I immediately started writing on this book instead. Though it's turned into a more arduous project than I could ever have imagined, I'm glad I did, because it's also moved me into an alignment that I wouldn't have thought possible. The question above has the power to help us do that.

Once the project is identified it's then given the highest priority each day, for as much time as is appropriate. Work on other things is handled in a context of giving priority to that. Perhaps we schedule it first, or at the most effective time each day. We give it the top priority even if we can only spare ten minutes on it.

Even just ten minutes daily on something that really matters to us can make a tremendous difference over time.

When we create a primary project directly related to our life-theme, it's as if we've concentrated our energy into one large boat, which then creates a large wake. It pulls many things towards it, attracts many energies of various kinds to lend support in the chosen direction. Instead of many small boats with different wakes, and perhaps different directions, there's one boat, one direction, one large wake with many different wavelets in it.

Then our other projects, and other matters that need attention, become part of that large wake. Taking care of these other, smaller projects actually becomes a source of support for the larger one. And the major project, in turn, becomes a source of support for the smaller ones.

It can all begin working together.

The Everyday

$\mathscr{F}$OCUSING ON THE important, and a primary project, is vital to begin to translate our creative vision into a practical, everyday affair. The willingness to get into the nitty-gritty of our dreams, into the day-by-dayness of them, is as important as the willingness to dream.

In our modern society the idea of the quick-fix seems to have taken hold. We've been conditioned by our culture to want instant solutions, instant shortcuts. If we have a medical problem we swallow a pill or take a shot; if we're bored we turn on the TV; if we want enlightenment it's available in a weekend seminar.

Our movies often reflect this view as well. Day-by-day effort seems to play little part. In most film biographies the hero or heroine seems to have an inspiration at some point, after which the goal is soon achieved.

It can be tempting to think that a large or worthy goal can be achieved simply by coming up with some masterstroke. And indeed, sometimes it does work that way. Sometimes we can manifest things with great rapidity and ease.

But most of the time it's not the sudden swift action, the great act, or the glamorous masterstroke that brings us to the goal. Rather, it's holding to our vision through the patient, committed, daily application of effort. Our vision comes true from making a renewed commitment, day-by-day, to do what needs to be done that day.

Not that great or inspired acts aren't helpful when they occur; they are. But they can't be relied upon to occur, and usually they're not enough. It's the ordinary, "nothing special" process each day that helps our vision grow into reality.

Imagine a farmer. The farmer will plant in the spring, cultivate in the summer, harvest in the fall. Is there some way to shortcut this process? Can he forget to plant in the spring, go fishing in the summer, and then, by some stroke of brilliant vision, harvest in the fall?

No. There's a process to go through; and it takes time and daily effort. The farmer cannot "quick-fix" this process. He may sow with mechanical planters, but he can't neglect to sow. He may water with automatic irrigation, but he can't neglect to water. He may hire others to help him, but he still has the responsibility. To be a farmer he must ensure, one way or another, that his plants get what they need each day.

He reaps what he sows.

As the farmer knows, that day-to-day process is usually not glamorous. In our own day-to-day process, often there will be very little that's romantic about it. Many days we won't feel like doing it, or we'll be assailed by doubts and difficulties. Right there is where our commitment comes in.

The film *Brother Sun, Sister Moon* differs from most film biographies in that it shows a process. Francis of Assissi, at a certain point in life, had a vision. He wanted to try something new, a new way of living. To begin, he gave away his possessions and renounced his inheritance. But then what? How to express his vision into the world?

What he does at this crucial point in the film is what he actually did in real life. He undertook a small primary project to begin on his vision. He translated his vision into the very down-to-earth process of rebuilding a little rundown church outside of town. As he labored each day to rebuild this church, his vision slowly began to come to life.

At this point in the film Francis is feeling very aligned, very in-harmony for the first time. Inside he's feeling very flowing, effortless, free. But he's expressing it on the outside with patient, steady, hard work, stone by stone.

In other words, he's found a way to begin to express his vision in a day-by-day way. In the film, a song now expresses very beautifully the process of this future saint—and of each of us as well. The gist of it is this:

If we want our dream to be, build it slowly, each day. Work heartfully. Great things come from small beginnings.

Goals

*I*N PUTTING PRIMARY things first each day, it's quite valuable to have some sort of plan. Planning is something that we all do, but sometimes we just do it in our heads. The real question is whether to write our plan down and give it some structure. In my experience, it helps tremendously to do so.

We sometimes avoid written planning because we feel that it means locking ourselves in and losing flexibility. This concern is legitimate, but it usually arises from having the wrong kind of plan—one that's rigid and over-scheduled. What usually happens is that such a plan is finally abandoned in frustration.

Sometimes we concentrate on tight schedules and the day's To-Do list. The danger of such daily planning is that it has an automatic tendency to focus upon the urgent, upon simply meeting today's appointments and problems. It's easy to lose perspective that way.

More effective is to use a weekly plan. Planning by the week affords us more perspective, allows us to schedule our time with greater flexibility, and helps us plan with an eye on fulfilling our long-term goals. In that sense it's planning from inner to outer.

Weekly planning also has another advantage, in that many of us already take a couple of days off each weekend to recharge in some way. This affords a natural time to plan for the coming week.

It's been said that management is effectively walking upon a path, while leadership is choosing the right path to walk upon. A weekly planning session serves both functions. We're exercising leadership by reviewing our *goals,* and also exercising good management by seeing how we can best implement those goals this week.

Thus it's valuable to set aside a little time each week, perhaps an hour or two on the weekend, to have a planning session. Let's imagine we're at one now:

The first thing is to review our life-theme (chapter 3). We start with a clean sheet or computer screen, and rewrite it. The purpose of rewriting it is to give us the opportunity to take a fresh look. Perhaps a clearer wording will emerge, or perhaps the theme has evolved in some way.

The next thing is to review the list of goals under our life-theme, and rewrite those as well. Ideally, the list will be just a handful. Again, the idea is to look anew and try to ensure that our list of goals is as clear and congruent as we can make it.

We can make use of an interesting phenomenon in doing this. As we visualized during the week, our pictures may have evolved somewhat. Indeed, if we began visualizing fairly recently, the evolution during the preceding week may have been quite dramatic. If we've been visualizing a long time, on the other hand, our pictures may have stabilized for a while.

Whichever it is, by rewriting our list of goals we have the opportunity to record any evolution in our pictures that may have occurred in the last week. And again, it allows us to take another conscious look. We're a bit different from who we were last week—we've learned some things, experienced some things. Are these goals still the right ones for us?

In fact, when I began to experiment with visualizing I rewrote my list of goals daily at first—that's how fast the whole thing was evolving.

This conscious re-thinking and rewriting of our goals is very beneficial. Even though the list may look about the same as last week's, subtle changes in emphasis may occur. Even if there are no changes at all, we've reconfirmed that these are the right goals for us.

Projects

$\mathcal{N}$ow it's time, in our planning session, to create one or more *projects* for our goals. To do that, let's examine what a project is and how it differs from a goal.

A goal, one aligned with our life-theme, is similar to a role that we choose. For example, let's say one of our goals is to be a good mother. In essence, that's a role we want to play. It's something we want to be.

A project, on the other hand, is a measurable milestone which occurs as part of that goal. It's a physical occurrence. If our goal is being a good mother, our project right now might be bearing a healthy baby in March. If one of our goals is being an entrepreneur, our current project might be finishing business school or raising a certain sum of money.

Other examples: If our goal is to be a veterinarian, a current project might be to open our own clinic. If our goal is being a biologist, our current project might be getting an A in Biology 101 or it might be discovering how RNA polymerase works. If our goal is to live a nurturing lifestyle, our current project might be to move to a new location by summer.

A goal can sometimes last a lifetime, such as "being and feeling healthy and vital." Or it might last a good part of a lifetime, such as "being a good mother." It's a life role that doesn't necessarily have an ending. We might decide a goal is unsuitable for us now and exchange it for another, but while we have the goal it can go on and on.

A project, in contrast, always has an end point by which we know that it's over. "I got into that college." "I learned how to do a flip turn in the pool." "I opened a new store." Indeed, the clearest sign of a project is the end point by which we know that it's done.

However, it's not always true that every project can be given a deadline. Einstein, for example, in the early years of this century gave himself a project of working out the special theory of relativity. Yet he couldn't give it a deadline because he couldn't predict when or if he might be able to discover it. Though it couldn't have a deadline it was a great project, and came to an end upon publication in 1905.

Sometimes a project will have a natural deadline, such as the date for submission of a holiday ad campaign, or the opening night of a play. When it doesn't, should we assign our own deadline?

One guideline is that if we can clearly see the steps to completion of a project, then a deadline is helpful. But if we're not clear on how it's going to be accomplished, a deadline may be a hindrance. Then we want the situation to be more fluid and open, so we're not trying to push the river.

In our planning session, once we've finished reviewing our goals then we can assign a current project to each one. And, as with our life-theme and goals, it's helpful to rewrite our project under each goal so that we can take another look. A goal may have changed, for instance, or a project may have ended last week, or we may want to change the emphasis in a project.

If we feel unclear about distilling a goal into a current project, it's often helpful to ask ourselves about what Barbara Sher calls the *touchstone* of our goal. That is to say, what is the emotional core of it? What do we hope to get from it? What is the point of our goal?

If we want to be an actress, for instance, our touchstone might be a longing for glamour or it might be a desire to move an audience through good acting. The different touchstones would probably lead to different projects.

A good final test for any project is to ask:

If I could have it right now, would I take it?

Imagine being already engaged in it—would you truly want it? Using this test can help us identify projects that are appropriate, aligned, and in harmony with our purpose and goals. And as always, it doesn't matter too much what we start with. The very act of starting on a project will tend to clarify for us whether it's an appropriate project right now.

At this point in our planning session we now have a rewritten life-theme, a related handful of goals, and a current project for each goal. And from our projects one is designated as the *primary project*, the one given first priority each day, even if it's only for a few minutes at first.

That primary project may not be foremost in terms of time, but it's primary in terms of the importance we give to it. Giving it that importance helps to ensure that we water the plant that we really want to grow each day.

Pictures

$\mathcal{A}$LL WE NEED do now is add a one-line description of one or two *pictures* for each goal and project to have an updated visualization list for the coming week.

Let's take an example: Say we have a goal of being healthy and vital, and that our current project for this goal is to become a vegetarian. Then that part of our visualization list might look like this:

Goal: Being healthy and vital
Image—Taking a walk, feeling wonderful
Project: Becoming a vegetarian
Image—Enjoying great vegetarian meals
Image—Enjoying vegetarian potluck

The images or pictures above are just a sample; others could have served as well. What matters is that the pictures feel right, and help to bring the goal or project to life in our imagination. Indeed, it's sometimes good to experiment a bit with different images to see which ones feel best.

Descriptions of the images, as with goals and projects, are good when they're simple. Rather than trying to describe all the details of each picture on paper, it's best to let a few words stand for, and key in, a detailed image in our mind.

Note too that the pictures don't include a deadline. In my experience it's best not to have a deadline in the images themselves. If for any reason the deadline is not met, there's a tendency to conclude that visualization isn't working and to lose confidence in it or abandon it.

It's usually better to work with deadlines, when we do, in our everyday working on the project. In other words, we plan and work with deadlines when that's appropriate, but visualize without them. That way, if the deadline passes and we haven't brought the project completely into being, we can continue visualizing it just as before.

Even if we have a second project for a particular goal, it's usually wise to keep the total number of projects for all of our goals to about half a dozen. This simple list—a primary project along with a few congruent secondary projects—helps us concentrate our energy and yet keep some balance in the different dimensions of our life.

Of all the actions we take each day, probably the most important are the inner ones that don't look active at all. Meditation and visualizing, in particular, have a tremendous influence on both our inner mind-states and our effectiveness in the world. Here's where we really water the roots that are the base of our life-plant.

For this reason it's very valuable to convert these two inner practices to a daily and habitual routine, like breakfast or brushing our teeth.

As with anything else, in doing so we have the option of trying to use willpower to get ourselves to do something we feel is desirable. But there's a better way—we can put them at the top of our visualization list.

In other words, we can make our first visualization each day be to picture ourselves sitting mindfully and visualizing each day. You may find that these particular visualizations are more easily done in a third-person or impersonal mode, as if you're seeing yourself on a screen.

Meditation and visualizing make an ideal combination; they go wonderfully together. And first thing in the morning is a good time for the combination. An excellent practice, especially if one has to go to work, is to do the combination in the morning for a few minutes each, and then sit mindfully for a longer period at night.

However, that's just an example. Whatever pattern we'd prefer to have, we simply make following that pattern our first visualization each day.

As we continue to visualize this top item each day, we'll find that we don't need to struggle or exert willpower to get ourselves to meditate or visualize. Both will begin to happen spontaneously and naturally, almost as if by themselves. We'll just find ourselves easily doing them.

Items

$\mathscr{T}$HE LAST PART of a planning session is to select an *item* or two for each of our projects. What's an item? It's that part of a project that we'll probably complete within the next week or two.

For instance, let's say we're in high school and have a goal of being an automotive designer. Our current project for that goal might be to get into design school, and we have a nice image of enjoying the school. Our items for that project right now might be researching what schools to apply to, and finishing a drawing for a design. Notice the latter:

We begin doing now some form of what we want to do.

If we do this for several projects, we might end up with five or ten items or so to be scheduled for the coming week. Though the items are short-term, they come from long-term goals, from what's important to us. Yet they're things we can do right now, this week.

Hopefully, some of our items will be about production capability—preventive maintenance, working on relationships and so on.

A typical entry might look like this:

Project: New cover design.
    Item—Learn new page layout feature.
    Item—Ask Sally about text changes.
    Item—Create new layout.

Our list of items is then used to make date/time entries on our calendar or computer for the next week. On a weekly schedule, we simply make appointments for each of our items. Each item is assigned a block of time during the week, such as 2 to 5 pm on Friday, or half an hour on weekday mornings or whatever.

It's important not to over-schedule our time. On the contrary, it's valuable to give ourselves free blocks of time at various points. Since we're not omniscient, unexpected things can and will arise; and when they do we want to be able to easily deal with them, to be flexible. A further reason for not scheduling ourselves too heavily is so that we can stay relaxed, our most productive state. A frantic, driven, or inflexible state of mind isn't usually the most creative or productive.

Somebody who needs our help may interrupt with a problem, for instance, and if it's appropriate we may need to be able to subordinate our schedule to a higher priority. Or an item might take longer than we think, or an unexpected event might happen. What we want, in Stephen Covey's memorable phrase, is a schedule flexible enough so we can focus on *results* and *people* rather than adherance to a rigid efficiency.

Also, when we schedule ourselves too heavily or rigidly, it's easy to become frustrated and just discard the schedule altogether, thus reverting back to a focus on the urgent, to the immediate fires and problems that compel our attention.

When we schedule ourselves well, though, we have a valuable tool. Then each item that we do means measurable progress towards our most important goals.

As mentioned before, there are two main elements in a commitment to our vision.

The first is planning, as a tool for helping us to remain focused on what's important and primary. That's what we've been looking at for the last few sections.

The second is perseverance, that is, continuing to carry out our plan.

Let's turn now to this second element—perseverance, or the actual walking on our path each day.

Staying Inspired

$\mathcal{B}$Y THE VERY nature of it, in walking upon our path each day we'll encounter obstacles, fears, doubts, and so forth. Perseverance is about including these things and continuing to take action anyway. The first step in this is small but vital— to stay inspired.

It needn't be a big deal. It just involves surrounding ourselves with reminders of what's true and important to us. To do that, we can bring together photos, drawings, notes and other things which represent our life-theme, goals or projects. This is sometimes called a *dreamboard* or a *treasure map,* and can act as a powerful support and reinforcement for us.

Part of our dreamboard can be sayings or ideas that we would like to be reminded of. They might be quotations from others, or fragments of lyrics that speak to us. They might be sayings of our own that sum up things we've learned. They can be a description of something we'd like to be. They can be anything at all that speaks to our spirit.

Photos of role models can be especially helpful on our dreamboard. As we go about our daily life, it's inspiring to be reminded that certain people have successfully walked a path similar to the one we'd like to walk on.

We might have role models for different dimensions. For instance, we might have a particular master as a spiritual model, a scientist as a livelihood model, our grandmother as a relationship model, and so on. Or there may simply be people, past or present, who have certain qualities we admire and would like to nurture in ourselves.

We can ask: Who are our role models? Whom would we most like to emulate? Is it one person, or do several people represent us best? What about them attracts us? What do their lives represent to us? Looking at such questions can help us become more clear about our own path.

Our dreamboard can be on a corkboard or a flat screen hanging on the wall perhaps. It can include pictures, notes, drawings, diagrams, affirmations and so on—anything that relates to our life-theme, goals and projects.

A dreamboard such as this can be very helpful because it serves as a continual reminder during the day, sometimes subconsiously, of the things that are important to us.

The idea is to have different facets of our life all pulling in the same direction—our goals, visualizations, role models, rewards, and so on. Cumulatively, these create a tremendous power and momentum drawing us towards expression of our truest self.

But a question: If we're really following our passion, why should aids such as dreamboards be necessary? If we're truly aligned, aren't things supposed to flow and almost seem to happen by themselves?

A different way of putting that question is this: How do we know the difference between persevering and fighting the river? Is there a time to give up? And if so, how do we know when that time has arrived?

Staying Aligned

*I*N ORDER TO look at that question, my experience with this book might be helpful. Though the inspiration for it was grand, though it feels very aligned, though a good picture of the end-result exists, still there's the writing every day.

And though there are moments of inspiration, most of the time the process is very mundane—stop-and-go, inch-by-inch. Some days it feels too difficult, as if I've bitten off more than I can chew. Other days there are external obstacles of one sort or another.

In other words, we can be feeling very aligned and still experience numerous difficulties. So the presence of difficulty, in itself, is not necessarily a sign that we're pursuing the wrong course. What is it then? Where is the line drawn between commitment and pig-headedness? How do we know when to persevere and when not to?

Let's take another example: Ross Perot, the well-known billionaire, founded his computer company on a thousand dollars and then set out to get his first service contract. Was his service snapped up? Not exactly. As I understand it, he got turned down by the first 80 companies to which he proposed his service.

Now he certainly could have felt justified if after the first 50 tries—or the first 35, or the first 20—he'd said to himself, "I guess I'm just not cut out for this." But he didn't. On the other hand, suppose he'd still been getting turned down at the 100th company? Or the 200th? How do we know when to keep going and when to quit?

The key is in whether we continue to feel really aligned with this goal or not. It's an internal sense of feeling called to what we're doing, a sense that we're on the right path even if it seems impractical or unrealistic.

But being aligned doesn't mean that we never have to retreat. Sometimes we do have to take a couple of steps back in order to take three forward later. We might have to drop our primary project back to an hour a day, or even just a few minutes. But if it's truly the right one, these are seen as just temporary setbacks.

On some level, we cannot be defeated unless we say we are. If we're following our right livelihood, fulfillment doesn't come when some end-result is achieved. On the contrary, fulfillment occurs every day just from the attempt to follow our deepest light. In that sense, we cannot fail.

When the goal is right the very process of attempting it feels right, necessary, beautiful. It's precisely that deep-down feeling of alignment that allows us to keep going through the details of the process even when they're mundane, stressful or tremendously challenging.

However, it's quite possible for something to be aligned at first and out of alignment later on. The goal or project that was right last year or last month may not necessarily be the right one now.

That's why it's extremely desirable to keep listening. What matters is not the degree of difficulty, but rather the degree of alignment felt internally. When we're still aligned there's a sense of things fitting together, no matter what may be happening externally.

And in some mysterious way existence does seem to support us when we're aligned—or at least it feels that way, even in the face of difficulties. We feel like we're blossoming and going in the right direction, even when the challenges are enormous.

When we're aligned, we feel more alive in doing what we do, even if it's difficult. That aliveness is the acid test. For many of us who feel chronically low in energy, the problem may not be physical. It may be because our aliveness is slowly dying by pursuing some goal, such as just making money, that perhaps is not our true calling.

If we're feeling that way, it may be time to quiet down and listen once again to our silent stillness inside, our inner guide which seems in some mysterious way to know so much more than our rational mind does. Otherwise, without such continuing alignment, our attempts at commitment feel like using willpower on ourselves. Then one part of us is trying to force or dominate another part; we're divided.

Conversely, when we become aligned again a sublime persevering energy surges up in us. It feels as if we've tapped into a much larger supply of energy, which in fact we have, though it doesn't always come in the form that we expect. Because now our love for what we're doing is released. It's this love which ultimately enables us to move through whatever difficulties and details are encountered.

Staying aligned also means a letting-go of the outcome, a trust in existence. When we can do that, it just feels like we're following the path of least resistance.

Sometimes old goals and projects do fall away. But at other times, that continuing let-go and trust in existence can appear outwardly to others as something else—paradoxically, as a strong perseverance.

Welcoming Failures

*W*HAT IF, WHEN we consider really doing what we love, we feel fear? Suppose we lack self-confidence? Suppose we're afraid of failing—what then? What can we do about the fear of failure?

Let's rephrase that question:

How can we get self-confidence?

Fortunately, it's not a mysterious force that we either magically have or don't have. On the contrary, it's a prosaic, practical kind of thing, and fortunately, having it does not depend upon being raised in the right family or getting ten years of therapy. Where does self-confidence essentially come from then?

It comes from the willingness to confront failure.

Do we feel self-confident about tying our shoelaces? Of course, we've done it thousands of times; that's why we feel self-confident about it. But can we remember the very first time we tried to tie our shoes? The sense of uncertainty, the nervousness? And we probably didn't make it on the first try or the second or even the tenth.

Suppose we'd said after the first attempt, "Well, I don't have enough self-confidence, I better give up trying to tie my shoes." It would have been a self-fulfilling prophecy. But we didn't give up. We kept going and learned to tie our shoes, so much so that we don't even think of it in terms of self-confidence.

Yet our willingness to face repeated failure in tying our shoes was the basis of our current self-confidence about it.

What about walking? We don't think of walking in terms of self-confidence either; we just do it. We feel quite confident about walking. Yet there was a time when we failed again and again in walking.

Watch children first learning to walk. They get up, fall down, get up, fall down. Take a step forward, fall down; another step, fall down again. They fall down hundreds of times in the process of learning to walk. Now suppose they thought each time, "I'm a failure, I can't do this, I give up"? None of us would ever walk.

The interesting part in all this is that each failure, each mistake, gets the child closer to the end-goal of walking. Far from being sidetracks or obstacles, each "failure" is a necessary part of reaching the goal.

The important point about "failure" is to learn from it and keep going. It only really becomes failure if we give up. Which is why it's not always a good idea to change our goal when we're feeling down, discouraged or scared.

Once we're over the low point or the rough spot we can examine our goal to see if it's really what we want. But if we give up when we're feeling uncertain or down, we'll never reach our dreams. Because there will always be such times on the way to any goal.

There's a great true story about Jack Kennedy when he was running for President. It was very early in the campaign, and he flew out one morning to a mid-western state where he was met at the airport by an old friend who'd recently been appointed campaign chairman for the state.

As they drove towards the first rally Kennedy's friend turned to him and said, "Jack, there's something I need to tell you. I have a confession to make."

"What's that?"

"Well, to tell you the truth, I really don't have any idea how to be campaign chairman for this state."

And Jack said, "I know how you feel. I really don't have any idea how to run for President, either."

Then he added: "But hell, let's do it anyway."

Stories are legion of people who have kept going in the face of failure, uncertainty and difficulties. Edison failed almost ten thousand times before successfully inventing the incandescent light bulb. Hershey created his famous chocolate company on the seventh try—he had gone bankrupt on the first six.

Abraham Lincoln certainly knew about failure and the criticism that can come with it. During his term of office he was constantly derided in the press as a monkey, a buffoon, a stupid gorilla—our greatest president!

Beset by unending problems in the Civil War, Lincoln simply kept faith by doing the best that he knew how to do. He said, "I do the very best I know how...and I mean to keep on doing so until the end. If the end brings me out all right, then what is said about me won't matter. And if it brings me out wrong, ten angels swearing I was right will make no difference."

I don't know about you, but that quote sends chills up my spine. Such a great soul.

Let's do what Abraham Lincoln did:

Let's get up every morning, do the very best we know how to do, water whatever we feel is right and beautiful, and then let the outcome be determined by existence.

Imperfection

NEXT TO THE fear of complete failure, our biggest fear is probably that we won't be able to do it right. That we'll finish it, but it won't be good enough.

Is there an antidote to our fear of inadequacy? Yes.

The antidote is to welcome imperfection.

How? One good way, as Barbara Sher recommends, is to lower our standards temporarily. Doing that is like a secret key that we can use whenever it seems that we won't be able to persevere. It allows us to keep going by taking the pressure off. Higher standards can always be reconsidered later.

We can lower our standards in either of two ways—by reducing our expectations about quantity or quality. Suppose we have to finish a thesis or project to get our degree, but we're afraid of it. Instead of working on it six hours a day, we can plan three hours working on it, or two, or one. Instead of four pages a day we can set an objective of one or two pages—whatever it takes to get started, or restarted. These are ways of reducing quantity.

We can also tell ourselves that the writing doesn't need to be good right now, that's it's just a preliminary draft or a trial run. I use it all the time. Whenever I run across an extra-hard part I remind myself that it doesn't need to be all that good right now. And if I get really bogged down, sometimes I'll just skip a particular section altogether and resolve to come back to it some other time.

Do we feel we're on the right track but not doing good enough? Let's lower our standards temporarily. If we're trying to raise $20,000 for the festival and it's not happening, let's lower the item temporarily to $5,000, or $1,000, or $100—whatever it takes to get a success or two.

Because that one success, no matter how little, leads to the next, and that one leads to the next, and so on. The idea is to create small successes and then build on them. Instead of focusing on what we can't do, we focus on what we *can* do right now—and let it grow. It's a form of watering the plant we want.

Actors and actresses use this a great deal. They don't expect to give a riveting performance on the very first read-through. On the contrary, they expect their performance to be perfunctory at first. They expect that, they build it in. They allow for mistakes.

Similarly, we can avoid letting perfectionism stop us by deliberately allowing for mistakes and imperfection. Mistakes are honorable because they mean that we're moving out of our comfort zone. They mean that we're trying something new, or going towards the limits of what we can do right now.

We can actually make it a goal to do something badly if necessary. We can make it our goal to make ten bad phone calls today, or make a bad drawing. We just do whatever small, manageable steps we can do. When we do that, we're like the small child learning to walk for the first time. Our eventual success is actually founded on our imperfections, mistakes and failures—and our perseverance in the face of them.

Our sense of imperfection can come in many forms. We may feel that we're not good enough. We may feel we don't deserve a particular goal. We may feel that it's just hopeless to pursue it. Or we may marshal our arguments: "I can't do it because I'm (take your pick) too young, too old, too tall, too short, too poor, too educated, too ignorant..." and so on.

As with affirmations (discussed in chapter 5), all such thoughts can be called *secondaries,* that is, secondary things that are at cross-purposes to the primary thing. A secondary is anything that comes up as an internal obstacle when we focus on a goal or project (or affirmation).

The thing to do with secondaries is to accept them, let them be there, but see them also as just thoughts—and then get on with it. "Okay, I'm too young to do this, and I'm going to do it anyway." Or "I'm supposed to be too uneducated and poor to do this, but so what, I'll just do it anyway."

We can create a positive climate of acceptance of our goals by the way that we talk about them. "I may seem too young to do this, but I can do it," or "I can follow my dream," or "I can bring my true nature to life."

Any energy spent on resisting or suppressing secondary thoughts and feelings just gives them more energy. Instead we can redirect our energy on what we *do* want to do—and then go do it. We're watering what we want instead of watering why it can't be done.

In other words, an internal secondary is no different in principle from an external obstacle. We can spend a great deal of energy figuring out why we can't do something, or just get

227

going and do it anyway. History is suffused with stories about people who made a difference in spite of various shortcomings and inadequacies.

A very good way of working with such secondaries is to emphasize them. For instance, as Barbara Sher says, we can take a sheet of paper and headline it: Why It Can't Be Done. Then we put down all our negative feelings. Now that those feelings are externalized, we can see them more objectively. In writing them down, we begin to see that they're not the whole story, that our alignment counts for much more.

Or we can exaggerate. Suppose when we think of going to college the secondary comes up, "I don't have the money to do it." We can say out loud and exaggerate, "That's right, I'll never have the money no matter what I do; in fact, I'll never be able to accomplish anything because of this."

Paradoxically, such emphasis brings those thoughts and feelings more fully to awareness, and thus actually diminishes their power. Rather than trying to fight them we've opened to them, given them full expression. Thus we're more able to see them for what they are instead of identifying with them.

Emphasizing a secondary is simply a form of becoming more conscious of it. When we become aware of barriers in ourselves we can be mindful of them, as with other sensations in the mind. In that process they will either diminish or their relationship to us will change.

Then we refocus on our path with renewed strength.

Rewarding Progress

THE FINAL ELEMENT of perseverence is the act of *rewarding progress.* That is, we reinforce positive behavior in ourselves. We stroke the positive; we give the swing repeated pushes in the direction it's already going. By doing that we're creating and reinforcing good habits.

Good habits help us tremendously in persevering. Like other forms of energy, habits are neutral. They can help us or hurt us, can be used wisely or foolishly; it's completely up to us. But by consciously choosing habits that support our path, we're greatly empowered in walking on it.

In physics there's a concept called *inertia,* which refers to a body's tendency to keep doing whatever it's doing unless an external force acts upon it.

Habits are like that. When a new habit is just getting started, it needs extra doses of attention and consciousness—the equivalent of the external force. It needs to overcome the inertia of the status quo, the old way of doing things. Once the new habit is established, though, it takes on an inertia of its own.

But it's not necessary to break old, detrimental habits before establishing new and constructive ones. Here, too, we can seek to turn on a light instead of fighting with darkness. Rather than trying to break detrimental habits we can simply focus on establishing beneficial ones instead. Then the old, unproductive ones fall by the wayside from neglect.

Instead of struggling to eliminate procrastination, for instance, we can form the habit of doing what's important today and put our attention *there*.

Rather than trying to stop eating junk foods we can focus on the new habit of eating a healthy diet. If we focus our attention on supportive, positive habits, the old habits die from lack of attention.

It's starving the problem and feeding the opportunity. It's watering a different plant.

Habits can be thought of as positive conditioning that we do for ourselves. The basic feature of positive conditioning is that some event or action is rewarded; that is, it's associated with tension-reduction of some kind.

Let's recall Pavlov's experiment: A dog is brought into a room and a bell is rung. A few seconds later a dish of food is brought to the dog. As the dish is brought the dog salivates, wags its tail, etc. And as the food is eaten by the dog, the dog slowly relaxes. There's a reduction of tension.

The interesting part about this experiment is that the dog's brain then associates together everything that happened. The food itself, the unconditioned responses of salivation, tail wagging, etc. all become associated in the animal's brain with the sound of the bell.

As the procedure is repeated, the association between the bell and the natural responses increases. Soon the ringing bell alone will cause the dog to salivate, wag its tail and, most importantly, experience tension-reduction. The animal's brain has learned to associate together all of these things.

This knowledge can be put to use in acquiring new, more supportive habits. We repeatedly associate some desired behavior with tension-reduction.

For example, let's say we've decided to become a concert pianist. We want to establish a habit of practicing each day for several hours. The more we're in a state of relaxation while we're practicing, the more we'll look forward to returning to it each day.

Further, we can reinforce productive habits by creating a system of deliberate rewards for milestones along the way. The idea is to set up periodic reinforcements for interim accomplishment.

All that matters about these rewards is that we find them gratifying. Rewards for small milestones could be such things as reading or a cookie or a walk—whatever feels like a reward. For larger milestones we can set up larger rewards.

One of the best rewards is a clearly perceived sense of progress. This is the principle of biofeedback—setting up a feedback system so that we can clearly see when we're moving in the right direction. Something as simple as using a weight scale is an illustration of a feedback system. If we make a chart of each day's weight we've then improved the visibility of the feedback, and thus the effectiveness.

While working on this book, for example, I had the feedback of the pages and chapters completed for each draft. That alone was a strong motivator. Though it may seem too simple, the mere act of setting up measurable milestones of progress—and meeting them—is very empowering.

Often a little thought will show us how we can break a project down so that we can recognize such milestones along the way. The natural reinforcement of achieving milestones is then supplemented by setting up a series of rewards. To use my example again: Every completed writing session gets rewarded with a small walk, a tiny snack, a few minutes of light reading, or whatever feels appealing.

When the day's writing or editing is finished I might deliberately take a drive or read a magazine before going on with the rest of the day. And I have the unspoken feeling that it's a reward and I enjoy it all the more.

A successful week—three writing sessions completed each day for five days—or finishing a chapter, or successfully rewriting an area of difficulty and so on, bring larger rewards. Examples might be a special dinner, seeing a special film or play, a special trip or whatever.

Such rewards might seem a little silly, but they have one terrific virtue—they work like crazy. They really do help us to create good habits and persevere in our vision.

There's a saying that encapsulates all this:

Sow a habit, reap a character.
Sow a character, reap a destiny.

Taking Action

THE FINAL STEP of commitment is to just go ahead and do it. As L. Ron Hubbard said, "Morale depends upon productivity." The sense of making progress each day is, in itself, an important factor in persevering. There are times when we persevere just because of momentum, just because we're already involved in doing it.

When we're through visualizing, planning, preparing, doing whatever we have to do to deal with our fears, then what's left is just to get started—every day. What's left is to take action each day, and just getting started is probably the hardest part of that.

Barbara Sher puts it wonderfully:

Do it right...do it wrong...but do it.

Accomplishing anything is like learning to swim. We can study and prepare for it on dry land, but sooner or later we have to actually get in the water; there's no substitute for that. It doesn't matter that our actions aren't perfect. What matters is just that we begin, we take action, we commit once again to walking on our path today.

The other factors discussed in this chapter all just help to ensure that we take this final and essential step—action. They're the engine that propels our process each day, that helps us to act.

When we act, our focus shifts from ourselves to the task at hand, from our inner fears and outer obstacles to the task that's in front of us, waiting to be acted on.

Though it's been heard many times, it's worth repeating Lao Tzu here: "The longest journey begins with a single step." A goal that may seem almost impossible today seems less so as we take another step, and another, towards it.

Maybe we can give our most important goal just a few minutes a day right now. That's okay, then we give it just a few minutes. But we can give it something; we can begin.

If we're a school teacher and we want to have a horse ranch we can begin taking steps to get that first horse. If we're a waiter and we'd rather sell real estate, we can start talking to agents. If we want to learn to give more we can begin by just sending a card to someone. But we can begin.

Each step we take builds up momentum. Step by step, that momentum grows stronger. Each day that we meditate or visualize or walk towards our goals, etc. makes it that much more likely that we'll repeat those things again tomorrow.

Finally we find ourselves in a place we couldn't have dreamed of before. Each day that we take the steps we can take that day, we're painting our painting. We're walking the path towards our truest self. We're progressing on Don Juan's "path with a heart."

Aristotle said: "We are what we repeatedly do."

The way we spend each day is the way we spend our life. When we do what we can this day, that in itself is our truest reward—knowing that we're walking our path.

Each goal brings obstacles and challenges, of course. But by keeping our aligned vision in sight, and continuing to stay committed to it, we can walk that part of our path that's appropriate for today.

Then our success doesn't depend on how we feel each day. It's not dependent on our impulses, or good luck. We can get up each day and continue to reinforce our vision. We can do what we can. By focusing on the possible each day, the seemingly impossible can come into view.

Houdini, perhaps the greatest stage-magician ever, was once asked by a reporter for a definition of magic. His reply is quite interesting:

"Magic?" he said. "Magic is practice."

BOOK 5

Inner Heart

EQUANIMITY

Book 5, Inner Heart, is about
healing our own inner wounds,
the effect of that on our love
and relationships, and how to
go about that process.

Balance Your Boat

𝒜 BOAT CANNOT move very well in the water if it's unbalanced, if it's not stable. If it's a sailboat it may be leaning over in the wind, but to proceed it still must somehow be in equilibrium. The same is true for us.

This principle could be called *Stability Creates Success,* because it means that whenever greater inner stability can be achieved, greater external flexibility is possible. Flexibility, the ability to adapt to circumstances in creative ways, is fundamental to the prospects of success in any area.

For example, why did the mammals survive when the dinosaurs perished? One significant factor is that mammals developed an ability to stabilize their internal temperature.

The metabolic chemical reactions taking place inside many dinosaurs sped up and slowed down in accordance with the outside temperature. If the outside temperature dropped, the dinosaur's internal life-process would slow down. When a giant meteor hit 65 million years ago and the earth's temperature fell drastically, the dinosaurs suffered extinction.

Yet the early mammals managed to survive that event. Why? In part, because the stable internal temperature allowed them to adapt to a wider range of temperatures outside. Their metabolic chemistry continued to function even when the earth grew cold. Their greater internal stability allowed them more flexibility to adapt to external events.

Another example is the rise of the vertebrates about 350 million ago. The development of an internal skeleton gave the vertebrate animal much greater stability, allowing it to become more mobile, complex, and resistant to predation. So it could survive in a wider range of external circumstances.

A third example might be the severe drought which began occurring several million years ago in Africa, causing the forests and jungles to thin out dramatically. Our ancestors responded very successfully to this threat by coming out of the trees and beginning to live down on the grassy plains, where danger was more prevalent.

How could they survive in this harsher environment? By evolving a rational brain which could, for the first time, form a stable internal model of the outside world, and thus creatively analyze it.

No longer was the brain entirely subject to instinctual stimulus-response with its external environment. It could now reflect and respond. This greater internal stability brought about a dramatic increase in flexibility and resourcefulness towards the outside world.

This principle holds just as true in our own efforts to be more adaptable and resourceful about our life. If we develop and maintain greater inner stability in some way, we'll automatically have greater adaptability to the world and thus a greater probability of success with it.

When we work on improving our diet, for example, we're increasing the inner stability—the health—of our body. Greater bodily stability and harmony, in turn, increase our potential resourcefulness in adapting to our environment.

Another example: When we meditate we develop more internal stability. So we tend to be more appropriate towards the outer world, to maturely respond, to have the presence of mind to follow our inner wisdom.

Becoming more stable inside involves breaking the symmetry between the inside and outside, a constant theme in the development of the universe. The outside may fluctuate, but the inside does not have to slavishly follow it as much. There's more response and less reaction, more choice and less mechanicalness. We're more able to resourcefully respond.

In following this principle, then, anything we can do to increase our inner stability will also lift our flexibility and probability of success. Stability creates success.

For instance, if we're facing a crisis it's often best to remain where we are and keep our tools and resources at hand. It's often good to produce something, a project that can help us remain focused. It's good to meditate in stillness, and so on. All such practices increase our stability and thus our chances of successfully meeting a crisis.

Like any good principle, this one can be widely applied But the challenges that we feel most deeply in life often arise from our own conditioning. So let's begin there:

Wounded Child

$\mathcal{O}$UR NATURAL SELF is spontaneous, loving, creative, open. Just watch an infant, who is still residing in that early natural self—open, affectionate, spontaneous, and so on. We were all completely that way once. What happens to us?

What happens is that inevitably we become wounded by the world in various ways. And the younger we are the more vulnerable we are, so our early family or caretakers tend to wound us the most. Even the most loving childhood will inevitably include some mistakes, some unmet expectations, some accidents and so on. A certain amount of loss and pain seems to be built into the fabric of life. So even the best of childhoods will inadvertently wound us to some extent.

And of course some children are abused in various ways, physically, emotionally or sexually. We can also be wounded, innocently or otherwise, by schools, society, other children, prejudice, religion and many other things. I personally have never met anyone who was not carrying some wounds from childhood. We all seem to have them to some extent.

What happens to us when we're wounded? Modern psychology describes a process of "schemas," or competing centers of influence in the brain. L Ron Hubbard talked of "engrams" created by early trauma. Harvey Jackins and others describe a process of "distress," and I think his view in this area is especially clear. The ideas in this section are partly based on his fine work.

Imagine that an infant and its mother are separated in a crowded shopping mall. And let's say the mother and child are reunited after a few minutes, so the child's bad experience is intense but short. What will the infant do?

The child has a natural repair process which will go into effect immediately. It will cry and cry and cry, if the mother lets it. If the mother is attentive and aware but not distressed by the child's crying, then the child will keep crying until the process is all done. And when it's done, the child will once again be happy, enthusiastic, affectionate, spontaneous, and so on, just as before.

In other words, the crying is an outer manifestation of an inner repair process. When this process is completed the child is drained of distress, able to normally store information about what happened, and ready to continue its existence in a natural and spontaneous way.

What often happens, though, is that the child's distress stimulates the caretaker's own distress patterns—picked up mostly from their own childhoods—and the caretaker cannot stay relaxed while the child cries and its organism repairs itself. Instead the crying alarms, threatens or irritates, and the caretaker or others try to get the child to stop crying.

We've all experienced variations of this: "There, there, don't cry, it's all right." Or "Stop your crying or I'll give you something to cry about." Or "Look, see the pretty picture." There's a thousand variations, but the net result is that the child is not allowed to finish crying, to complete the natural process of internal repair.

Because the child is forced to stop this natural process, the experience gets stored as a *wound* in the unconscious. It's uncompleted. The child contracts a little, becomes a little more shut down, a little less spontaneous and alive.

The next time the mother needs to leave the child with someone else, things may become difficult. The emotional recording of the old upset is going to be triggered and the child will cry and be upset again. In psychological terms the child undergoes a *spontaneous regression* back to the earlier incident, reliving it again—emotionally—through the present incident.

But the story goes further than that. Because the repair process was incomplete, a *pattern* (also called *schema* or *engram* and other names as well) forms in the unconscious mind that seeks to recreate itself. A chain of similar incidents will be scripted or facilitated by the unconscious mind, which seeks to recreate the original incident, duplicate the feelings of that incomplete experience, and complete them this time.

If we look carefully, we'll see certain patterns recurring again and again in our lives. Usually we think of these things as bad luck, unfortunate circumstances, coincidences, etc. We have a good reason every time we lose a relationship, or every time we arrive late, feel abandoned, or lose our temper, for instance. But the same kind of thing keeps happening.

We start on the road to our freedom when we begin to see that these recurring patterns in our life are, for the most part, self-created. Though ultimately liberating, it's a difficult notion to face—and I ought to know.

I was somewhere in my mid-twenties when I started to realize that I got angry at people a lot. I always had a good reason, but there was a pattern: I was irritated a lot. Suddenly one day I saw that I was involved in creating the situations that made me angry.

It was quite a big moment in my life. I had a glimpse for the first time that I was not some puppet on a string, helplessly reacting to my past or to events, but rather the creator—or rather, the co-creator—of what was happening to me.

Of course I would have to have this insight again and again, in new situations and at deeper levels over the years. Nevertheless, it was when I first saw that pattern and started to own it that it began to gradually lessen. Though it's humbling and painful, it's also great news to begin to observe some life-pattern that we're involved in creating, because if we're creating it one way then we can create it some other way.

Sure, others make their contributions to whatever is going on. But, tempting as it is, it doesn't help us to see where others need to work on themselves. Perhaps they do, but so what? Seeing that isn't going to help *us*. What helps us is to see what *our* contribution is—to work on ourselves.

Whenever we first notice a pattern it's going to seem very reasonable that we have it. We're going to feel very, very justified in having it. The reasons for each occurrence will be good. It requires a degree of insight and humility on our part to admit that maybe we're helping to create these repetitive patterns in our life that seem to be unfortunately happening to us because of circumstances.

I was perhaps 33 when I identified manipulation as an issue in my life. The insight occurred when I happened to spend an afternoon with an unusually flowing person and I suddenly saw the contrast in our behaviors.

It wasn't an easy insight. It was difficult to confess to myself that I was being rigid, controlling, and manipulative with others. It was a terrible moment to look into myself and see that, but it was also the way out. By seeing and admitting for the first time what I was doing, for the very first time I also began to have some choice about whether I wanted to be that way or not.

By the way, I've had to make such confessions to myself many times. The first time we see something is simply the first time; we'll have to see it again and again. The good news is, once we truly start identifying a pattern in our life, it's on its way out. It may take years, and many more episodes of insight under varying conditions, but that pattern is on its way to eventually being history.

Seeing into the patterns of anger or manipulation, for instance, didn't mean that I'd never be angry or controlling again—far from it, as friends could tell you—but rather, that I'd slowly become more conscious about those things and thus gradually lessen them as a factor in my life.

Becoming conscious of various areas of unconsciousness within ourselves is like a purifying flame. In the loving gaze of consciousness, those things that are natural to our being stay with us and are strengthened; those things that are part of our wounds gradually dissipate, or to put it more accurately, they gradually integrate into our consciousness. Then they become simple memories instead of emotionally-charged unconscious directives.

That is why, in any serious work on our relationships, we have to begin with ourselves.

It's fine to think that other people should change, but that won't help *our* growth. We can be very well-intentioned and even skillful with others, yet to the extent that we're still running old patterns on them, still acting out unconscious childhood wounds upon them, our relationships are going to suffer. And so are we.

With this background, let's go back to the child now. What other natural healing responses does the child have?

If she's badly frightened—and someone is there who will be attentive and relaxed and willing to let her go through whatever she needs to—the child will start to spontaneously tremble and scream and perspire from a cold skin. She'll keep this up for quite a long time, and then, as with the crying, it will be done. Then she'll resume being happy and affectionate and creative; she'll have no emotional residue left over from the incident.

If the child is frustrated about something, she will again discharge the distress if allowed to. She'll do this by making angry noises and sharp physical movements and perspiring from a warm skin. In other words, she'll throw a "temper tantrum." If not stopped or frustrated in this discharge, she'll once again heal herself and resume being happy, relaxed and cooperative.

If a child is ridiculed or embarrassed in some way, he'll seek out a chance to talk about it if a relaxed and attentive adult is available. If that adult will refrain from giving advice but will merely listen with attention, the child will relate the experience repeatedly.

Finally he'll start joking and laughing about it. He'll laugh more and more until the tension of the embarrassment is completely gone. Once again, he'll be completely healed of that incident.

In all these ways, our body-mind organism knows how to heal itself from traumatic experiences if allowed to do so. But most of the time when we were wounded, we were not allowed to discharge the distress. We were not allowed to shake, tremble, scream, cry, make angry noises, talk without being evaluated or advised, and so on.

Because the wound was incompletely healed, it will be retained in the unconscious, along with the other wounds that were unhealed. These form our present-day patterns as adults, the ways in which we compulsively create and act out our old unconscious scripts from the past.

This hidden-away pain is the unexperienced, uncooked, undigested part of our experience.

How do we heal it now? Basically, by being willing to experience the unexperienced pain that is there.

Mindfulness

$\mathcal{M}$OST OF OUR internal stored pain is hidden away from our consciousness. It is kept away precisely because it is painful; unconscious mechanisms are trying to protect us. Thus our inner pain is not normally felt in its true intensity, but rather as a kind of chronic background disjointedness.

Mindfulness, discussed also in chapter 1, is a process of being willing to sit down in silence and truly take a look at the disjointedness inside, truly feel it, truly experience it. When we just sit there in silence, without distracting ourselves in any way, but just allowing our attention to carefully and calmly observe our own inner process, that is when the pain slowly starts revealing itself.

Mindfulness is mentioned first among ways to heal our pain because, in my experience, it is the most powerful and profound game in town. I've never come across anything that can match the power of mindful awareness, long-term, to bring about beneficial changes at the deepest level.

Its real power is *processional,* that is, its effects slowly cumulate if we keep it up. It has immediate benefits, of course, such as more equanimity, more sense of humor, more ability to respond instead of react. However, its long-term effect is even greater and involves our self-identity—but it's subtle, like changes in our face in the mirror over time.

Because its deepest effects take place very gradually, it is easy to feel that we're not making much progress and that our mindfulness practice is not working. For that reason, we'll be tempted many times to give it up.

Another giving-up factor occurs also. After we've been practicing mindfulness for a time, life will start going more smoothly, we'll seem to be more lucky, things will flow more. We may begin to feel that we possess a natural gift for handling the events of life. Who needs daily mindfulness sitting? This thought too will tempt us to give up the practice.

A third giving-up factor, ironically, is that things may seem to get worse for awhile. The pain that's been suppressed will start surfacing into consciousness. In fact, we're no more distressed than before, but it may seem as if we are for a time because we'll be *more aware of it* when our over-reactions and distress patterns act out.

For these reasons, it's helpful to make a commitment that we're going to practice mindfulness for a certain period of time and not try to evaluate the results right away.

What is mindfulness? Basically, it's being willing to sit down and be still for a while. No activity, no goal in mind; just a willingness to sit there and witness our own inner process for a period of time. And it's desirable if we can do this without getting caught up in comparisons—"Yesterday went well but today not well," or "I'm not sure if I'm making any progress," etc. Such comparisons obscure the pure witnessing that we're trying to do.

Let's say we were to spend some time each day, say 45 minutes or so, sitting in pure mindfulness meditation. Let's see briefly what would be involved:

The first thing would be to pick some physical position where we can let our body be still for awhile. Frequent shifts in position, frequent scratching, writing down thoughts, even trips to the bathroom can become an occupation. Anything at all can be used as a means of supplying distractions to our consciousness and keeping us busy.

So we want to find a position where we can let our body be still for awhile, and yet stay attentive. As a practical matter, this usually means a form of sitting. We can sit on a cushion in one of the classic meditation postures, or we can sit in a chair. We can even lie down, though we're much more likely to become drowsy that way.

The next thing is either to close our eyes, or to gaze slightly out-of-focus at some nearby surface, such as the floor or a wall. The idea is to reduce visual stimulation, to reduce the amount of visual input coming in. Since we want to pay attention to our inner process, minimal outer distractions are desirable. Nevertheless, any outer distractions that do occur are watched just like any other phenomena going on.

The last preparatory thing is ensuring that there's no particular thing that we're concentrating on, such as a quote or a mantra or an image or even a teacher. It's not a time for dwelling on sublime ideas or visions or mantras, as valuable as they may be, but rather to have truly *no occupation*.

The idea is to allow a kind of let-go—to let whatever wants to go on in the mind go on, without trying to control it. But then, to be very attentive to what's going on, without getting identified with it. These are the basic conditions.

When this practice is deepened, what happens is quite fascinating. As mentioned, various psychic wounds lie hidden and incomplete in the unconscious. Like all other entities in the universe, including us, what they are basically seeking is attention and appreciation.

When we sit silently in mindfulness, suddenly a great spaciousness is made available. We're no longer distracting our consciousness with the myriads of things that we distract ourselves with. Our consciousness, our attention, is available. In that spaciousness, our unconscious mind begins to send up things to consciousness to be noticed—hidden-away things, normally suppressed out of awareness:

Memories, feelings, thoughts of old losses, frustrations, fears, griefs. Fantasies of various kinds, which can be either positive or negative, rapturous or terrifying, or anything in between. Sexual fantasies. Incredible rages, unbearable griefs, tremendous guilts, terrifying fears, and so on.

Inside each one of us are some very, very intense things which will come up and be healed if we persist long enough in creating a safe, non-distracting, non-reactive, loving space for them to appear.

What those pains want is simply our loving attention. They want to be able to come up into consciousness and be noticed, accepted, loved—just like what we would want. When we provide that accepting and non-reactive attention, it's exactly like the attention that the baby needed from the mother in order to discharge distress. We provide that loving, relaxed attention to ourselves now.

The situation can be compared to a dog kept down in a dark basement. The dog barks and howls fiercely. Of course it does; it wants to get out, it wants to experience the sun, it wants to be free. If we let it up, give it a good bath and some loving attention, it will run around for awhile and then will probably curl up at our feet and go to sleep.

Our wounds are like that. A particular chain of wounds may need to come up many times, each time at a little deeper level. Each time it completes a little more of what it was unable to complete in the past, and a little more energy rejoins consciousness. So our consciousness grows a little bit larger and more spacious, and our unconsciousness grows a little bit smaller and less influential.

Most of the time, however, it's not a matter of high drama. Initially at least, much time will be spent watching the mind wondering why in the world it's doing this, fantasizing about the next meal, things like that.

The real pain doesn't come up for awhile, until practice deepens. A mindfulness meditation retreat can be useful for bringing up deeper material. Or perhaps more time spent with each day's sitting. But one way or another, if we keep on, everything does come up to be attended to. Eventually, every old conditioning surfaces if we persist long enough.

Gradually healing our wounds like this is not dramatic, but it can do more for our life and our relationships than just about anything else we can do. Therapy can help, relationship skills can help, many things in this chapter can help, but the sword that cuts the deepest is mindfulness.

It's so powerful that eventually we can see even the whole clinging and grasping of our mind-mechanism, even the whole mistaken identity about who we are as a separate entity—everything.

By increasing our ability to step back and look at our own unconscious material, mindfulness helps us to become more conscious. And that profoundly affects every aspect of our experience of our life.

Mindfulness II

So IF WE sit down and relax and let ourselves be just unoccupied but attentive for awhile, at some point a natural watching of our inner process will arise, if we have the seed of knowing about it. We can be in solitary confinement for ten years and never become mindful if we don't know that mindfulness exists and so begin noticing it.

But if you can read this sentence you have the seed, because you know that such a thing as mindfulness exists and is possible. In fact, it will arise naturally if we just create the time and space for it to do so—sitting silently for a period each day—and then recognize it as it begins.

As we sit unoccupied in silence, we gradually become more and more observant. Since so little is happening on the outside to distract us, we become more easily aware of what's happening on the inside. The beautiful night stars are there in the daytime too, but only when the bright sun goes down can we truly see them. When our bright activity and distractions go down, we can observe our starry insides better.

We begin by noticing our breath, perhaps at the belly as it moves in and out with each breath. As we do so, we come into the present moment, where all spiritual realms begin. The breath is about the immediate, the present. It's not about the past or the future; it has no baggage of opinions and ideas. Noticing the breath grounds us into the present. Using that anchor, we can then expand awareness out from there.

If we want to go into the deeper stages of mindfulness, it's desirable to go on a retreat at some point. On a mindful retreat, we can be away from the distractions of ordinary life and have the opportunity to sit quietly in mindfulness for days or weeks at a time. Our practice will deepen.

As it does, various obstacles will come up. Perhaps the most prominent one is physical pain, which will definitely intrude sooner or later. Some of it will arise just from sitting still for long periods. But more significantly, it also arises because physical pain is part of what needs to be released from the unconscious.

Physical pain comes from places of hidden tension and holding, hidden blockages in the face, neck, shoulders, back—from almost anywhere in the body. These tensions can release in various ways, as spasms, vibrations, or in conjunction with intense memories from the past.

As with anything else, our job is to observe this pain without buying-in and without aversion, without resistance and without distraction. The idea is to let our attention be soft and gentle around the pain, to investigate it, to explore it with our loving attention instead of recoiling from it.

If we do recoil, that is an element of *the five hindrances* described by the Buddha, and re-described by Jack Kornfield, a teacher of mindfulness:

The first hindrance is *aversion,* which can be described as any feeling that wants to push away experience. In response to what comes up we can feel fear or anger or dislike, for example. In the past we've used this feeling of aversion to push away our experience, but now we want to just watch benevolently whatever is there.

The second hindrance is *desire,* which is the opposite of the first. Here we want to grasp and hold on to things in the mind. We might have a very rapturous experience one day and the next day we want to repeat it. We may want to follow a train of thought. When we cling like this, we're no longer open to our experience, to whatever's there, since we're trying to go in a particular direction again.

The third hindrance is *restlessness* or *agitation.* In some sittings we'll feel uptight, or that we can't calm down, or that we don't have the right position, etc. Or we'll feel worried or remorseful about something. Naturally, we watch this too.

If it gets bad, it's often good to surrender further into it. One time I was in a horrifying mindstate which was filled with glaring neon lights, buzzsaw noises and devilish forces and it became apparent that I would be there forever—a real nightmare. Finally I said, "This is God too" and surrendered into it and was willing to see God in that form forever—and it lifted.

The fourth hindrance is *dullness* or *sleepiness,* and is the opposite of the third. If we get very sleepy, taking deep breaths or getting up and walking outside is usually helpful. And above all, to watch it with loving attention. Quite often this restores the mind to alertness.

What we really want is to investigate the nature of sleepiness just as we would do with anger or lust or greed if they came up.

This is much different from thinking or analyzing it—"Why am I sleepy right now?"—which leads nowhere. Real investigation of something is just a pure observation of it in order to see into its nature.

The fifth hindrance is *doubt*. Here the mind thinks it's not making any progress, that it's not the right day, that there's work to be done, that some other practice would be better, or whatever. Doubt, too, can be watched. And it's helpful to inspire ourselves by reading or seeing or hearing people who are wiser than we are.

In working with the hindrances, our basic job is to open to them, to open our heart and let them in, as with all our other experience. Often it's the most difficult obstacles that teach us the most when we can finally open to them. Instead of running away, which we've done for so long, now we bring our gentle and balanced and loving attention to everything.

A mindfulness retreat can be done privately or in a group. A group is recommended because we get the support of the group and the personal example of the teacher. An evolved teacher can be just invaluable, particularly in helping us avoid various dead ends in which we go astray by getting identified with something.

A note about daily sitting:

For many people the best time for sitting practice seems to be early in the morning, when we first get up. Especially if we're a "morning person," sitting as the first thing we do each day is good because we're fresh and alert. And it also helps in setting the tone of the whole day.

The potential downside of morning sitting is the pitfall of "getting it done." Since most of us have a number of matters to take care of each day, at the beginning of the day there can be a subtle pressure to be done with our sitting so we can get on to other things. "First I'll get mindfulness done, then I'll do this..."

An alternative is to sit at night, when the day is done. For the most part the world is winding down or has gone to sleep, our own busy-ness has ended, and if we feel like going on a bit longer we can do so.

Some people find it a bit easier at night to get into the patient, goal-less observation that characterizes mindfulness. The potential risk in night sitting is that we may be tired and less alert at the end of the day, and thus more prone to daydreaming and drowsiness.

As always, watching our own experience will help us to see what's right for us. We all have our own rhythms. And of course, we can always do both.

A story: My Irish grandmother, Katie Grace, who was my first teacher and like a saint to me, was widely known among her family and friends as an unusually peaceful and loving person. Yet she worked incredibly hard from early morning to night raising nine children.

"How did she do it?" I used to ask my mother. And one time I learned something that felt intuitively right: I found out that grandma used to go out on the front porch every night, after everyone else had gone to sleep, and just sit there in the darkness for an hour or two...

A distinction can be drawn between *pure mindfulness* and what can be called *directed mindfulness.*

Pure mindfulness, as we've seen, means that we're open to whatever experience presents itself, without trying in any way to control or direct that experience. Though it works more gradually than anything else, in the end it seems to cut deeper too. It creates the purest, emptiest space to allow our ego-separateness to come into view.

Directed mindfulness, in contrast, works more quickly in certain ways. It directs our attention to certain facets of our experience or alters our experience in some way, while still retaining the characteristic feature of observing our process without getting caught up or "hooked" by it.

In the next few sections we'll discuss certain types of personal work that can be done using directed mindfulness.

Body Scanning

*T*HE FIRST KIND of directed mindfulness is known as *body scanning,* and it means putting our focus on the body and sweeping our attention systematically through it. As Jon Kabat-Zinn reminds us, this practice is particularly desirable if we're in pain or experiencing great tension or stress, because it helps us more readily handle them.

In many ways our heart, our emotional life, is closer to the body than the mind. When we're angry we feel it in our body as a hot, burning sensation; when we experience fear we feel clammy; when we feel deep grief our body is often racked with sobs; and so on. Every psychic wound from our past has a physical component, a pattern of tension held in the body. And every current problem is represented in the physical body as well, as we'll see a little later.

That is why focusing on the body can be so helpful, because psychic wounds that are hidden away and potentially difficult to access are sometimes surprisingly available at a kinesthetic level, and can be healed using that modality. By focusing on kinesthetic sensations, as the body scan does, we can often gain access to all areas of our inner life.

The basic idea of the body scan is that we start at one end of the body and then slowly and systematically move our attention through each area of the body until we have moved through the whole organism. Then, if we wish, we can repeat the scan one or more times.

The process is kind of like the projection of a movie. Though the movie seems continuous, it's actually a succession of still frames. Body scanning is like that. Our attention stays for awhile on a certain area, then moves to the next one and observes that for awhile, and so forth. For instance, the phrase "Scan down the arm" means a stop-and-go focusing on the shoulder, then the upper arm, then the elbow, the forearm, the wrist, and so on.

The body scan can be done sitting or lying down. It's often good to do it lying down, while remembering that we want to be awake and alert. We lie down, relax, close our eyes, and start. Though it can be done effectively either way, the time-honored method is to start at the top of the head and move slowly down to the feet.

So we just bring our attention to the top of our head and see what it feels like there. No need to analyze what it feels like. Rather, we just let our attention gently rest in that place, in the pure physical sensation. Whatever that is—heat, cold, itching, tension, pain, numbness or whatever—we attempt to experience it with equanimity. Sometimes we'll seem to feel nothing, in which case that's our experience at that moment.

From the top of the head we can let our attention move to our forehead. We notice in detail whatever physical sensations are there. If we get distracted by thoughts or emotions or other sensations, we just gently bring our attention back to the area of the body that we're focusing on. We bring a loving, balanced, non-reactive attention to it.

From there we proceed systematically through the eyes, the nose, the mouth and chin, the sides and back of the head, and on through the rest of the body, ending in the left or right foot. More important than the particular route we take is that we make sure to cover in detail each area of the body.

Though the body scan can greatly reduce tension in the body, tension-reduction is not really what it's about. Rather, it's about noticing what the body really feels like, what the actuality of the body is like.

The first thing we'll probably notice is that we're not nearly as well-acquainted with our body as we thought. For many, even for avid exercisers, the body scan is the first time in our life that we actually start to feel truly alive and at home in our body. Suddenly we're going beyond habitual thoughts and insecurities about our body to the actual body itself.

The first few body scans usually result in a greater sense of tingling and aliveness in the body. As we continue day by day, however, we find that deeper layers emerge. Deep-seated pains begin to show up, hidden knots of tension, sometimes with tendrils extending through the body. These can be quite mystifying, since they often seem to have no relation to any physical system that we know about.

Sooner or later, the body scan becomes an exercise in facing our pain. These hidden pains very much affect our life, but we're usually quite unaware of them. Now they reveal themselves. Or we may be diseased and have strong physical pain already. In either case, how we choose to approach this pain is crucial.

Instead of pulling away from it, recoiling from it, hating it, we can try a different approach. We go further into the pain instead, we soften around it, open to it, investigate it with pure attention.

Sometimes there's an area that we have difficulty with. Sometimes we find it quite difficult, for whatever reason, to focus directly on a particular pain by itself. In that case a good idea is to continue our systematic scans, moving gently through the area of pain each time. We notice our approach to the pain, then the pain itself as we sweep through it, and then our moving-away. By doing this over and over, we can gradually focus directly on the pain itself.

At other times the exact opposite occurs: The pain seems to compel our attention, making it seem difficult or impossible to focus on anything else. Then the best thing is to forget the scan and focus directly upon the pain. We want to make its acquaintance, to directly investigate its nature.

In effect, since love and attention are intimately related, we're sending love to the pain. As we do so, as our attention deepens, we'll notice that the nature of the pain changes. Instead of being just a solid mass, it seems to dissolve, or move, or change shape or texture from one moment to the next. Sometimes it disappears altogether.

And even when the pain remains, we usually discover that our relationship to it has changed. Our relationship to it becomes softer, more detached, more compassionate.

Breathwork

ANOTHER WAY OF looking at mindfulness is from the view of classical deconditioning:

In the classic experiment, a bell is rung and a dog is given an electric shock. It howls, it runs around, it shows the tense signs of fight-or-flight. After a few such trials the dog is said to be *negatively conditioned;* that is, the ringing bell alone now causes the dog to show signs of distress. Let's say we now wanted to *decondition* the dog. How would we do it?

What we'd do is first give the dog a bowl of food. While it was eating, and thus experiencing a reduction of tension, we'd ring the bell faintly. Next time when the dog was eating we'd ring the bell again but slightly louder. Each time we fed the dog we'd ring the bell a little bit louder.

Pretty soon the animal would exhibit signs of *positive conditioning;* now the ringing bell would cause it to salivate and wag its tail. The negative conditioning is deconditioned, in effect, by gradually replacing it with a positive—that is, tension-reducing—conditioning to the same stimulus.

Recent research shows that the most essential element of this process is the presence of an *atmosphere of tension-reduction* in which the stimulus is then repeatedly presented. Why mention this? Because our own negative conditioning is essentially the same. In classical terms, to decondition our wounds we must present the negative stimuli again in an atmosphere of tension-reduction.

The wounding incidents that were our original negative stimuli have been internalized as incompletely-experienced memories. Whenever we can bring them up in some way and experience them in an atmosphere of tension-reduction, we'll be deconditioning them.

Interestingly, that is a way of viewing what's happening when we sit in mindfulness. Any sort of mindfulness practice will sooner or later bring up repressed material, which will be *re-experienced* in the relaxing atmosphere of non-judgmental attention. So when we just observe, "doing nothing," material is being deconditioned. Just in the process of being silent and aware, particularly over a period of time, deconditioning occurs.

And as we slowly loosen our conditionings by watching them, the mind gradually becomes calmer. And we can watch with more equanimity when storms do take place in the mind. We can watch our desires and aversions without necessarily being hooked by them. Being more free from our robotic conditioning, we tend to choose more appropriate and balanced actions, which have a profoundly beneficial effect on our life and relationships.

For this deconditioning process to work, unconscious material must be surfaced into consciousness. Mindfulness and body scanning both do this. A third way, with names from "rebirthing" to "vivation" to "breath of fire" and many others, can be included here under the title *breathwork*.

Engineers use a concept called the *signal-to-noise* ratio. For instance, a clear TV picture is said to have a high such ratio. A distant and fuzzy picture is said to have a low signal-to-noise. In deconditioning our mind, we're essentially trying to increase the ratio between the *signal*—the unconscious material—and the *noise*—our usual inner and outer activity—so as to better observe the former.

There are two good ways to do this. The first way is to reduce the amount of noise, or distracting activity, so that the signal can be better noticed. Mindfulness and body scanning both could be said to accomplish this.

The second way is to increase the strength of the signal itself. We could say that this is what breathwork does. We're moving away from pure mindfulness a little more here. While scanning involves just the deliberate moving of our attention, in breathwork we're altering a basic physiological process, so there's more "doingness" going on.

Nevertheless, breathwork is a very natural method because we're not trying to control what material we're going to look at. We're letting the unconscious control that.

Though *pranayama*, or yogic work with the breath, is thousands of years old, modern-day breathwork seems to have originated with Leonard Orr. Significant contributions have also been made by Jim Leonard, Phil Laut, Sondra Ray, Stan Grof and, as is usually the case, many others.

Breathwork involves doing some extra breathing while still staying mindful. By temporarily increasing our breathing, a natural healing process in the body seems to be called forth, and material which might normally be quite subtle is brought more clearly into awareness. The "signal" increases.

A higher rate of oxygen-CO_2 exchange can be brought about by increasing either the volume or the frequency of each breath. By altering these factors during the process of breathwork we can achieve pretty good control over the intensity with which subconscious material is presented to us.

The preliminaries are just to lie down, close our eyes, get comfortable, and make sure there are no articles such as belts, etc. which might block full and easy breathing. It's nice to have a blanket because we may feel cold at certain points. A glass of water is handy because our throat may get dry.

We begin by just taking bigger and deeper breaths while keeping our rate of breathing at a normal pace. This *slow and full* breathing is the basic engine of breathwork. We want to stay mindful while we're breathing, we want to observe our sensations in detail, and that's easier to do when we're breathing slowly and fully. Breathing fast also increases our air-CO_2 exchange, but is somewhat more distracting.

Generally speaking, we want to reach a plateau where things start happening. This plateau is normally signaled by a tingling sensation in the body. We want to increase our breathing enough to reach this plateau, which usually takes 5 to 20 minutes, and then continue it enough to maintain the plateau until the process is finished.

It's also possible, if we start our breathwork while we're feeling emotionally charged up, to reach the plateau almost immediately. I remember the first time I began a breathwork session while I was feeling sad; the process brought me to tears within 60 seconds.

In fact, it's a great idea to do breathwork when we're feeling emotional, because then some unconscious material is already close to the surface and more easily accessible.

It's useful to think of our breathing during breathwork as *circular,* that is, continuously going. By eliminating the gaps between outbreath and inbreath, and inbreath and outbreath, our breathing is automatically increased.

It's also important to stay as relaxed as possible during the process. By doing so, we satisfy the essential element of deconditioning—that the negative stimulus is presented in an atmosphere of tension-reduction.

To facilitate this, we let go on the outbreath. It takes care of itself. Any effort is made on the inbreath. We "pull" on the inbreath and then let the exhale happen by itself. The idea is not to huff and puff and make a big effort, but rather, to simply connect up the inbreaths and outbreaths, and then pull in more air than usual on the inbreath.

In the first few sessions, a not-unusual occurence is to experience *tetany,* a temporary cramping or paralysis which often occurs in the hands or feet, but can occur in the arms, legs, mouth or wherever we've been holding tension.

If this happens, just keep on breathing and observe it like any other phenomenon. It's sometimes an indication that we're pushing the exhale, in which case it's good to let the exhale relax more. It can last up to half an hour or more, but in any event will integrate before the session is over.

In breathwork it's also helpful to breathe only through our mouth, or if our nose has a good airflow and we prefer it, only through our nose. Mixing the two, breathing in through the nose and out through the mouth for instance, can be a bit distracting and so tends to reduce mindfulness.

This section has discussed the basic mechanics of doing breathwork. Now let's look at the other aspect of it, at what's going on internally:

Breathwork II

So we're breathing more for a while, and things start coming up into consciousness. What then? The guideline now is to be willing to "take what we get." Whatever sensations or feelings come up are exactly what should be there, exactly what needs to be looked at the most in that moment. Even if we're feeling nothing, or numb, that's precisely what we need to be observing.

And what we do is apply our old friend mindfulness to the situation. Breathwork is working to surface certain things normally hidden in the unconscious, and our job is simply to fully experience and lovingly witness whatever is happening without getting lost in it.

What comes up might be feelings of tension at certain places in the body, it might be a burning in the eyes, it might be feelings of loneliness, it might be a memory from long ago—it could be any of a million things. Whatever it is, we investigate it not by thinking about it but by just giving it our full attention.

We don't need to know what the meaning of something is. No rational analysis is necessary or desirable. If a pain in our back comes up, we don't need to know what that represents psychologically. We may or may not get psychological insights corresponding to what we're feeling physically, but it doesn't matter if we do or not. It can heal without us knowing what it "means." Welcome what we get.

Whatever is most noticeable is focused on just as if we were sitting in pure mindfulness. We just observe it with an accepting detachment, and as we do so it begins to integrate. This wounded energy from the unconscious archive rejoins the energy of consciousness, integrates into consciousness. Our consciousness gets a little bit larger. It's really a beautiful process, and I highly recommend it.

Two common hindrances can and almost certainly will be encountered at various points, so let's talk about them. The first is that certain material will try to get you to "go away" in some way, either by feeling dull, or feeling like you should stop because it's not working or because you could be doing better things, or by writing down great ideas that you get, or by day-dreaming, or whatever.

The most common "going away" from our experience is probably a feeling of intense sleepiness or numbness to block the experience of whatever is underneath it.

When we find ourselves "going away" in some way—and we have to realize that we're doing that—the remedy is to breathe full and fast, that is, to keep breathing fully but increase the speed of our breathing. This tends to wake us up and bring us more into the present. And if sleepiness gets too great, it doesn't hurt to sit up, or get up and walk around while still breathing and observing.

The second potential hindrance is that things start feeling too intense. If our mindfulness is well enough developed, anything can be watched. Nevertheless, there may be times when we'd like to turn down the volume a bit.

This is accomplished by breathing fast and shallow. Fast and shallow breathing lowers the intensity and starts tuning us in to the inherent pleasure of our body. Then, when it feels right to do so, we can return to slow and full breathing to resume the usual process.

We could lower the intensity by returning to slow and shallow breathing—our normal type of breathing—but that's not desirable. This type of breathing acts to inhibit sensation; so what will happen is that the material being presented will go back into suppression and will not integrate.

To get the real benefit of a breathwork session, it's important to keep going until the material is integrated and the process reaches a natural end. We know that we're at the natural end because we feel wonderful, our body feels aglow with pleasure, and we're in good spirits.

It's good to continue until we get to that point, which can take anywhere from a few minutes to several hours. Most usual is an hour or two, and the longer sessions tend to be in the beginning.

It's pretty common to have our rational mind try to convince us that the session is over before it actually is, so it's good to be on the lookout for that and not get suckered into ending the session prematurely. If we find ourselves sort of wondering if it's over, it's not. We'll feel aglow when it is.

It's valuable in breathwork to create a positive context for the material coming up. If we start rejecting, resisting, or condemning our experience, we're either going to have a hard time or the process isn't going to work.

To this end, a suggestion is sometimes made to gather a personal repertory of positive contexts that can be used to help create acceptance of uncomfortable material. Gratitude, surrender, finding a way to enjoy it, etc. are often cited as examples of such contexts. We can even keep a statement in mind such as, "I'm grateful for all my experience," or "This too is part of life's beauty," or "I open to the pleasure of this."

There are many good contexts such as this, and they can all do the job. However, it should be said that anyone with some practice in pure mindfulness already has experience in creating the fundamental positive context—complete acceptance of whatever is happening without getting lost in it. For this reason, it can be helpful to practice daily body scanning or sitting in mindfulness for a few weeks before beginning breathwork. Learning to bring non-reactive, loving attention to all phenomena is the very essence of a positive context.

Working with a breathwork coach is recommended, particularly in the first few sessions. When we feel like stopping, they'll help us to go on. If it gets too intense, they'll help us modify our breath to tone it down. They'll help us create a positive context for material that we want to reject or resist. And finally, it just helps a lot to have another caring human being there.

If you can't get a coach, for whatever reason, can you learn to do breathwork on your own? Yes, you can, but it may be difficult. To prove that it could be done, I deliberately taught myself how to do it—and then later did sessions with coaches to see what I missed.

When teaching myself, I had some rough times in the beginning—times when I wanted to stop, times when it seemed too intense, times when I had trouble not getting caught up in the drama. If you must do it alone, you'll need to be very, very willing to experience whatever is there.

That willingness is ultimately the key, as Jim Leonard so ably points out. If we're willing to experience our experience, if we're willing to keep going, if we're willing to have it happen, then it will. And it'll be the right thing. Indeed, willingness is the key to any kind of growth work on ourselves. If we're truly willing, everything else falls into place.

Naming

*T*HIS SECTION IS based on the pioneering work of Eugene Gendlin, who calls his method *focusing*. I usually call it *naming* because focusing, to me, is part of a dimension which a number of people have described, though not with Gendlin's precision, and which concerns *the power of naming something to increase awareness of it*. Naming, in effect, is a way of increasing the "signal," while then using mindfulness to integrate the material brought up.

Gendlin and his associates intensely studied, on videotape, thousands of therapeutic sessions. The work of various counselors and methods was examined, and this question was asked: What do these various therapeutic processes have in common when they are going well and producing results for the client?

They found that not only was there a common process going on when therapy went well, but that this skill could be learned and used on one's own. We choose a current problem and then use this method to work with it.

In naming, therefore, we add yet a little more doingness to pure mindfulness, because now for the first time we are choosing what material to focus on. Nevertheless it's quite a natural process because the actual healing is done, as with other mindful processes, by our own organism.

We begin by reviewing the problems that are currently competing for our attention. We ask, "What's preventing me from feeling completely wonderful right now?" Of course, if we included every conceivable problem the list might be very long indeed, so we concentrate on just the half dozen or so that are most significant or troubling. We briefly review each significant problem and then say, in effect, "Yes, that's there, but I'm going to set that aside for now."

Then we choose one problem and bring it to the fore-front. We ask, "What does this problem feel like in my body? What is the felt sense of this?" In asking this question, we're not seeking to analyze the problem intellectually. We're not even seeking to feel it emotionally. Rather, we're seeking a deeper level; we want to sense it physically, in our body.

Another factor is that we want to sense the whole of the problem, the totality of it. All of its history, all of the people involved, all of our past efforts to solve it, how we feel about it, what we think about it, everything. But again, we don't seek to analyze any of this.

Instead, we use mindfulness to explore the sense of what the problem, taken as a whole, feels like in our body. Most often this felt sense will come up somewhere in our torso, perhaps the chest or belly, but it can appear anywhere, or even be a pattern scattered over different places in the body. Whatever it is, we pay careful attention to it. By doing so, it increases in our awareness.

Then we ask *the body* to come up with a one- or two-word name or handle to describe the problem. We might even verbalize it by saying something like, "What is the name of this felt sense?" or "What is the quality of this?"

277

Note that we don't ask our rational mind for this name, nor do we accept whatever quick name the mind might come up with. We want the name to come from deeper within our organism, and so we patiently wait for the body itself to suggest a name. This might take perhaps half a minute or so.

A one-word or two-word name will sooner or later float into our consciousness, such as "guilty" or "hopeless" or "frustrated sadness," or whatever it might be. And what we do then is check our reaction to it. If it's the right name we'll feel a kind of "Yes!" quality about it.

Have you ever tried to remember a word or somebody's name and it was on the tip of your tongue, but you couldn't quite remember it? And words would come, but you'd say, "No, that's not it." And then the right word or name would come and there'd be this feeling of certainty and alignment suddenly and you'd say, "Yes—that's it!"

That's the feeling we'll have when the name for the felt sense is the right one. And if it's not the right one yet, we can ask again, "What is the name for the felt sense of this whole problem?" And then patiently wait until the real name comes, the one where we feel a little internal shift, a little inner "click" where we spontaneously feel, "Yes, that's it."

What we do then is resonate back and forth between the name and the felt sense. We say the name and use it to deepen our experience, to call it forth even more. We do this a few times, deepening the experience as much as possible. In effect, naming is an aid for deepening our mindfulness about certain material.

Next we can do a variation on the theme. Substituting our felt-sense name in the blank, we can ask a question such as, "What is it about all this that makes it _____?" or "What makes the whole problem so _____?" or "What is this _____?" or "What is the worst of this?" This quite often brings about a "shift" in our sense of the problem.

If we don't feel a slight shift inside, we can ask an alternate kind of question such as, "What does this felt sense want or need?" or "What would be moving forward for this felt sense?" or "What would make it feel okay?" or "What would be right for this?"

Again we are using a device to focus our attention yet deeper upon the material. As our mindfulness dwells steadily on the felt sense of the problem—without getting caught in wanting, aversion, analysis, acting out, or anything that takes us away from pure observation—a natural internal healing process is enabled.

In some ways, this is the same natural healing process as discussed in earlier sections, only this time directed towards a specific current problem. Somehow, our organism knows what "healthy" is, knows how to go towards greater balance and harmony and equanimity. What it essentially needs from us is our spaciousness, our pure attention. That is the catalyst that enables the process to work.

Though the process itself works underground, we feel the end-result—a kind of internal shift in the body. This shift is again that "Aha" feeling, and is accompanied by a new name or handle coming up in response to our question. Whenever we get such a shift, we might pause for a little while and receive it, savor it, acknowledge it. We're reinforcing the good result we received.

Then we use the new name to start the process over again: We resonate between the new name and the new felt sense, thus deepening the felt sense, and so on. During a session, which might last 15 or 20 minutes, we can go through a number of such shifts in this way, some large and some small. Then it's time to leave it for another day. It'll be right where it was when we come back to it.

As with pure mindfulness, body scanning, and breathwork, the description above is more complicated than the process itself. In actual practice the process doesn't seem to have separate steps but to be a smooth flow. We get a new name, resonate with it, ask a question about it, get a new name, and so on, all flowing together. "Shifts" can come at any point in the process, and each one represents progress with the problem.

We might very well ask how we can make progress on a real-world problem simply by focusing on it internally. How does that change the problem in the external world? Well, it doesn't, at least not right away. But often the best way to make major progress in the external world is by starting with the way we look at things internally.

Believe me, a series of good focusing/naming sessions can do wonders for a problem. We'll have a new perspective, or be less divided and more integrated about it, or we'll see the next step to take or whatever.

And most importantly, we'll experience it differently, we'll have a different relationship to it. That has great value in itself and also, almost inevitably, leads to major changes in the external world.

Naming II

*N*AMING IS EXTENSIVELY used in various methods and traditions. For instance, Ron Kurtz' hakomi therapy uses a process called *tracking*, where the therapist will name the person's experience as accurately as possible in a word or a few words, in order to deepen the client's process.

If a client recounts a sad story, the therapist might say something such as, "Sad, huh." At another time the response might be, "Feeling scared now, huh." This simple naming by another human being often helps to precipitate the client more deeply into his or her process, while increasing rapport by demonstrating that the therapist is tracking or following the client's experience.

In our everyday life, correctly naming what's happening is a wonderful device that helps us honor our experience. If we're feeling under the weather, for instance, and content ourselves with saying, "I'm just tired," we miss the opportunity to see what is really there. If we're a little patient we might say to ourselves something like, "I'm feeling rejected by MaryAnn." That correct naming allows us to proceed further into our experience, to begin integrating it instead of suppressing it, and to see what we need.

Many approaches to personal growth talk about the importance of our *self-identification*, which to me is another aspect of naming. There is a world of difference in how we name our experience. For example, if we say, "I'm a failed actor who managed to start a restaurant" it's much less empowering than if we say "I'm a successful businessman."

As Hyatt and Gottlieb point out, if we're asked "Who are you?" we're very likely to give a few *labels,* and those labels will reveal a lot about how we see ourselves. Because of the tremendous effect of such labels, it's very worthwhile to spend some time creating a label for ourselves that adequately expresses our best sense of who we are and who we can be. As they say, "All of us behave according to what we say we are... Labels can empower us to act, or they can keep us stuck."

For example, at a certain point in my life I decided to label myself as a "winner," because I wanted to emphasize that area of my life more. But as time passed and I did indeed become more successful, I started to see that what was really important to me was to be a "healer."

So I changed the label of who I was and what was important to me. To be more accurate, I gave myself both labels, but put "healer" first. (Indeed, it's because "healer" was higher in the hierarchy that I put aside some needed money-making projects to begin this book some years ago.)

As luck would have it, the very day that I recognized my new self-label, I went to visit an acquaintance who was going into anaphylactic shock as my car pulled up. He lived out in the country, far from a hospital, was perspiring and frightened, and I had no experience of it. But because of my new identification I quickly devised a method which brought him out of it. We were lucky; but the experience did demonstrate the power of our labels.

Sometimes such labels are referred to as *values*, but it's very similar. The idea is that we're trying to identify what's important to us, who we are in our own eyes, because it has a profound effect on how we feel and behave. The right labels can help us reveal and bring out our potential. For instance, if we've failed in several businesses, there could be quite a difference in our future depending on whether we label ourselves as a "failure" or an "entrepreneur-in-the-making."

I very much recommend spending some time making lists of empowering self-labels, defining what they mean, and then winnowing them down to one or a few that represent what's important to you.

In my own case, after some experimentation I finally settled on four labels that I worked with for awhile: master, healer, lover, winner. Of course, they had personal meanings: "master" to me meant someone becoming more conscious; "healer" someone attempting to contribute; "lover" someone learning to open their heart; "winner" someone doing well and enjoying life. That was what was important to me.

Those labels could just as easily have been phrased as values: consciousness, healing, loving, winning. More important than the form was the fact that these were meaningful words to me. They represented in brief, easily-remembered symbolic form what I wanted to be, the qualities I wanted to bring out in myself. And I found them very helpful.

And as both Tony Robbins and Jim Leonard point out (though they use different terminology systems), all decision-making really comes down to values clarification, to knowing what's important to us. If we have a clear sense of that, a clear sense of those values which we're drawn to, decision-making becomes greatly simplified.

One other thing should be mentioned about our self-identification. The primary direction is inner to outer—that is, what goes on in our inner life, where we put our attention, essentially determines our outer life. But that's not to say that the latter doesn't influence the former; it does.

Every time we act in a new way, no matter how small, it has an effect on our image of who we are and what we're capable of. So it's also important to have the courage to begin acting in new ways, perhaps small ones to begin with, that are consistent with our new labels or values.

When we name our current experience and important values accurately, the effect is actually transformative. We can discover this in our own lives.

Affirming

Affirmations CAN BE thought of as an extended form of self-identification, of who or what we are, and what we'd like our life to be like. In my opinion, affirmations are not as powerful as visualizations, because they involve concepts and so don't reach into the oldest parts of the brain—which process images—the way images can.

So for a while I didn't use them. And was I mistaken. They can be extremely powerful in clarifying what we want and where we're going, in aligning the rational brain with the older parts of our brain, and not least, in helping to conjure up empowering images.

An affirmation is simply a positive statement about some aspect of our life. The affirmation itself has great value, and perhaps of equal value is our reaction to it.

These internal reactions, which I call *secondaries*, are brought up from the unconscious by the affirmation and can then be mindfully observed and integrated just like any other unconscious material. It can also be helpful to write down the secondaries to make them more external.

For example, suppose we use the affirmation, "I have wonderful relationships." If we have any problems at all with relationships, a little voice is going to say something like, "Oh yeah? What about Pat? What about my children?" Whatever the exact words, it's a disagreement with our positive statement. Such secondaries announce the arrival of *the critic*.

The critic is just a metaphor. Actually, there are a number of voices in our heads, voices that can be critical of us in various ways. These voices represent people from our past who became internalized at some point. Our brain bought into certain criticisms so much, particularly those that came from our early caretakers, that it took them and brought them inside! Now they live within us as part of our wounds.

Our wounds essentially have three components: the *kinesthetic*, the *auditory*, and the *visual*. The kinesthetic is about what we feel (sensations or emotions); the auditory, words and sounds that we hear; the visual, what we see.

Each of our wounds has components of all three. For example, if we experience traumatic physical pain at some point, we feel the pain and a corresponding emotion, we hear certain internal conclusions about what happened, and of course we see what happened. All of these components, what we felt and heard and saw, are stored as our memory of what happened.

For healing our wounds, pure mindfulness brings up and integrates all three components. It's the most gradual but also the most thorough process, and indeed, can take us all the way to complete awakening.

Next most important is the kinesthetic level, precisely because it's the feeling level. Thus after mindfulness, the early methods of this chapter were body scanning and breathwork, both of which emphasize the kinesthetic. In the auditory area, where we are now, naming and affirming are found. Farther along, methods for the visual area are considered.

The critic, being a metaphor for all the negative voices inside us, is in the auditory area. And affirmations are one of the best ways to reach it and bring it to the surface where it can be observed and integrated.

So when we say or write an affirmation such as "I have great relationships," if we're mindful we'll notice that there are voices in our unconscious that don't agree, secondaries such as, "Nobody really cares about me" or "How come so-and-so left me?" We want to surface these secondaries into the light of consciousness.

The way to start is to make a list of problem areas in our life, and then formulate them into statements such as, "I keep messing up intimate relationships." Then through a simple inversion, we turn the statement into a nurturing affirmation: "I have a wonderful love life."

What we can do then is write that affirmation on the top line of a sheet of paper or a computer screen, and then pay close attention to the internal secondary that arises, such as "I don't have enough confidence with men," or whatever. We write down that secondary on the second line, and at the same time observe it internally. We experience it, we're mindful of it; we accept it being there.

Then on the next line we write the affirmation once more: "I have a wonderful love life." And again the same or another secondary will come up from the unconscious, some statement that doesn't agree, such as "Other people have a wonderful love life, not me." We write that down under the affirmation.

Then we write down the affirmation again on line five, etc., and just keep going like that until we feel complete for the present. By systematically surfacing the critic in this way, there's less and less resistance to our affirmations, and they can begin to manifest more in our life.

A safeguard concerning visualization also applies here: We should make and use affirmations about ourselves only, not about others. Just as we would not want someone else to try to infringe on our freedom, so we don't want to infringe on others' freedom, even if our intention seems beneficial.

Any attempt to do otherwise is coercive and, in the last analysis, is just another power trip. More to the point, it won't work, because trying to manipulate others leads our energy in a contracted direction, and thus works counter to the life we're affirming. Our most effective work is always on ourselves.

Affirming II

$\mathcal{I}$'M A GREAT believer in being quite outrageous with affirmations. We simply assert what we'd like to be true, even if it seems doubtful or downright impossible. That is, when creating affirmations, we don't pay attention to how possible it seems. We just ask ourselves what we'd really like.

For instance, concerning the subject matter of this chapter we might say, "I love my feelings." This is a general-purpose affirmation which helps us honor our feelings, honor our work in integrating unconscious material, and counter our normal rejection and suppression of painful feelings. It also leads us in the direction of opening to whatever pleasure is in this moment. And in fact, that's another excellent affirmation: "I open to the pleasure in this moment."

It's great fun to play with affirmations. It's very open-ended, the possibilities are limitless, and you'll soon find that you're having a great time creating and trying out the most promising ones. This is an excellent area in which to apply the Japanese concept of *kaizen*—constant improvement.

Over time I've tried to clarify what the most helpful general affirmations might be, ones that any of us could find beneficial. The best one I can think of is this: "I love my life." It starts right out with the feeling that opens our hearts the most. We might have a wonderful life and yet not love it, not be able to appreciate it. We might have many great things in our life, yet be unable to appreciate what we have.

So "I love my life" affirms the love in our heart, it helps us look at our life with gratitude, it says that we're finding life fulfilling and passionate, it says that our life is going in the right direction, it affirms the privilege that our life is. All of these things are affirmed. It can even be used as a mantra, that is, continuously repeated inside for a period of time, with excellent results.

It seems like we've already been given the greatest gift that life has to offer, which is life itself. We already possess the greatest gift; what matters is opening to it. So the most fulfilling general-purpose affirmations that I've been able to identify all start with the formulation, "I love..." Daily work with these is, in my opinion, transformative.

I love my life.
I love my feelings.
I love people.
I love my work.
I love my family and friends.
I love everything in this beautiful world.
I love my love life.
I love my success.
I love my flaws and mistakes.
I love the mystery.
I love my home and community.
I love every moment of my life.
I love you, _____ (your first name).
I profoundly love and accept myself.

That's just a start. From there we can branch out to wherever our imagination takes us:

I am so lucky.
I attract my true soulmate.
My life is wonderful.
My life makes a difference.
My work progresses steadily and well.
I feel relaxed and wonderful.
I feel tremendous peace inside.
I follow my joyful impulses.
Everything is a gift.
Everything is a gift.
Everything is a gift.

Another use of affirmations is when we have challenges. For instance, if my computer broke down and I was having trouble getting it to work right, I might create a short-term affirmation such as, "My computer is working great and I enjoy working on it." This creates, at the least, a very clear outcome for the brain of what would be desirable. Can you feel the images forming in response to that affirmation?

And then there's my current favorite: "Writing this book is the greatest fun in the world."

Healing Visions

A WAY OF using visualization to help heal our psychic wounds and improve our relationships can be called *inner dialogue.* There may be a number of people in our life that we have not had resolutions with—people who we feel have hurt us in some way, but with whom we have not been able to communicate our deepest feelings, for whatever reason.

It can be anyone with whom we've had unsatisfactory experiences or an unsatisfactory relationship. Perhaps we were too little to adequately communicate our feelings. Perhaps we were too intimidated to do it, or the person is dead now, or we don't know where they are. Or perhaps we want to resolve it externally but wisely choose to work in an inner way first. Whatever the reason, inner dialogue can help us complete that communication, with very effective results.

To begin, we choose the person that we'd like to work with on an energy level. We sit or lie down, relax, close our eyes. Then we imagine ourselves and that person together. If they're dead or gone, we can just imagine them as we knew them. It's good to imagine ourselves with them in a beautiful spot somewhere, perhaps on a beach or in a meadow or anyplace that we would find inspiring and comfortable.

Then we imagine that person and ourselves having a conversation. We can pour out all the things we've been holding in, perhaps for a long time. We can scream and shout, we can express our terrible grief and hurt, we can cry or be angry or blaming or whatever we like. This is catharsis time and we can take our finger completely off the edit button. Whatever it is, we can let it out!

It is worth noting, however, that this is not the way we would want to approach such a conversation in real life. In real life this style would be called "dumping" on the other person and would be rather unproductive. (In chapter 6, real-life interactions are looked at.)

Sometimes, and this can be especially true with people who have wounded us deeply, we still find the other person so intimidating that we can't truly express ourselves yet. If so, we can imagine the other person being physically smaller than us. We just make them smaller and smaller in our imagination until we find ourselves completely without fear in expressing our feelings. By the way, they listen and hear us out without interruption—isn't imagination great?

When we're done, then the other person answers and says whatever they like. It's very likely that they also have resentments against us that have been incompletely expressed. So let's let them express it, the reasons, the hurts, the rage, all of it. If it's too difficult to listen to, just make them smaller until you can listen. If you're like me, you may learn a great deal by really listening to them, perhaps for the first time.

We hear them out without interruption, and then we reply. Then we hear their reply, we respond again, and so on back and forth until the process is finished. If we don't have time to let it finish, we can always put it aside and come back to it tomorrow; it'll be right where we left it.

We'll notice a remarkable thing as the dialogue between us and the other person continues: Our communication with each other will gradually calm down. Eventually, as our true selves emerge in the dialogue, it will even become loving. The beauty that we once saw in that person, perhaps long ago, we see again. And they may again see the beauty in us.

This inner process with that person can be repeated as many time as necessary until there's little or no emotional charge on them. When it's over, we can imagine walking on the beach with them, or giving them a hug, or telling them we love them. When we feel loving, or at least somewhat relaxed towards them, then, if it's appropriate, we're much more ready to have a constructive dialogue with them in person.

It's very healing to have such inner dialogues with our parents or caretakers, our spouses, partners, siblings, friends, business associates, etc. Unexpressed hurts or resentments can be there even in a good relationship, let alone deteriorated ones. By letting the unexpressed be expressed on both sides in this utterly safe imaginary environment, almost always we'll find that we can understand that person better and see them once again with our heart.

It needs to be mentioned that seeing someone with our heart does not in any way prevent us from setting proper boundaries with them. It doesn't mean that we need to allow abuse, buy into destructive patterns, condone manipulation or whatever. Seeing people with our heart just means that we'll spontaneously tend to act in ways that will promote greater harmony and well-being for all concerned.

Another way of using the visual modality in our healing process is to work with current problems. What we do is sit or lie down, close our eyes, relax, and then imagine the problem. We see briefly scenes in front of us representing the problem, then we ask our deepest self to give us an *imaginary symbol* which represents the healing of the problem.

Then we wait, and a symbol will emerge. It will usually be something we see, but it may be something we hear or feel, or even all three. Whatever it is, we can take a few minutes each day to bathe our healing symbol in a golden, loving light, in our own healing energy.

Another very effective use of visual energy is to work with *drawings*. For instance, we can make a drawing of our life right now. What it looks like can tell us about ourselves. What does the drawing say? Is it bright or dark? How are people included? What's most prominent? What's missing?

In a few days, we can make another drawing of our life. What's similar to the first drawing? What's different? What's most prominent this time? How are things connected? How does the drawing feel? If it had a voice, what would it say? What does it need? And so on.

Other interesting drawings are infancy, childhood, young adulthood, current problems, the future, our love life, our work life, what we'd like our life to be like, and so on. It can be illuminating to make these drawings with our non-dominant hand, which brings out our inner child more. An immense amount can be learned just by feeling, studying and comparing such different drawings.

Finally, it's fascinating to make a diagram of our *parts*. It's a wonderful metaphor to imagine what our psychic parts are inside, and then draw them. There are no rules whatever for how this is supposed to look, and in fact it will vary widely from one person to the next.

What do you think are the parts inside of you? Is there a controller? A critic? A creator? A lover? A pleasure-seeker? A sufferer? A fighter? The possibilities are endless.

When we've drawn our parts, it's good to just look at them for awhile. What's included? What's left out? What are the connections? What does each part want? What is each part trying to accomplish for us? Is there some way that this could be accomplished more constructively?

We may want to modify a part or create a new one. How? By waving our magic wand. We get the agreement of the other parts to work with this new part. We ask if there's a part that disagrees, and if so, how it might be accommodated. We ask the creative part to suggest ways that the purpose could be accomplished in a better way, and so on.

This is a very creative metaphor, and the idea is to play with these parts until they represent what we'd like. Can such metaphorical play be effective? Very much so, just like inner dialogue, affirmations, symbols, etc., all of which are different forms of metaphor. In each we're adding something to our bare experience, but in a way that's useful and constructive.

Another wonderful use of healing images is to imagine someone that we're having a problem with, and then to send love to them.

The thing is not to worry about getting love *from* them, but just to send love *to* them. From nothing, we conjure up all the love in our heart. We imagine what it would feel like to be really loving. We then imagine that person in our mind's eye and direct all that love to them, bathe them in it.

Of course, the greatest effect of sending such love to another is on ourselves.

Forgiveness

$\mathcal{S}$ENDING LOVE TO another can be a preliminary step to *forgiveness*—sometimes it helps us to get the emotional wheels moving—but preferably it is an ongoing part of our forgiveness of ourselves and others.

Forgiveness is essential, of course, because our hearts are contracted to the extent that we cannot forgive something or someone.

The danger, though, is in forgiving too easily or too soon. Sound strange? What it's good to avoid, in my opinion, is a kind of "whitewash" forgiveness, where we forgive someone on the surface but deep down still harbor resentment towards them. In other words, we want our forgiveness to be deep and genuine; then it has a truly profound effect.

Every time we heal even a little of one of our psychic wounds, it has an effect on our overall ability to forgive. Whenever any unconscious energy rejoins consciousness, our heart becomes a little more open. Thus in helping us to heal, each of the methods described in this chapter also helps us to forgive. And conversely, when we can forgive we help to heal our basic wounds.

Before talking about forgiveness, a few words should be mentioned about the front porch to forgiveness—apology. This is about when we're simply wrong, when we've clearly hurt another in some way but we're tempted to be self-righteous about it.

Sometimes, even with the best of intentions, we hurt others. Just in the nature of things, we're going to make withdrawals from our emotional capital with others from time to time. Sometimes we're just human; we're just not as intelligent or skillful or conscious or heartful as we'd like to be.

Having made more than my share of such inadvertent withdrawals, I've found that usually the simplest and the best thing to do is to just apologize, and the sooner the better. When we can do so, we benefit not only the other person, but also ourselves.

By apologizing we let go of *self-righteousness,* a form of suffering that happens when we make others wrong. In order to cling to self-righteousness, we have to build walls. When we build a wall against somebody or something, we think we're locking out pain, but actually we're locking it in.

For one thing, we have less energy. A psychic wall is dynamic and requires energy to maintain itself. This is energy unavailable to the rest of our organism, diminishing to that extent our vitality and aliveness.

Second, our consciousness is smaller, less spacious. Bliss increases as the limits of our consciousness grow more flimsy, as we begin to taste the oceanic consciousness that our small consciousness resides in. When we build walls, to that extent we build up a kind of mental cage and restrict our access to the larger consciousness. We're living in a much more limited psychic environment.

Third, a self-righteous state of mind is a suffering state of mind because it means that we're attached, we're insisting on a particular point of view. Self-righteous insistence is the essence of suffering, because it means we're stuck somewhere. We're no longer as free to move; we're not flowing with the river as much.

The larger in spirit we allow ourselves to be, the more easily we can apologize when it's appropriate. Then we can let go more easily. We've done what we can; we don't have to hold onto that pain anymore. We've cleansed our hearts, helped to heal a portion of ourselves, and a portion of the world as well.

Forgiveness II

$\mathcal{T}$o SPECIFICALLY APPROACH forgiveness, a good way to start is with a *life history*. It's very instructive to sit down and write out the story of our life. We could ask this question: If we described the ten or twenty most influential events in our life, what would they be? From that, we ask: Who hurt us the most, and how, and when? Then we ask: Who are the people in our life history that we most need to forgive?

Then, if we like, we can pick someone from that group and first do some inner dialogue with them. After that, we might want to write a *five-part letter* to them. This excellent type of letter is advocated by Jeanne Miller and Phil Laut.

A letter need not necessarily be sent. Lincoln wrote many letters complaining to people about this and that, and then would throw them in the fire. Great healing can come just from expressing ourselves as we would truly want to, and for that purpose any form of letter will do.

On the other hand, if we potentially want to send the letter, more skill is called for. Otherwise we're just "dumping," discharging our emotional garbage onto someone else, with predictable results.

A five-part letter has a reasonable chance of producing a good result if sent. But a precaution: The good intent of a five-part letter can be ruined by emphasizing the "negative" part of the letter over the "positive" part. If we refrain from that, the results can be quite encouraging.

Such a letter allows us to express even very difficult things and yet sometimes—no guarantees—leaves the other person saying that they actually enjoyed reading it. Often our attitude towards the person will undergo some change just by writing the letter to them, whether it's sent or not. And if it is sent, it can potentially be even more healing.

We begin the letter, to and about this other person, by a salutation and then perhaps a brief explanation of what we're doing. Then we begin a sentence: "Something I'm grateful for...." and finish it by writing something we're grateful for about them. And sometimes we might add an explanatory sentence or two.

Then we start a new paragraph and sentence and write: "Something I'm grateful for...." and finish the sentence. And then another sentence: "Something I'm grateful for...." and so on. We're telling the person things we may never have told them before, all the things we're grateful for about them. We continue like this, starting and finishing sentences in that form, until we feel complete with it.

Then we start a second type of sentence: "Something I'd like to be forgiven for...." and complete the sentence. And another: "Something I'd like to be forgiven for...." and we complete it. And once again, we keep going like that until we feel complete.

Then we do the same with the third type of sentence, "Something I would like to forgive...." and the fourth, "Something I want...." and the fifth, "Something I love about you...." So the letter has this form:

Something I'm grateful for....
Something I'd like to be forgiven for....
Something I'd like to forgive....
Something I want....
Something I love about you....

Note something interesting: The letter begins and ends with positive statements. It starts with things we're grateful for and continues with things we'd like to be forgiven for. So by the time the person gets to the most difficult part—things we'd like to forgive—they're ready to read it, they're in the right frame of mind to read it.

Then following that are things we'd like to see, which is neutral-to-positive, and things we love about them, which is very positive. So the letter is at least 75% positive. Moreover, it's a chance for us to remember what we love and are grateful for about that person. That works on our own heart.

Finally, the letter is not accusatory. It doesn't say, "You did this and so you're a thus-and-so." Instead it says something a bit more skillful: "Something I'd like to forgive is...." Whatever it is, we're already saying that we'd like to forgive it, if we can, and move on.

Writing such a letter, whether sent or not, can create quite a shift. That's particularly true if we've been doing some inner work on this person, perhaps some breathwork or inner dialogue or a "raw" letter first. At some point we'll feel a shift in how we feel about them, how we see them; we'll suddenly have more humor and compassion about it all.

Again, taking steps towards forgiveness doesn't mean we have to lay down and be a victim. It doesn't mean that we can't set appropriate boundaries. It doesn't mean that we can't take care of ourselves.

As Ken Keyes says, we can love another person without necessarily buying into their act. We just look into our hearts and do whatever seems right from that place. And how that's going to look isn't necessarily predictable.

Forgiveness is about our heart. It's an inner thing, it's not about what we do externally. Our inner forgiveness may or may not be followed by some external action. But if our heart is right, and if our forgiveness is genuine, then whatever we do externally, if anything, will tend to be right too. It will tend towards greater harmony.

In many ways, the most important act of forgiveness is to forgive ourselves: So let's ask ourselves a question now, one based on an idea by Harvey Jackins:

Given your heritage and childhood and upbringing, given your background and education and all the experiences you've been through, isn't it true that you've done the very best you could at every moment of your life?

Though it may not have been very good or very empowering, wasn't it the best you knew how to do at that time? Didn't you make the best decisions you were capable of at each moment? If you could have made better decisions at any moment, wouldn't you have done so? If you had known how to be more skillful or more conscious at any moment, wouldn't you have done so?

Everyone I've ever asked those questions of has replied, "Yes." And the reason is this: The simple truth is that you did the best you knew how to do. If you could have done it better at any moment, you would have. If you'd known how to be more skillful, more loving, more compassionate, more aware, you would have been.

When we truly see this, we can forgive ourselves; we can let ourselves off the torture rack at last. What we did may not have been very enlightened sometimes, but it was the best we could do at the time.

In my own case, I've committed many unconscious acts in my life: thoughtless acts where I've hurt someone. Yet even then, I was doing the best I knew how to do. At each moment I was making the best decisions I knew how to make.

True forgiveness is seeing that this is true for all of us. It's true for you and me and everybody. We're all in the same boat. We've all done the best we knew how to do at every moment, even when it wasn't adequate.

And yes, it's even true for the people who wounded us. They were doing the best they knew how to do, too. It may not have been good enough at times, but still, if they'd truly known in their bones how to do it better, they would have. We all would have.

To really see this is to just forgive everybody, including those who wounded us, including ourselves—everybody. It's understanding that we're all seeking the light in our own way. Sometimes it's more apparent than at other times, but we're all groping towards it as best we can.

When we work to heal our inner wounds, we're also healing our basic ability to relate. Then we can more easily see the light in ourselves and others. That light is there in each of us, and as we focus on it we help it to become more manifest in the world. Then our own heart, and the heart in others, are both increasingly revealed.

BOOK **6**
Outer Heart
APPRECIATION

Book 6, Outer Heart, is about
bringing the golden rule to life
in practical terms, and thus how
to bring more love and beauty
into our relationships.

The Golden Rule

*W*HO HAS NOT heard of Jesus' famous golden rule?

Do unto others as we would have them do unto us.

Instinctively we recognize its beauty, its power, its elegance. Yet somehow too it seems a bit impractical, more suited perhaps to an extraordinary being like Jesus or to an ideal world somewhere than to the everyday nitty-gritty of *this* life.

"Okay, so how I'd like so-and-so to treat me is to give me all their money. So does that mean I should give them all my money?" It seems impractical. We honor the golden rule, but we don't want to give it much thought in our practical affairs because, damnit, we have to live in the real world.

But perhaps our problem with the golden rule is that we don't really understand it the way that Jesus intended.

Let's look at it once again, in more modern language this time:

Treat others as we would like to be treated.

And how would we like to be treated?

If we like chocolate ice cream and Tom likes vanilla, and Tom wants to practice the golden rule towards us, does he give us vanilla ice cream because that's what he likes? No, he gives us chocolate, because that's *our* preference.

In other words he doesn't say to himself, "How I'd like to be treated is to receive vanilla ice cream, so that's what I'll give you." No, he thinks of *us* and what we'd like; he gives us chocolate.

What does it mean then:

"—as we would like to be treated"?

It means that the first desire of our heart is simply to be understood and appreciated. And to be treated by others from that understanding and appreciation.

Our greatest psychological need from others is to be appreciated, affirmed, valued, understood. We want to feel that we matter, that we have a worth, that we're cared about, that we "make sense." We consider our greatest friends to be those who understand us, who appreciate us, who accept us just as we are.

We want people to empathize with us, to appreciate and understand our beauty and points of view, and if they act towards us to do so based on that empathy. If others are going to practice the golden rule towards us, they're going to have to appreciate who we really are first.

But that same appreciation is exactly what others want as well. So a translation of the golden rule becomes:

Treat others based on an appreciation of them.

I almost used "understanding" in that last sentence, but upon reflection it doesn't seem to go far enough. We can feel that we "understand" someone and yet still not feel benevolent towards them.

This is a little different. It's about being willing to look into the core of someone and see what's right about them, what's beautiful about them, what's good about them, and respond to that and nurture it and treat them based upon it.

When we can do that, our relationships will take care of themselves.

That's really all this chapter has to say. But let's break it down into a few details anyway, just for fun.

Before we begin, let's remember that appreciation and understanding don't mean agreement. What we really want from others is not for them to agree with us, but simply to look into our heart, to see from our lens for a little while, and above all, to see the beauty that is at the core of each of us.

Seek to Understand

At the bottom of appreciation is understanding. Understanding is so important because it forms the kernel, the very basis for appreciation.

The key concept of really trying to *understand* other people, as opposed to some technique for getting along better with them, didn't enter my consciousness until I read Stephen Covey's landmark synthesis, *The Seven Habits of Highly Effective People,* in 1989. Then I got it, and it's made such a difference. The sections on "understanding" and "listening" here are based on my own experience now, but derive any poetry in their ideas from Dr. Covey's seminal work.

Let's mention here, too, the psychologist and humanist Carl Rogers, who apparently discovered in the 1950's the idea of *reflective* or *empathic listening.* This remarkable contributor seems also to have been the first to use encounter groups.

Understanding is so vital because it forms the basis of all other things that we do in relation to other people. Without it, we cannot hope to really practice the golden rule towards others, and our relationships cannot really attain the richness and beauty that we're capable of.

What's needed is to really look into someone's being and see what's beautiful and right about them. When we give someone that gift, they almost can't help but respond. Most fundamentally, we understand others by *seeking to understand them.* We love others by *seeking to love them.*

"Seek and ye shall find," Jesus said. When seeking to understand another, what are we really doing?

We're seeking to comprehend what's important to them.

If we're trying to rebuild a relationship with our son or daughter, say, and they're into the internet right now, it's not going to do much good to take them to the theater because we're interested in Shakespeare.

Instead, we can look at them carefully enough to see what's important to them. We might show them a new website we found, or share creating a family home page with them, or go with them to an internet tradeshow. Again, what we're really doing, in Stephen Covey's masterful phrase, is making what's important to the other person important to us.

I love to give good examples about people I've learned from. Once I heard Tony Robbins describe what he did on his wedding anniversary. His wife, he knew, loved anything that was romantic and exotic. So on that day they took a stroll along the beach together at sunset. As they walked they started hearing, from the cliffs above, sounds of drums. They took a path up the cliff to see what was going on. At the top they found a table set for dinner, with a band suddenly playing romantic music, and a waiter ready to take their order!

He made what was important to her important to him.

In order to best understand the details of understanding and appreciation, let's first look at an interesting metaphor that serves as a very good thermometer in measuring the state of our relationships with others:

Emotional Accounts

*W*HAT DOES IT take for understanding to deepen between two people? What does it take for someone to really open up and tell us about themselves? Is there something so important to people that our desire to understand them depends upon it?

Stephen Covey talks about a great metaphor called the *emotional bank account,* which conveys very clearly a simple yet profound idea about what relationships are based on.

The emotional bank account is like a financial bank account, only it measures how we're doing with another person. And the fascinating thing about it is that it measures not how much love they feel for us, but rather, how much *trust* they feel in us. Its unit of measure is trust, not love, and that represents an extremely valuable lesson about relationships.

This lesson is that the caring or regard that we have for another is founded in a bedrock of trust. If we're beginning to trust someone less we're beginning to become more guarded. If our trust is diminishing, we may still love them but we'll tend to be less open, less vulnerable. And others react the same way if their trust in us is diminishing.

So understanding between us and another ultimately depends upon something else—the trust between us. Many romances founder upon this principle: The trust becomes so damaged that, even though some love may still be there, the couple can no longer function well together.

The saying, "It's greater to be trusted than to be loved," expresses this wisdom: That those people we trust more and more we come to love more. It feels safe to love them; there's no conflict between our trust and our feelings.

So if we want to be good at loving other people, we must first become trustworthy. No tricks or gimmicks will do, because over time people do sense where we're really coming from. In general, people trust us more as we become more worthy of their trust.

The emotional bank account is a metaphor to measure someone's trust in us. It measures how dependably safe they feel around us. But how do we know how high or how low the account is?

We know by using our intuition, our inner sense of what is so. If we just ask ourselves where our emotional bank account is with someone—and we're mindful—the answer will come with great reliability.

As an experiment, let's imagine several different people in our life and ask ourselves how our emotional bank account is with each of them, on a scale of zero to a hundred. With a little practice we'll find that our intuition knows immediately where we stand with someone else.

When we make continuing deposits with another person through integrity, appreciation, understanding and so on, we build up a reserve in our emotional bank account with that person. Their trust towards us increases. Conversely, if we act insincere, critical, insensitive, etc. the account goes down, because withdrawals are being made from it.

When the account is high, communication between two people is easy, spontaneous, understanding. They get our meaning even if it isn't phrased right. If there's a misunderstanding, we get the benefit of the doubt. Because they trust us, people are willing to open up more. In consequence, we come to understand them a lot better.

If we make a mistake with that person, it's overlooked, forgiven, discounted. If we make a serious mistake, they'll trust us enough to share it with us and work it out rather than build resentment or disconnect. When issues arise, they're resolved in a spirit of love.

When we have a high account with another person, we have a lot of flexibility with them. Goodwill prevails because of that underlying trust. In friendship, romance, marriage it allows for deeper and deeper intimacy: They feel and we feel "I trust you enough to show you more of the real me, to be myself around you. I trust that you can accept even those parts of me that seem unlovable."

If the emotional bank account falls into the medium range, communication suffers. Now it's not so free and easy. Certain subjects are touchy or need to be avoided. Trust is still there, though less so. Mistakes are considered more seriously, because there's less of a reserve to draw upon. But still, things are usually resolved satisfactorily, and the relationship gives a certain amount of fulfillment.

In a couple, this level looks like accommodation. They respect and tolerate each other, but the real aliveness, softness and vulnerability is missing except for occasional moments.

When the emotional bank account becomes low, we have to be careful of what we say. We're walking on eggshells. Often we put what we want to say into writing to make sure we'll be heard. There are strong feelings of resentment and being misunderstood. Tension smolders, and often there are battles, arguments. Verbal defensiveness alternates with emotional withdrawals and cold war. Self-righteousness is very prominent.

When the account sinks lower and becomes overdrawn, the situation often ends up in open warfare. A couple will refuse to speak to each other, or go to court and confess each other's sins. There is active mistrust. Bad motives are assumed, and words or actions are interpreted through a negative filter. The parties tend to demonize each other.

The emotional bank account is an example of reaping what we sow. If we belittle others, condemn them, blow up at them, take advantage, act deceptively and so on, we're making withdrawals in the account and its balance is falling lower.

It's good to understand that rebuilding an emotional bank account takes time. We can't just see the error of our ways and expect some relationship to suddenly get better, though that is occasionally possible.

Usually there is no quick fix, since trust tends to build slowly but fall quickly, like financial markets. "It slides faster than it glides," as the saying goes. So it takes time to rebuild. Accounts fall low because of large or repeated withdrawals, and we can't just snap our fingers and fill up the account again. But we *can* make a start.

Raising the level of an emotional bank account is a process, like growing a crop. It takes time. It usually gets restored slowly, a gradual process of making periodic deposits into the account while doing our best to avoid those things that cause withdrawals.

Let's keep this metaphor of the emotional bank account in mind as we examine the details concerning understanding and appreciating other people, and thus practicing the golden rule with them.

Listening

$\mathscr{G}$OOD LISTENING IS the essence of understanding. If good understanding is the key to appreciation, then in turn, good listening is the key to understanding.

I used to think that the core of good conversation was thinking up witty and interesting things to say. Thus while other people were talking I would be busy thinking up some clever reply. I was astonished to gradually realise that all this had almost nothing to do with conversing with another, let alone communing with another.

What's the essence of good conversation then?

It's about listening so carefully to the other person that we really get what they're communicating. Then our reply or comment, believe it or not, comes without any forethought on our part.

Rather, our response comes from inside us, directly from the organism itself, and if we've listened well enough our comment or reply tends to be harmonious, interesting and appropriate—*even though we expended no effort to try to make it that way.* It just happens by itself if we've been receptive enough.

Such listening is meant in the broadest sense, and is in no way confined to only understanding the words. It means taking in the other person, opening up to them on all levels and in every dimension we can. It means honoring them, valuing who they are and what they're trying to express.

Such listening is in some ways an external counterpart to sitting in mindfulness. When we sit silently in mindfulness, we're receptive to whatever comes up, to whatever wants to fill up the space of our consciousness. No attempt to control.

Good listening has the same characteristics. It might be described as external mindfulness—mindfulness applied to the other person.

The first question we might ask is: What prevents us? Is there something that gets in the way of good listening, and if so, what is it?

The greatest barrier to good listening comes in trying to *impose our own agenda on the other person's expression.*

Let me tell you a story: When I went to college we had these eating clubs, kind of like fraternities, and each year at a certain time the upperclassmen in the clubs would interview the sophomores who wanted to join. Each interview would be one-on-one, and would take about 15 to 20 minutes.

When I was an upperclassman and it was my turn to conduct some of these interviews, I would sit down with a sophomore and say something like, "So, what are you really like, anyway?" or "Why should you join this club?"

Can you hear the arrogance? In those days I had no idea how to even make small talk, let alone have a heart-to-heart conversation, and besides, since we only had a few minutes I thought the whole idea was to "get to the point."

But we can't really "get right to the point" with human beings. It's too direct, too violent, too harsh. We may very well get an answer, but we won't see the real person.

Only by being receptive, spacious, patient, and a good listener can we hope to contact the real person. Otherwise, we'll get the public face, the canned reply, defensiveness or whatever, but not the being.

We all have layers and layers to our persona, like the layers of an onion, and only when we feel really safe do we begin to peel the outer layers away to reveal the deeper ones underneath. When we impose our own agenda on what someone is trying to convey, we shut off this process. And then the real person or the real problem stays hidden.

For example, I had a great love one time where my chief complaint was that she wouldn't communicate her feelings. Yet every time she did try to communicate her truth about something I would get defensive, reactive and self-righteous.

Naturally she couldn't share her real feelings with me for very long, couldn't peel the onion anymore because it just wasn't safe to do so. And so resentment built up and she left one day, while I grieved and wondered why I was always meeting people who didn't really share their feelings.

Silly, eh? But the tendency to react instead of respond is widespread. We want to jump right in and set people straight, figure out the problem, share our experience and so on.

But if we haven't given the other the spaciousness to be comfortable, to open up to their real feelings or to the real problem, our replies will simply be irrelevant. We'll be coming from our conditioning, looking through our personal lens and mistaking it for theirs. And the other will feel frustrated and misunderstood. They'll feel that we "just don't get it."

Let's see if we can learn from some of the mistakes I made in those club interviews, ways in which I was blocking real communication:

The first way was that I was *asking directive questions*, that is, probing. I'd interrupt somebody in the middle of what they were saying and ask them something concerning what *I* wanted to know about. Examples of this are:

"Why did you do that?"

"What about your finances?"

"Are you and Jane splitting up?"

Here we're forcing the other to communicate through our own agenda. We're asking questions to direct the course of what they're expressing. We want to get to the heart of the matter right away.

But that's like pulling on a plant to make it grow faster; it just destroys the plant. Similarly, a person's ability to open up with us can't be forced or directed. It can only develop in its own time, as they trust us more.

When we probe we're using force. We're controlling, directing, manipulating, and people turn away inside. We can ask probing questions all day long and get nowhere. People may be polite, but they close down inside. We haven't shown respect for their own process.

The second mistake I made was *judging and evaluating*. We can call this "J&E" for short, and it expresses our need to interpret for other people, to let them know our analysis of what they're saying. J&E shuts people down inside because it doesn't allow them to open up at their own speed.

Examples are:

"You've got it all wrong."

"That's your Oedipus complex."

"I told you that would create trouble."

When we interpret for others we're not giving them a lot of psychological space. Now they've got to deal with our interpretations. Feeling judged, they usually either clam up or start arguing about the point. Either way, real understanding is blocked. We're coming from our own autobiography and trying to impose it on others instead of truly seeking to understand them.

The third mistake I made was *giving unsolicited advice.* Examples are:

"I know exactly what you need."

"Here's what I would do."

"Let me tell you what happened to me."

Again we're putting the emphasis on us, on our filters, our experience, our evaluations. Because the real problem is often not revealed immediately, in effect we're prescribing without a proper diagnosis.

When we jump in with advice, we're looking at our own intentions and motives and using them to interpret what a deposit for the other would be. We're looking through our own history and then projecting onto others what we think they need or want based on our needs or wants.

The fourth mistake was *emotional defensiveness.* This happens when someone is talking about us or our tribe or our ideas or whatever, and we interpret what they say in such a way that we feel that we have to defend ourselves or our point of view, and/or attack them or their point of view. You can imagine what this does to the other person's willingness to open up and share their real self.

Whenever we block understanding through reactivity or defensiveness, then, we'll be wondering why the other is so uncooperative, uncommunicative or uninteresting. Sometimes we're so desperate to be understood ourselves that we don't take the time to listen and understand the other first.

Any kind of coercion or controlling behavior towards others is a waste of time for a number of reasons, one of which is that we never get to see the real person. We don't see the love and beauty and generosity that can be there.

The only way to truly understand another person is simply to listen. People are anxious to tell us what's in their heart if only they can trust us enough, if only we make it safe enough for them, if only we give them enough spaciousness.

The essence of the golden rule, in my opinion, is that we give others *first* what we'd like to have ourselves.

Listening II

$\mathscr{S}$EEKING TO UNDERSTAND another, to appreciate another, has to come from the heart. We have to really be seeking to see the beauty in them, to understand their point of view, not just feigning interest. We let them show us how they view the world. Not to agree or disagree, but simply to understand.

When we listen well enough to understand another, it's an incalculable gift. Then we're saying, in effect, "I value you enough to lay my framework aside for a moment and really listen so that I can comprehend and appreciate you."

In doing that, we open ourselves up to being influenced by the other. That's the risk, that we too can be influenced. So having a little stillness inside helps greatly in good listening. Then we can listen to other points of view without feeling a need to react. Without a little stillness, we cling to our own positions and paradigms, afraid to let go of them even for a moment.

Hence the importance once again of mindfulness, of becoming more aware of our own internal process. It slowly allows us to see our positions as positions, our conditionings as conditionings, so we don't have to cling to them so tightly. As our inner stability grows we can be flexible enough to look, for a moment, through someone else's lens.

People do want to open up. Without exception we have hurt and pain and humiliation inside, things we don't think we can share, things about us that we don't think are lovable. And we have experiences and feelings of great beauty that also need a receptive atmosphere to be shared.

When someone is secure enough to give us lots of space and safety in which to express ourselves, we blossom. We share our feelings; we become more real, more ourselves. We can explore our heart, share who we are. It's a great gift when we receive it. And it's something that we can give to others. And following the golden rule, we can give it first.

Good listening is one of those things that seems like wandering through pea soup until we get it, and then it seems so simple and so obvious that we wonder why we didn't get it long before—but it's still like pea soup until we get it.

Basically, we just give up our agendas and any need to control and just open up to the other person, really tune in to them. Good listening is much more than reflective listening, but reflective listening is a great place to start—because in order to reflect back to somebody what they're saying, we have to really listen, perhaps for the first time.

The first level in reflective listening is to *summarize the content*. Basically, we listen to what someone says and repeat it back to them.

"I don't want to put up with your being late anymore! You're late too often!"

"You don't like my being late so much."

Summarizing the content represents a great advance, because in order to mimic we must first listen. When I started out, I was so unused to actually listening to other people that it was all I could do just to let go of the intense urge to reply right away. The best I could manage was to repeat back a few phrases here and there. Yet even that was a tremendous shift for me.

Summarizing what someone else is saying causes us to listen more intently. We have to comprehend the meaning of what is being said in order to summarize it. However, we're still at a rational level.

One thing to avoid is the *back-handed summary,* where we rephrase something in a negative or prejudicial way:

"I don't want to put up with your being late anymore. You're late too often!"

"You're impatient so you can't tolerate a little lateness."

This last reply is not reflective listening, of course, but actually a counter-argument under the guise of listening well. The person's words are being twisted against them. Far from creating openness and spaciousness, this kind of reply will really shut it down.

Rather, what we want is to summarize someone's point of view so accurately and so truly that it's better than they might do it themselves.

The second level of listening is to *reflect the feeling.*

"I don't want to put up with your being late anymore! You're late too often!"

"You're feeling frustrated."

People communicate in many dimensions at once, and often the least of it is words. We also communicate through facial expressions, body language, posture, gestures, eyes, tone and timbre of voice, volume and so on. Distancing behavior, cold silence, etc., also communicate.

To really listen well, then, we tune in on every level that we can. Not just to what someone's saying, but to how they're saying it: the context, the feelings, the sensory messages.

We're trying to really see through their lens, and to do that we have to listen not just with our ears but with our being. We don't need to have specialized knowledge in order to do that. We just need to be sincerely attentive, to use our intuition to hear the communication that's coming "between the lines."

On the third level we combine these components. We *summarize the content and reflect the feeling*.

"I don't want to put up with your being late anymore! You're late too often!"

"You're feeling upset that I'm late so often."

Now we're finally getting to the heart of the matter. Now we're reflecting back to someone on both a rational and a feeling level, using our analytical right brain and our intuitive left one as well.

Of course, it's not the words we say but where we're coming from when we say them that makes the difference. Even if our skills at good listening aren't well developed yet, if we're sincerely seeking to understand others, they'll get it.

The interesting thing is that when we sincerely attempt to understand, we make it possible for the other person to be more authentic around us. The barrier between what they're saying and what they'd like to say begins to dissolve.

Then they can begin to really be themselves. They feel so relieved because instead of encountering resistance they're encountering another human heart. In such a space, not just communication but a real communion can occur.

Once a friend was visiting me for a weekend, and when she arrived she was quite angry but wouldn't say anything. I asked her what was wrong, and she said a few words but was still hesitant. I just listened and sometimes reflected back to her some of her feelings and thoughts.

I listened intently, giving her lots of space to express herself, and suddenly a torrent of words and feeling came out and the real issue emerged, which was quite different from the ostensible one. The *real* issue was speedily resolved, and we felt much closer.

When we don't use good listening, oftentimes we'll be dealing with an issue which isn't even the real issue, but the issue which feels safe enough to talk about. Naturally, since it isn't the real issue, it doesn't resolve satisfactorily

When we attempt to understand people and appreciate the beauty in them, when we create safety and space for them, their trust and confidence in us increases and they often begin to work through the actual issues that concern them.

Listening III

$\mathscr{G}$OOD LISTENING IS especially important when the other person is being reactive.

For instance, suppose someone asks for our advice on some matter. And we give it, but notice that their response to our advice is reactive. Then it's a good idea to go back to reflective listening:

Let's say we've been asked about a debt problem and we respond, "How about going to a credit counselor who can call up all the creditors and maybe schedule small payments for awhile?" And we hear the reply, "What are you talking about? I don't have any money for payments!"

When a person responds reactively, any further advice is useless. When someone is feeling reactive they simply cannot listen to advice. It only creates ill will and a feeling of being misunderstood. So in such a situation good listening is once again called for, and we might say something like:

"So you feel trapped, like you have no alternatives."

"Exactly," they say, "that's it. It's a feeling of being very confined and limited. I have a little income, you see, but not nearly enough to take care of these bills."

Now the person is calming down a bit, and at some point they'll again become receptive instead of reactive:

"Well, do you really feel a credit counselor could help?"

Since the response is not emotionally charged now, our advice is once again appropriate:

"Well, I was in the same situation once and that course of action was very helpful to me."

Another example of this is when we're accused of something. Let's say our mate turns to us and starts telling us how upset they are that we don't help around the house enough. Our usual response to this might be to state defensively that they don't appreciate all the things we do, or counter-accuse that they're not affectionate enough, or whatever.

Will any of that help? Not at all. It will just lead to an argument, perhaps the latest in a long line. This approach gets the primal and emotional brains inflamed, with predictably poor results. What will help is to apply good listening to the situation. Instead of responding back emotionally, we can simply reflect back what they're saying and expressing until they calm down. Sometimes it requires a lot of patience, but they will calm down eventually.

At that point we can tell our side of the story and it will be listened to. If the other becomes reactive again, we once again revert to good listening. In actual practice, you'll find at this point that even your responses take place in a context of deep and true listening. In this way very charged scenes can often be defused and dealt with in a positive way.

Many people find that it's quite a relief to have something constructive available when a potential argument arises. Instead of reacting back, or feeling helpless and resentful, we can just use the energy in this constructive way, which tends to promote a heartful and fruitful discussion. It's one of the most valuable things we can know how to do.

This is part of a larger aspect of good listening, which is knowing when to use it. There are times when the most appropriate thing is simply to say nothing, or to nod, or reply with a single word—times when reflecting back to someone would be an intrusion, an interruption.

Only we can know when those times are. By attempting to really tune in, to understand and appreciate that person, we'll intuitively know the right thing to do. Techniques are just a starting point, like training wheels. The real essence is to come from a quiet, understanding heart.

Sometimes the best thing to do is just to be with someone silently, to show them respect, to let a silent communion of hearts occur. This is particularly helpful with those who are ill. Studies have shown that just being together with someone in silence, with no words, can bring about a profound sense of togetherness and communion.

If someone is semi-conscious or anxious or preoccupied with pain, we can deepen the communion by synchronizing our breath. We just let our breath fall into rhythm with theirs. If the breathing is very fast, we can synchronize with alternate breaths. If we breathe with someone and then gradually slow our own breath down, their breath will also calm down. And studies show that breathing more slowly is strongly correlated with relaxation of anxiety.

Whether someone wants to talk or be silent, the idea is to give that greatest of gifts—our acceptance, understanding, appreciation—and give it first.

Listening IV

A FINAL ASPECT of good listening, which can be called *empathic talking*, is to talk for the other when that's appropriate. It's a willingness to gently express someone else's point of view for them when that's desirable.

For instance, empathic talking is quite useful when a relationship has become so seriously damaged that the parties are no longer talking. Or two sides in a negotiation can reach a place where they think a resolution of their differences is not possible.

Our normal reaction in such situations is to be silently hostile, or to react with sarcastic or angry outbursts confessing the sins of the other. This only makes matters worse. A more effective alternative is to practice empathic talking. Empathic talking means to talk for the other, to express their feelings and point of view better than they would themselves.

A friend who owns a small business once over-reacted and publicly berated an employee, who since then had been courteous but distant. They had once been good friends, and my friend had tried everything she could to repair it, but nothing had worked. We discussed it, and she decided to try empathic talking.

They went out for lunch, and my friend took the occasion to express what her employee's point of view might have been. She took her time, and went into it in detail. "I guess you felt this..." "You must have felt that..."

The effect was miraculous. Suddenly her employee was willing to really talk about the incident, expressing his bitterness. My friend responded with good listening, and later, expressed what had happened from her point of view. The conflict was resolved; the relationship was restored.

If we're patient enough using empathic talking, usually the other person will eventually start talking again themselves. Why? Because we won't get it quite right. As they feel more comfortable and understood they'll start to correct us: "Yes you got that, but you missed this..." or "That's sort of it, but I really felt like this..."

In empathic talking we'll never get it perfect. We're not that person, so our expression of their views or feelings will never quite match up. But if we're close enough, a dialogue can begin once more and a true resolution becomes possible. It can also be used in a negotiation where the two sides have grown skeptical or far apart. The idea is to present the other side's point of view better than they would themselves.

I have a friend who had severe difficulties obtaining a critical license. He had to appear before a panel which had already turned him down once before. This time he decided to go into the meeting and present the panel's point of view as they would themselves before presenting his own viewpoint.

And he did. He calmly, patiently, respectfully presented *their* point of view, showing deep understanding of the panel's concerns. And then when he presented his own point of view he did so in the context of that understanding.

He received the license.

When someone has died, or it's no longer possible to communicate with them, or we find it difficult to empathize with someone, we can seek to heal things on an inner level by inner dialogue. Or we can use a variation of empathic talking which we might call *empathic writing*. We write an imaginary letter from them to us.

In it, we express their point of view, how they must have felt. Writing this letter from them to us greatly increases our understanding of the other person. It breaks us out of our own limited point of view, and helps us see both sides. That in turn helps us to forgive and let go, releasing some of our energy for a better purpose.

Another fine use of empathic talking is when we're with someone who has had a loss. Ellen Kriedman talks about this. For instance, if a bride is left at the altar we might be tempted to say something like, "It's good you found out now" or "I always thought he was no good." Such expressions, though well-meaning, will only make the person feel worse.

Instead we can use empathic talking, and validate their feelings: "I'm so sorry. You must be feeling awful, so let down." Such simple validation, along with just holding the person if appropriate, comforts them much more than any brilliant words we could say. No need to be brilliant to be helpful. We can just validate someone's feelings at such a time, just be there for them.

If someone's child dies, for instance, we need not say how lucky that they still have other children. Though well-intentioned, uplifting expressions at such a time only hurt rather than help, because the person feels even more isolated in their grief. Instead we can hold them, tell them how sorry we are, that they must be going through hell. We can just be there with them.

These are the aspects of good listening. Again, the real miracle is wrought not by technique but by our true empathy, by our sincere attempt to appreciate the beauty in someone, to see through their lens and understand them.

Good listening is vital to using the golden rule, because it allows us to understand and appreciate someone else, and then to act towards them based on that. It is what all of us most desire from others.

Non-reactiveness

*R*EACTIVITY CREATES KARMA. "Karma" here doesn't mean anything mystical; just the seeming fact that everything we do creates waves, ripples that then have to be dealt with. As long as we're *reactive*—responding from conditioning—we tend to create situations that then feel negative to us. And when they happen, it feels like we're the victim of them.

As long as we put the responsibility for how we're feeling "out there," we feel more or less victimized. But it took me a long time to realize that our feelings are not about reality; our feelings are just about our feelings.

When we begin to see how reactive we actually are, and that our viewpoints about things don't necessarily represent the whole "truth," our reactiveness gradually lessens. Because now we're beginning to watch our reactions *as* reactions, our viewpoints *as* just viewpoints. This lessening of reactivity very much affects our relationships with others.

In appreciating others and seeing their beauty, and in responding from that seeing, the next element after listening is being non-reactive, briefly referred to earlier.

Every kind of work on ourselves that we do tends to heal our emotional wounds and thus decrease our reactivity long-term. Such a process is uniquely valuable, but happens gradually, almost imperceptibly. In the meantime, we can help ourselves a great deal by consciously choosing to be more non-reactive in our relationships.

The reason for this is that nothing lowers an emotional bank account faster than an emotional over-reaction. If we blow up at somebody, harshly accuse them, act jealous and so on, large withdrawals are occurring. When we feel a negative emotional charge *and act upon it*, we damage ourselves and others, and create negative ripples (karma) to deal with.

Therefore an important element of good relationships is damage control. It's similar to Hippocrates' prescription to physicians in ancient Greece, "First do no harm." Ken Keyes says it like this: "First get centered, *then* act." If we're being emotionally reactive in a relationship, the other person is going to find it very difficult to feel safe around us.

Thus when we're feeling charged up and negative inside our first order of business should be to regain our center, some feeling of equilibrium. And meanwhile, to refrain if possible from making decisions—or acting upon them—because such decisions or actions will almost certainly be unskillful and thus create further enturbulence and problems.

George Gurdjieff, the awakened master who taught in Paris earlier in this century, talked about a piece of advice his father gave him that helped greatly in his progress. "When you're feeling upset," he said, "wait 24 hours before you do anything." It's a way of breaking the pattern of reactivity.

Just in the nature of things we'll sometimes encounter situations that push our buttons. We'll find ourselves feeling emotionally charged and tempted to do something, to act out or act upon our upset. What should we do when we're right in the middle of it?

Ordinarily there are two alternatives when we're feeling emotionally upset. The first alternative is that we *sit on the emotion* in some way—we suppress it, we distract ourselves, we minimize it or pretend that it's not there. These are ways of not looking at the emotion, not dealing with it, not feeling it. They are ways of rejecting our experience.

The problem with that strategy is that it leads to more wounding. Energy doesn't just disappear; it has to go somewhere. When something is not welcome in our consciousness, it goes to the unconscious. From there it will mechanically keep trying to act out in our life.

Just as we can listen to and appreciate others without necessarily agreeing with them, so also can we listen to and appreciate negative impulses and fantasies and thoughts inside ourselves without needing to buy into them or act them out. We can just observe them, be aware of them.

Only when our negative impulses are given a respectful but detached hearing in consciousness can they lie down and, so to speak, go to sleep. While they're being ignored or repressed, though, they're a source of reactivity. They affect our behavior in unconscious patterns that, until we begin to see them, we're unaware of.

The other traditional alternative is to *act out the upset,* let it out, express it. We buy into the upset. Firing up our self-righteousness, we express our emotional charge in words or actions. This is sometimes called "dumping our garbage," because that's about what we're doing. We're dumping our raw woundedness onto another person.

In a way, it's a step up from suppression because we're at least expressing how we feel. But as you've probably noticed, this strategy also doesn't work very well. We take actions we regret later, we lower people's trust in us, we damage relationships. When we act out our greed, anger, fear, etc., we hurt others and ourselves. And our mindfulness doesn't increase at all, so we're just as likely to be reactive next time.

There's a third alternative, however, which is to work out the energy in private. Then perhaps we express it to the other in some constructive way, or perhaps not. Osho, an awakened master, put it something like this:

Our positivity is for sharing with others;

Our negativity is our own business.

This doesn't mean to suppress our feelings. Rather, it's a question of how we deal with them. If our emotional charge is a light one, it's usually appropriate to express our feelings then and there, so long as we can do it constructively. But if the emotional charge is heavier, it's beneficial to try to work with it privately first.

There are many ways to work with energy, as discussed in chapter 5. For example, we can sit down and be mindful of it, watch it, investigate it without thinking about it. If we're very upset and identified, it's often useful to watch it in the body. What are the sensations like at a physical level?

Or we can talk it out with a friend, or work at a deeper level with a therapist. Just as a child, when traumatized, will automatically work out the negative energy if an interested and non-reactive adult is present, so too will we tend to work it out by talking or emoting if someone is there who can be receptive but doesn't try to probe or offer advice.

We can also do breathwork or naming or any of the other processes described in chapter 5. Sometimes just a short period of breathwork can make quite a difference.

Another good way is to work with the upset in a safe, physical way. We can pound the bed with a plastic bat, punch or kick a pillow, yelling while we're doing it. We can cry out our grief or exaggerate shaking with fear. In other words, we express the energy in a raw and unedited way, but privately and safely. We get the energy out, but without being ugly or unskillful with another.

If we don't have an opportunity to first work out the energy in private, then our challenge is greater. If we must deal with such a situation real-time, then our best friends are mindfulness and reflective listening.

In any given situation, by applying enough mindfulness to our inner experience we can wake up from unconsciousness right in the middle of the upset—or even better, before it gets going. Like anything else the knack of this gets easier with practice.

When we begin doing this—watching our patterns and conditioning as they're happening—we won't wake up right away. We'll probably wake up three days later and go, "Mmm, that wasn't too skillful." Then we'll start waking up a day later, an hour later, ten minutes later, etc. It's quite a moment the first time we wake up right in the middle of an upset. It's like, "Wow, where have I been for the last five minutes?"

Eventually, we can bring enough skill and mindfulness to most situations, most of the time, that they become less likely to upset us in the first place—though this should not be confused with suppressing our feelings.

Once we've worked with and integrated our reactive energy enough, it's often helpful to communicate with the other about it. But as Harville Hendrix says, any discussion of a troublesome issue should be by appointment only, so that the other doesn't feel ambushed. Or as Ellen Kriedman puts it, timing is very important when discussing feelings.

We can say, "I'd like to talk with you about something. Would this be a good time?" If not, then a mutually agreeable time is set up. But either way, the idea is to first remove some of the charge before attempting to communicate about it.

My friend Kristine taught me a lot about this when we were together. If something was concerning her she'd work on her energy privately first, then wait for an appropriate time and say something like, "This has been bothering me. Can we talk about it?"

When we talk about it, the essential thing is to express our feelings without dumping. It helps very much to focus on "I" sentences rather than "you" sentences, feelings rather than accusations. There's a world of difference between saying, "I've been feeling concerned about thus-and-so" and "You are a dirty bastard for thus-and-so." Hear the difference? Above all, avoid personal attacks.

The idea is to avoid activating the other person's old-brain fight-or-flight response, or your own for that matter.

Because once that happens, the situation becomes much less likely to resolve constructively. As Gary Smalley says, even if we're discussing a problem or upset with another person, we always want to show that we honor and respect them.

Finally, it's important in any discussion or disagreement never to call the relationship itself into question. If we say to our spouse in a moment of reactivity, "This really makes me doubtful about our relationship," we're making the other feel a lot less safe. It's a very large withdrawal.

Instead, let's use every disagreement as an opportunity. Let's give the other such respect that even in disagreement they know that we honor and value them.

Non-reactiveness II

A GOOD PART of being non-reactive is to develop what can be called *large-mindedness*. What that means is to be consciously senior to our conditioning, consciously senior to any form of pettiness or small-mindedness.

Because it happens upstream, where we assign meaning and interpretation to things, it's not a suppression of feelings. Rather, it's holding our perceptions in a larger perspective; it's reframing events from a larger point of view. It's being above petty ego concerns. Again, we don't want to suppress feelings or be unmindful of them; so if feelings do arise, we need to skillfully deal with them.

But if we can intervene further upstream, we'll observe that reactivity arises in the first place because of the meaning that we attach to events. By reframing our perspective, by looking through a larger, less ego-driven lens, the meaning often changes. And with it, our feelings.

The United States' two greatest presidents possessed the characteristic of large-mindedness to an extraordinary degree. A couple of examples:

During America's Revolutionary War, when George Washington was commanding the desperate colonial army, a letter from his second-in-command to his third-in-command was accidentally opened and given to Washington. The letter spoke in bitter terms of Washington's utter incompetence and general stupidity.

Now how do you suppose Washington reacted to this letter? Fire the general? Demote him? Rant and rave to him, or about him? Be petty or mean-spirited in some way? Nope. What Washington did was simply send the letter on to its intended recipient with a short note apologizing for having inadvertently opened it. That's all; he just overlooked it.

That's a large-minded person.

Abraham Lincoln had tremendous large-mindedness as well. One time Lincoln sat next to a woman on a train, who told him that he was one of the ugliest men she'd ever seen in her life. And Lincoln's response? His response was to ask her what she thought he ought to do about that. "Well," she said, "you could stay home."

Lincoln used to tell this story on himself—he liked her answer. He was large enough to like her answer and find it humorous. He was a person who could rise above pettiness and ego rather than getting trapped in it.

So a large-minded person chooses not to take offense easily. As the late Ken Keyes said,

"We cause as much suffering in the world when we *take* offense as when we *give* offense."

Yet we can ask the question: Where's the line between being large-minded and suppressing our feelings?

There's a balance in life which can only be called an art form. On the one hand, we want to be real and share ourselves with people. Yet we don't want to dump on others destructive over-reactions based on childhood conditioning. We want to be real, but also appreciative and understanding.

When we feel fanatically self-righteous, often our feelings are not really about the other person or the supposed issues. The over-reaction is the clue that we are probably re-stimulating earlier wounds. The most useful thing we can do at that point is to watch. Here's the conditioning in full flower, right in front of us; here's our chance to really observe it.

Whatever the situation, our most skillful act is to first open to it, soften to it, listen to it. Then it has the space to potentially transform. As the Buddha said, hatred can never stop hatred; only love can stop hatred. That applies to our internal feelings and rejected parts as much as it applies to external people and situations.

As Stephen Levine mentions, if we're feeling unbearable grief, we can let the resistances go and die into the grief, experience it, honor it, until we feel a rebirth of wholeness and love. If we're feeling unbearable frustration or fear, we can let the feelings come in, allow them inside, surrender to what they have to teach. Then our heart opens and we feel things in a different way. Then we can more easily be larger than our situations.

When we're ready to share something honestly without destructive judgments and condemnations, when we're ready to share our feelings without adding charge or attack to them, then our sharing will tend to lead towards harmonious and beneficial results. Then we're acting skillfully.

It's very helpful to observe our *true* feelings. The feeling on the surface could be anger, say: "You're always home late from the office!" But underneath that may be a feeling of hurt:

"I really enjoy our time together and I feel a sense of loss when we don't get to spend time together at dinner." Sharing our truest feelings is usually much more effective.

And, as mentioned previously, if the other person gets emotionally reactive, the best thing to do is good listening. This is especially true if someone starts projecting negative qualities onto us. As Harville Hendrix says, defending against such projections only confirms them in the eye of the accuser.

So in such a situation, instead of getting emotionally reactive ourselves, we can try to understand: "So what you're saying is..." In so doing we're using a more skillful response, one more likely to bring about a constructive resolution.

The final aspect of non-reactiveness is to be consistent in our caring. It's not enough to care about others. We have to be consistent about it if we would win their trust. If we're warm sometimes and cold others, if we send double messages, if our words are high-minded but our actions are not, if we're polite sometimes and sarcastic other times, the account with that person is being lowered. They sense that something is wrong, that we're not being congruent.

When we are inconsistent with another, it's usually because we're emotionally reactive at times. If we act pleasant most of the time but hostile now and then, the trust level still tends to go down. The person says to themselves, "Which mode can I trust? Which mode is real?"

For example, once I knew an acquaintance and we were becoming friends. For months I saw him occasionally and was always friendly; but once, out of unconscious conditioning, I was angry and hostile about a misunderstanding. From then on, not surprisingly, he kept his distance.

When we're safe to be around most of the time, but occasionally unsafe, we're perceived as generally unsafe. So it's worth keeping in mind that in five minutes we can destroy months of deposits. It's perfectly okay to have disagreements, of course; it's how we do it that makes all the difference.

It's important for others to feel that we're consistently safe because it allows trust to build, it allows people to open up. It doesn't mean that we never feel down or have bad days, but just that our respect and caring can be counted on. The other person needs to know that those qualities aren't going to disappear suddenly if we're emotionally upset.

For instance, suppose our relationship with a child is damaged, and we've spent time rebuilding it by making deposits. Little things: We've given her a book on her favorite subject, perhaps, or we've taken her out for a walk, or we've offered to help on one of her projects. And suppose, because she doesn't respond right away, we then tell her that she doesn't appreciate the things we do for her. Right in that moment, we've just undone all the good things we've done.

When an emotional bank account is being rebuilt, we can make many deposits without seeing a change right away, but nevertheless those deposits add up if we don't undo them. That's where non-reactivity comes in. To build or rebuild an emotional bank account takes time, patience, equanimity and consistent evidence of caring.

Integrity

*T*HE THIRD ELEMENT of building trust and allowing us to enjoy the beauty of other people is *integrity*. When those around us are duplicitous or unreliable, we begin losing trust in them. When we are duplicitous or unreliable, people begin losing trust in us.

The word "integrity" comes from the same root as the word "integral," meaning harmonious and whole. When we have integrity there's a harmony, a congruence between our representations and reality. It means that we are of a whole, that our inner matches our outer, that our words match our actions. We're dependable and we talk straight.

We may be able to get away with being duplicitous or unreliable for a short time, with brief relationships or new acquaintances, but in the long run people sense who we are.

Emerson said this: "What you are shouts so loudly I can't hear what you say." William Jordan put it this way:

"Into the hands of every individual is given a marvelous power for good or evil—the silent, unconscious, unseen influence of his life. This is simply the constant radiation of what he really is, not what he pretends to be."

Our job is not to be saints or superhuman, but simply to do the best we can. When we do our best to come from integrity, we put out an unconscious radiation of that quality. We become more worthy of trust by others. Integrity, then, is about who we are rather than who we seem to be.

For instance, if Susan knows that we talk kindly about Bill to his face, and negatively and unkindly about him when he's not around, that may or may not affect her trust in Bill. But it will certainly affect her trust in *us*.

Or suppose that we betray confidences? If we say to Karen, "I know I shouldn't tell this, but...," she may enjoy the gossip, but she'll also know that we're likely to betray things *she* tells us in confidence as well. Her trust in us is lowered.

In talking about integrity, then, our emphasis can't be on narrow, legalistic rules to be rigidly applied. Rather, the emphasis must be on where we're coming from. How much wholeness is truly in our words and actions? The real test is an inner one: Is our heart in the right place?

In my opinion, life is so mysterious that it can never be truly contained within any set of concepts. So while some principles or paradigms may be more useful than others for a time, none can substitute for the light of awareness. To each situation we can learn to bring our heart and do what feels appropriate to it.

Integrity can be divided into two components—*telling the truth* and *keeping our word*. Werner Erhard has often emphasized these two notions, and I think rightly so. They can be thought of as two sides of the same coin: Being honest is seeing that our words conform to our actions. Keeping our word is seeing that our actions conform to our words. Let's consider both:

The larger sense of being honest is not just telling the truth, but to be as we seem to be—to act without hidden agendas or manipulations, to be up front with people, to show ourselves as we are. It can be tempting to manipulate or dissemble or pretend to be what we're not, but in the long run such behavior tends to damage not only our relationships, but ourselves as well.

How? In two ways, I believe:

First, it affects our *state of mind.* "Duplicity" comes from the same root as the word "duality," meaning to lack oneness, to be split, to be inharmonious. When we have secret motives, when we talk one way but behave in another, etc., we create divisions in ourselves that result in a less unified state of mind. We become less spacious inside.

An example: One time someone had been quite unkind to me for a while, and then suddenly a chance to get back at them came up. It would have been anonymous, reciprocal, even poetic, and all it would have taken was a phone call.

I went to lunch contemplating making the call, and had the good fortune to suddenly notice my state of mind—hard, tight, closed, cynical. In a flash of insight I knew that it would be more that way in my life if I took that action.

I decided not to make the call, and immediately felt a lightness: My state of mind became more open, expansive, innocent, loving. This is a primary link between our actions and our feelings—that skillful versus unskillful actions cause two different states of mind within us.

It seems to me that the greatest influence upon the next moment is this moment. If that's so, our present state of mind continually conditions future states of mind.

When we behave unskillfully we are more likely to think and behave that way in the future, thus perpetuating painful and contracted states of mind.

The second cost of unskillfulness is *future regret*. This second consequence happens in repose, and is very intriguing. At times in our life we tend to sit quietly and review it. This often happens when we become ill, or older, or as we face death. It can happen in a period of intense grief. It happens when we get past the beginning stages of mindfulness.

And what happens at such times of quiet review is that we experience pain for past actions in which we were unkind to others. We experience regret, and the more unloving the action the deeper and more painful the regret.

I remember a situation like that during a three-year period following a breakup of a deep relationship. Because of grief I was drawn to solitude, and past unskillful actions towards this person came back to haunt me. Unkind, selfish actions were very painful to remember.

Elderly friends have told me that near the end of life we don't recall our achievements so much as we recall acts of kindness or unkindness between us and others. I believe it, because such things certainly come up when we sit in mindfulness. Past unskillful actions become part of the "dark night of the soul" that we must traverse in order to awaken.

As true as all that is, the danger is that we can set up an ideal such as integrity and then find, when we can't live up to the ideal, that we either abandon it, become cynical, or put it in a category called "beautiful but unworkable ideas."

So I feel it's quite important to frame any desirable quality in a way that's do-able. Following the principle of reinforcement in chapter 4, we want to set up any goal in a realistic way that allows us to have and reinforce a series of successes. To that end, let's talk realistically now about telling the truth and keeping our word:

Integrity II

$\mathscr{F}$IRST, ARE THERE any exceptions to always telling the truth? Are we ever justified in not telling the truth? I believe the answer is "yes" to both questions.

Let's talk about three potential exceptions:

The first exception is when we're *under coercion*. This occurs when someone is damaging or attempting to damage us through force, especially immediate physical force. If someone is about to rape us, for instance, we're justified in lying to try to stop it. As another example, if we're being tortured by a police state we're justified in lying in order to attempt to save ourselves or others.

The second exception is when there's an *irreversible emergency*. If we come home one day and the trees in our yard are about to be bulldozed, we're justified in lying if necessary to try to save the trees. For even if the bulldozer operator later sees that he has the wrong address or instructions, it'll be too late if the trees are already down. Later, away from the heat of the emergency, the truth can and should be expressed.

The third potential exception is when telling the truth would *inflict needless pain or suffering*. If we meet someone who's badly disfigured there's no need to blurt out the "truth" of our shock. If our small child talks about Santa Claus or the tooth fairy, there's no need to rip such childhood fantasies away prematurely. Or when we're given a gift, we don't need to say it's not what we needed.

356

Instead, we can enlarge the frame of what we're looking at. If we think so, we can tell someone they have a beautiful spirit; or that it was thoughtful of them to give their gift. If our mate asks if they're looking old, what they may really want is to be reassured that they're still attractive to us.

The theme of these three exceptions is that we don't want "truth" that will likely cause hurt or damage. On the other hand, lying just to gain an advantage or to get what we want leads to the usual duplicitous results. Nor would it be skillful to use these exceptions not to tell the truth about our feelings when it's appropriate.

A good test might be something like this:

"Considering the whole situation, will what I'm about to say or do increase overall harmony?"

If not, let's let it go. When done appropriately, telling the gentle truth tends to decrease overall pain and suffering. The truth, *when told in a context of appreciation*, tends to be liberating and harmonizing.

The danger in the question above is the distortion that can happen if we imagine that the end justifies the means. Hitler thought he was justified in killing six million Jews because it would create the "greater good" of the Aryan state. A businessman might justify unethical business practices by saying to himself that he's going to give money to charity.

End-justifies-the-means thinking is dangerous because it can be used to justify any action whatever. We do well to avoid it because it has a strong tendency to harm others and contract our state of mind.

This can be phrased this way:

The means we use to attain an end
Is the actual end we achieve.

If we use love to bring about a better world, love is what we achieve. If we use condemnation, division, polarization to bring about a better world, we achieve condemnation, division, polarization. If we dissemble to achieve supposedly good ends, we achieve dissembling.

Cornucopia, a Miami growth center, taught me about the idea of "gentle honesty." I've seen "the truth" sometimes used as a weapon, to brutalize or harm others. Gentle honesty is a beneficent influence. The idea is to tell the truth—and to gain the liberation of spirit that it offers—but to do so in a gentle way, in a way that respects others.

Also, it's good to be *willing* to share our truth, but without forcing it onto others. We don't need to thrust our beliefs or innermost feelings onto everyone we meet on the elevator. Rather, we can share when it's appropriate, when we trust the other and they would like to go deeper with us. We can be willing when there's an atmosphere of open acceptance.

The other part of integrity lies in keeping agreements. One of the largest withdrawals we can make with another is to fail to keep an important commitment or promise. Conversely, when we keep our commitments, especially when this is done over a period of time, the trust that others have in us rises dramatically.

Once I had an elderly friend, Alfred, who was like a father. My trust in him kept increasing for several years before I realized what was partly behind it—simply, that he always did what he said he would do. I was struck by what a rare and beautiful quality that was.

Keeping promises and commitments is actually a form of honesty. It's seeing that our words and commitments are not spoken falsely. That being so, the most important part of keeping a promise or commitment is back in the beginning— being careful about what we commit to.

Being attentive to our words, to what we say we'll do, is the most important part of keeping our word. Because people often build their hopes on our commitments, it's kindness to consider them carefully before making them. That way, when we say we'll do something, people can depend upon it. This builds large reserves.

But occasionally, even when we've considered potential obstacles before committing, a situation arises where keeping the commitment would create big problems. Then it's good to approach the person and see if some other arrangement might be mutually agreeable. If so, cool. If not, often it's best to try to keep it anyway if at all possible.

As an added benefit, life gets much simpler when we just do what we say we'll do. Werner Erhard said that, and it has certainly been borne out in my experience. I've seen all kinds of screw-ups happen when I didn't just keep my word. Conversely, when I did keep it I would often get some great benefit that I didn't expect.

But the basic reason for keeping our word isn't because of such fortuitous outcomes, which may or may not happen. The basic reason is to honor ourselves and others. Let's talk about that now:

When we keep our word with others, it increases our ability to keep our word with ourselves. Making our word count with ourselves is extremely empowering. Then we can say "I'll get up at 7am tomorrow" or "I'll quit this habit" or "I'll get started on this project" and simply do it. That greatly affects our self-esteem and our trust in ourselves.

Keeping promises to ourselves is one thing; misusing them as a whip on ourselves is another. It's life-enhancing to be able to make and keep our word about things that we can definitely carry out, such as "I'll finish four pages each day" or "I'll be sober for today."

However, it's usually unwise to make promises about long-term targets, such as "I promise I'll make $100,000 next year" or "I promise this will be a hit album." That's actually a kind of mental flogging, trying to use force upon ourselves or the universe, thus creating internal and external disharmony. It's a form of insisting, opening the door to suffering, and the very opposite of listening to hear what wants to happen, of getting in alignment and letting-go of the outcome.

What we can do is visualize the goal or target, commit to it, build toward it, yet without trying to dominate ourselves or existence. If it's in the flow for us to reach a goal or target, we will. If our goals are aligned, events will tend toward their fulfillment. We don't need to force things.

In living from integrity, what matters is the intent—where we're coming from. We "come from" the truth, which doesn't mean we'll always succeed. Sometimes we'll try to be truthful and fail, or be unable to keep our word. When that happens, it's pointless to condemn ourselves. Rather, we can simply commit once again to living from integrity as best we are able.

In my opinion, what matters in every area is the attempt to keep sailing our boat in the right direction. We may or may not reach our goals—that's affected by some of the random storms of life. Yet if we keep doing our best to sail the boat in the right direction each day, we've already reached the most important goal. For the knowledge that we have tried to do what's worthwhile, consistently, day-after-day, is the essence of fulfillment.

Validation

$\mathscr{T}$HE FOURTH ELEMENT of having good relationships is to *validate others*. Though many have talked helpfully about this subject, Ellen Kriedman shows great mastery of it. Many of the ideas in these next two sections are based on her very insightful work.

All of us respond to sincere praise. We love to be valued and appreciated. When someone authentically tells us we did a good job or they appreciate something we did, we blossom inside. A seed of beauty is being watered. We tend to be even more skillful or appropriate or conscientious the next time.

And of course, this is just as true of others. When we recognize what is beautiful about others and sincerely express it, we make large deposits. Trust grows tremendously when someone can feel that we really appreciate them.

But to truly build trust, appreciation must be sincere. Sincere appreciation only comes from being willing to truly see what is valuable and beautiful about the other. Then our praise comes from the inside out, from a love that isn't trying to sell something.

One way of valuing others is to remember the little things. With people, little things are big things. Little slights, little discourtesies, little forms of disrespect can cause large withdrawals. They signal to others that they're not important, that they don't matter. This is something we're all sensitive to. Beneath our strong exteriors, we're all pretty tender inside.

Conversely, when we make continual small deposits, they add up. Little remembrances, little courtesies, small gifts, thoughtful acts eventually make a huge impact. They let the other person know that we care, that we value them.

This is especially so in our closest relationships. They require our most constant deposits, because when we're in close contact with others we can make withdrawals without even knowing it, through violating hidden expectations.

Expectations are always present—especially in close relationships—but often are not verbalized. Unawares, we can be violating these implicit expectations of others. Or we may be assuming that our own expectations are self-evident, and then become upset when they seem to be disregarded. So it's useful, as Stephen Covey emphasizes, to get expectations out on the table whenever possible.

Since we can be making unknown withdrawals in close relationships, continuing deposits help us to keep them in good health. Again, small things—kindnesses, remembrances, being on time, walks together, courtesies, giving assistance, and so on—over time create large effects.

My phrase for this is *patience and positivity*. Though it's simple, it's one of the most important things I've ever learned. Virtually anything that we want to accomplish in life, whether it's in relationships or in any other area, will be well served by patience and positivity.

Why? The patient application of positive energy in any area is like water flowing over stones. Even though stones are harder than water, eventually the water smoothes them.

Similarly, things that seem almost impossible can often be accomplished through continuing to patiently put positive energy into the situation.

This is especially true when rebuilding emotional bank accounts that have fallen unusually low. Even very estranged relationships can sometimes be restored when we put out small amounts of positive energy for as long as necessary. I've restored a number of relationships this way.

When doing this, it's important to do it without trying to speed up the process, find a shortcut, or push through to a conclusion. In relationships particularly, such things are often counter-productive. Again, our job is just to sail the boat in the right direction each day, as best we can, and then in great trust leave the outcome to existence itself.

Gary Smalley has talked effectively about this. To have good relationships, he says, we first honor people in our heart—and then that inner essence expresses on the outside in whatever way it does. We say inside, in effect, "I honor you, and will try to show you that I honor you, no matter what the state of our relationship, even if I need to contend with you or set up boundaries, I still honor you." And in our intimate relationships, we can try to show in every possible way that we honor the other person.

The basis of positive energy towards others is to get clear in our hearts that we honor every human being, every form of life, every form of consciousness—that we honor all of life, without exception. Albert Schweitzer, in a beautiful phrase, called this "reverence for life."

Validation II

$\mathscr{W}$E ALL NEED to feel that we're okay as we are. It's a food that we really cannot do without. Most of us have not gotten nearly enough appreciation and validation either as children or as adults.

So we project a confident exterior when possible, but inside we all have many wounds and self-doubts of various kinds. We've learned to insulate ourselves, to a degree, from lack of appreciation or active criticism, but inside we all crave to be appreciated just as we are. The person who can supply this appreciation will be welcome virtually anywhere, and will very much tend to have relationships that work.

A study at the University of Washington found that married couples that stayed together said, on average, about *five times more positive than negative* things to each other and about each other. In contrast, couples that broke up made, on average, *one-and-a-half times more negative than positive* statements to and about each other. Isn't that interesting?

But where do we find these positive traits in people? The answer is that we look for them. As Jesus said, we find what we're seeking. If we look for negative things, we'll find them. If we look for positive things, we'll find them.

In the early 1970's I worked as a software programmer for an accounting firm. A co-worker took an active dislike of me; of course I took an active dislike of him as well, and things rapidly went from bad to worse. We disliked each other.

But I began to wonder: What caused this, and what could be done about it? Was it just an immutable chemistry that could not really be changed? I examined my attitudes towards him and found that they were all highly negative and critical. To say the least, I was not impressed with him. And of course, he felt the same way about me. He thought I was a perfect fool. Was it destined to remain that way?

Just as an experiment, I decided to see if I could find some positive quality about him. I sat down with a big pad of paper and prepared to write down his good qualities, just for fun. And I couldn't find any! I was at an impasse. I persisted for awhile and finally found one—he showed up for work on time! Not much, but a start.

As an experiment, I kept looking. I noticed he was very organized; I could admire that. I kept looking. Eventually, I found all sorts of qualities that I could appreciate about him. And gradually, my general view of him started changing as well. I began feeling that he had some pretty neat qualities!

This different view started spilling over into comments from me to others about him, and later directly to him. Just little things, little positive comments. And they were sincere; I meant them.

For a while his behavior remained negative, but very gradually he started to change right before my eyes. He began to open up, and I discovered that he was an expert in several areas that interested me. He also turned out to be a fantastic storyteller. Though we didn't become the best of friends, we did come to like and appreciate each other.

That was quite a lesson for me.

I wish I could say that I remembered that lesson from then on, but of course I didn't. Many times over the years I forgot about it and reverted to my habitual conditioning of being critical and condemning. I ruined many relationships because of this. Yet even a history of poor relationships can be greatly improved with time and patience. So if you have that history now, take heart!

It's like there's a fork in the road. If we concentrate on people's shortcomings, their mistakes, their inadequacies, on where they fail to measure up, and so forth, those people—around us, at least—will tend to be shut-down, contracted, cold and cynical. Not terribly warm or responsive. The more intimate the relationship, the more true this will be.

On the other hand, if we raise people's value, if we notice their strengths, if we notice the little thoughtful things they do, if we praise their accomplishments and reinforce their capabilities, they will tend to be open, alive, spontaneous, appreciative of us and responsive to our needs. And again, this will tend to be even more true in intimate relationships.

As Ellen Kriedman says, we want to build people up; we don't want to ever tear them down. We want to reinforce what's true and beautiful about them. If we look, we'll find that every being has a core of magnificence.

Building people up does not mean lying to them, using empty flattery, or being insincere. This is something different, a change of focus: That when we sincerely look for the good and beautiful, we find it.

Why? Because, again, in this universe we find what we're seeking. *Wherever we put our attention we bring things into existence* in our consciousness. As we continue attention on some thought or feeling or perception, it becomes more true and real to us. In this sense we are creating reality all the time—our reality.

But in a deeper sense, we're just helping to reveal the truth. What's really happening when we notice the beauty in someone is we're helping to bring out the real, natural person, the naturally beautiful being who was there as a child before being wounded, and who is there now beneath the surface.

Watch what happens when you notice and reinforce people's strengths and capabilities. They become more loving, appreciative, fun-loving and intelligent right before your eyes. That's what we all were like before being wounded by life. That's the natural state of all of us.

We can change our point of view about other people by deliberately noticing what's good and capable and wonderful about them. But it's not enough. We must verbalize it as well. We must say out loud the positive things we are noticing. This simple verbal affirmation of others is more powerful than armies, and can accomplish miracles.

Since we're all inevitably wounded, we all have a gap between our wounded self and our natural core self. Who fills that gap? We can. We can do it internally by noticing and appreciating all the unwanted and wounded parts of ourselves, allowing them into consciousness. And externally we can do it by noticing and appreciating the good in others.

When appreciating others, or even correcting them, it's quite helpful to be specific.

The mind has a tendency to generalize, to go from "The lines aren't straight" to "You just aren't doing this right" to "You're not suited to graphics." This generalized invalidation creates big withdrawals. Instead, if we occasionally need to correct something, let's be specific and also say what we *do* want: "The lines need to be straight."

The same holds true for compliments. It's much more validating to be specific and expanded. Instead of saying "You look good," for instance, let's be generous with our words: "You look wonderful in that outfit. You just radiate in it. I love the color, and it brings out the color in your eyes."

Instead of "Good job" we can say: "That was a terrific job you did on the Murphy account. Not only did you bring the video in on budget, but your ideas for the voiceover were right on target."

Besides "I love you" we can add: "You just light up my life. I love the way you are. I'm so lucky to know you and have you in my life."

Can we overdo it? Give too much appreciation? In my experience, no. It's not possible to give too much appreciation, *if* it's sincere. Most of us, and especially those of us who seem negative to others, are almost completely starved of it.

We can make the difference. Let's not hold back in our short life. Let's shower people with appreciation. Let's really notice what they're doing right. Sometimes we may be the only person in someone's life who is doing so.

It's the extra things we do in life that really make an impression. It's when we go out of our way to appreciate the beauty in someone or reinforce their capabilities. It's when we take the trouble to wrap a gift and enclose a note with it. It's when we're asked to pick up the groceries and we gladly do it. It's remembering anniversaries or holidays in a special way.

It's when we go the extra mile, take the trouble, expend the extra time or energy or money on someone that they feel especially honored and valued. In all interactions we're either sending out the message "You are worthwhile" or "You are not worthwhile." Let's do everything possible to show people that they *are* worthwhile.

Too often our messages to each other are conditional, even when not stated: "I'll love you if you get the promotion." "I'll love you if you always look this good." "I'll love you if you cater to my needs." "I'll love you if..."

Imagine two people who have just fallen in love. Their love is unconditional. The other doesn't have to do anything to qualify for it. They're seen in their best light, and it brings out the best in them. They are each other's highest priority, and are willing to say so:

"What happens if I don't get the promotion?"

"As long as we're together, nothing else matters."

Or suppose our lover says, "Look at these wrinkles. Do you think I'm looking old?" We can understand that we're being tested here and expand our focus, so that we can be both truthful and supportive:

"In fact, you look more beautiful to me every day."

Oftentimes children get very conditional love messages too, stated or unstated: "I'll love you if you clean your room." "I'll love you if you do as I say." "I'll love you if you don't show anger." "I'll love you if..."

But imagine the love a mother feels for her newborn. It's unconditional. The child doesn't need to do anything to deserve it or qualify for it. Just its existence is enough. The mother's love is freely given; it's not dependent upon anything the baby does.

As much as we can, let's let our love for others be like that—unconditional, not dependent upon anything they do or don't do. Let's build people up, validate their feelings and strengths, reinforce their capabilities, show that we appreciate their incredible beauties.

That's what we would want.

By Jesus' magnificent insight, let's do it for others.

Win/win

*T*HE FIFTH ELEMENT of good relationships is to have *win/win agreements,* that is, agreements among parties where all parties win. Roger Fisher and William Ury, as well as Stephen Covey, have made very fine analyses of agreements and negotiations. The ideas in these next two sections are partly based on their penetrating work.

Win/win implies a great symmetry that is very much in accordance with the golden rule. It's not enough for us to win and them to lose, or for them to win and us to lose. Win/win means that we value and honor others and ourselves as well. Both matter. We strive for that outcome where both we and the other win.

Win/win starts with the skillful expression of views. If we try to press our own case first and make the other wrong, what results is lack of listening, failed marriages, unproductive negotiations. When we first seek to understand the other's point of view, the world changes.

But expressing our own point of view is just as important as hearing the other's viewpoint. What's critical is the order in which it's done. To keep silent about our own way of seeing things is to come from a lose/win paradigm, to be permissive and ineffectual.

When we don't communicate effectively about our own point of view, we store up emotion—hurt, resentment, etc. That can hurt the relationship as much as the other extreme, for it means that we'll grow distant inside. The relationship loses its joy, spontaneity, perhaps its existence.

Lose/win means being permissive and indulgent, going for popularity. Sometimes parents do that with children. Permissiveness, giving someone their way too much, is in itself a withdrawal from relationship, because it's a way of saying that we ourselves don't count. It's as much of an extreme as trying to dominate another.

In negotiations, the lose/win paradigm is to be a "nice guy," to be indulgent and intimidated. It's seen sometimes in people who don't want to make waves, who want to keep the peace at all costs, and it results in domination, victimization, and hidden resentments.

The win/lose paradigm, on the other hand, is the one that says we can only win at the expense of the other. It's the one that looks at life as a zero-sum game, where we win by beating another, forcing them to lose. Most of us are deeply scripted in this paradigm, having grown up surrounded by it. We've seen it in sports, law, dysfunctional families and many other places.

When we come from a win/lose paradigm, we're saying that we don't care what happens to the other, that we have to control, to manipulate, to win regardless of the cost. The cost is heavy. It results in loveless relationships, lost spontaneity, poor communication, cold silences and so on.

Most of all, the cost is loss of the possibility for creative synergy with others, for accomplishing things together that would be difficult or impossible separately. People's actions can be coerced; but their hearts, minds and most creative efforts cannot be.

So a win/win approach means balancing consideration and courage—consideration of the other with the courage to express our own point of view. It means being kind *and* brave. It balances respect for the desires of others with the fortitude to also actualize our own.

Win/win, since it looks for mutual benefit in all our dealings, thus involves a search to find *the creative alternative.* The creative alternative is the one that's not our position, not their position, not just a mediocre compromise, but a creative solution that allows for both sides to really benefit.

The first step in finding the creative alternative, in a slight modification of Fisher and Ury, is to *separate the feelings from the problem.* This is necessary because we have emotional brains underneath our rational ones, as covered in chapter 3. If we get caught up emotionally, everything deteriorates.

The best preventive for this is good listening. We listen carefully to the other's point of view. We seek to understand. We present their point of view before presenting our own. This tends to create the psychological space within which the negotiation can succeed.

It's often helpful to set up good listening as a kind of ground rule. First party A talks until they're done, while party B listens without interrupting. Then they reverse, and so on. Along these lines, some object can be designated as a *talking stick,* possession of which entitles the person to talk without interruption, and then pass the talking stick to the other.

This Native American procedure often allows even the most sensitive subjects to be discussed without degenerating into arguments, bad feelings or shouting matches.

If that can't be agreed upon, we can use a technique which Penelope Russianoff calls "To-you-To-me." We might say, "I know that to you this seems like a matter of monthly sales, but to me it's more of a personnel thing." Or, "I know that to you this is a matter of honor, but to me it seems more important to be practical."

The second step in a win/win process is to *identify the interests behind the positions.* What's the difference? Let's look at a classic example:

Imagine two people in a library. One wants the window open, the other wants it closed. They argue these positions back and forth. Now the librarian enters. She inquires why the one wants it open and learns that he seeks fresh air. She inquires why the other wants it closed and learns that he wants to avoid a draft. These are the underlying interests.

The arguers believe that the solution lies along a single continuum of positions—how much the window should be open. But the librarian focuses instead on their interests, on what they really want. Rather than focusing on intransigent positions, she seeks a third alternative. Pausing a moment, she then goes to the next room and opens a window. This provides fresh air without a draft, fulfilling both parties' interests.

To focus on what each side has said and done, to focus on accusations and extreme positions taken by both sides, is counter-productive. Trying to compromise such positions can seem impossible. Yet quite often the *underlying interests* can yield a solution.

In the Egyptian-Israeli peace treaty of 1978, the worst contention was over the Sinai Peninsula, which belonged to Egypt and had been occupied by Israel in the 1967 war. Egypt's position was that all of the Sinai must be returned; Israel's position was that at least part of it must be retained as a buffer. Again and again prospective boundary lines were drawn dividing the Sinai, but none of them worked.

What yielded a solution was to examine the interests underlying the positions. Egypt's interest was to preserve its historic territory; Israel's was that Egyptian tanks not be at its border. The solution worked out was to return the Sinai to Egypt but demilitarize large areas of it. This satisfied Egypt's need for sovereignty and Israel's need for security.

Because the interests involved are broader and more general than positions, they are more amenable to the creative solution, to the creative alternative.

How do we find out the other side's interests? Just by asking. Why do they want this? What are their basic concerns? Then we use good listening to really hear the answers; to listen to the fears, hopes and needs underlying the other side's positions. We satisfy the universal desire to be truly understood.

Then we share our own interests and concerns. If there is to be strong advocacy, here's the place for it. But rather than attacking people or their positions—always damaging—we can be vigorous instead in clarifying our interests.

It's often valuable to summarize both parties' view-points on separate sides of a whiteboard or computer screen or sheet of paper. We start by putting down the concerns of the other on one side. We use reflective listening to make sure that we understand their interests, and put those interests down as accurately as possible.

Then we put down our own concerns and interests on the other side of the whiteboard, paper or screen. Looking at both parties' interests side-by-side in this way often helps to foster better mutual understanding. That in turn tends to lead to the creative possibility.

Win/win II

$\mathcal{T}$HE THIRD PART of finding the creative alternative is to *invent options for mutual gain,* as many as possible. The most skillful negotiators are not the toughest, but rather, those who can figure out how to expand the pie before it's divided. It's this expansion that often leads to the creative solution.

The basic feature in creating more options is to separate the inventing process from the deciding process, so that our imaginations are not hindered. We separate the imaginative process of thinking up possible solutions from the judgmental process of selecting from among them.

In practice this means having a *brainstorming session.* We can brainstorm alone or jointly with the other side. If the latter, such a brainstorming session is explicitly distinguished from a negotiating session: We're not attempting to reach an agreement here, but to generate ideas.

All ideas from everyone, no matter how whimsical, are written down, because embedded in those whimsical suggestions will also be the ones that can lead to a solution. So we ask open-ended questions: How can we jointly gain? What options might a neutral party come up with? Are there some temporary options perhaps?

The most promising ideas are then worked with: How can this idea be made better? More realistic? How could it be carried out? Each idea is made as attractive as possible so that the parties have an expanded field of options.

Fourth, an option is selected *based on objective standards.* Why objective standards? Because they help to prevent back-sliding into a battle of wills as the negotiation concludes. Using standards of fairness, precedent, scientific merit, common practice and so on can assist the parties in keeping free of their emotions.

Let's say we're negotiating to buy a home. If a price can't be agreed upon, what we can do is look for ways to judge a price objectively. This could include independent appraisals, recent sale prices, etc. If there's a conflict of standards, we try to find an objective basis there too. We can ask which standard is most widely applied or has the greatest precedent.

Finding objective standards sometimes means setting up *a fair procedure.* The purpose of a fair procedure is to ensure that the same standard gets applied to both sides. The classic is two children dividing a cake between them—one gets to cut the cake, the other to make the first choice.

Another example: Before a divorcing couple decide on who gets the children they can decide what the visiting rights will be. That way they are both motivated to agree on fair rights. Another: If heirs have to divide a large number of heirlooms left to them collectively, they can take turns making their choices.

In difficult or multi-party negotiations, it's often good to use a *one-text plan.* A one-text plan simplifies the process of creating options and choosing one by starting right off with one document or plan. It's then modified by all parties while still remaining just one thing.

A married couple plan to build a new house, say. She wants traditional with a chimney and a bay window; he wants a ranch-style with a den and garage. They're disagreeing and are on the verge of drawing up two separate plans, which would only cement their separate positions. What to do?

Suppose the architect decided to use a one-text plan. She'd investigate the interests behind their positions: Why do you want the bay window? Why do you want the den? Then she'd draw up one plan, and invite criticism and suggestions from both sides.

Note that the husband and wife are jointly critiquing *one* plan instead of defending separate ones. Based on their suggestions, the architect draws up another plan—but still just one. She then invites suggestions on that plan, draws up yet another one, and keeps going until the final plan.

A variation of the one-text plan is what is sometimes called a *mission statement*, which is basically a life-theme for a family or organization. It sets out the purposes of a group of people living or working together. The key is to keep it as one document which is being created by all sides.

A family that draws up a joint mission statement has a common set of goals and a closer bond. It also has a greater commitment by each family member to carry out the jobs that flow from those goals, whether mowing the lawn or paying the mortgage.

In a small organization, everyone can meet and create a mission statement together. In a larger organization, people representing different areas can meet. When the main statement is formed, each area then meets separately to fashion their own statement based on the organization's overall one.

As Stephen Covey says, without involvement there's no commitment. The involvement process is as valuable as the end product, and is the key to its execution. The very act of arriving jointly at the group's purposes greatly increases the commitment of everyone to carry out their part of it.

Another variation of the one-text plan is *performance agreements*. These plans can be used between employers and employees, companies and suppliers, contractors and subcontractors, and so on—any two parties who need to interact to accomplish something.

A performance agreement has these elements:

Desired goals, which are clearly expressed and agreed upon by both parties. *Accountability,* which happens through periodic meetings to discuss results. The s*elf-evaluation* of performance in terms of the agreement. *Consequences,* which should be established in advance.

As an example, a programmer and a supervisor agree on specifications for a new program (desired goal). Twice a week they'll meet (accountability) and the programmer evaluates the program's progress (self-evaluation). Upon completion the programmer will get a bonus (consequences).

Within those parameters the programmer is now his own boss. How the program is written is his own business. The supervisor is not trying to supervise his every move nor come up with on-the-spot consequences. Such an agreement tends to liberate both parties.

In effect, the supervisor now becomes the programmer's first assistant, lending a hand with resources as needed and available. The worker is his own judge.

Performance agreements avoid the ineffectiveness and poor relationships of tight supervision, of: "Do this, do that." That's an inefficient process because it ties up the manager's energy and, even more important, doesn't release the potential for creative performance in the worker.

Performance agreements are a final example of synergy, of a win/win approach. Each party wins. Moreover, both the result and the relationship are equally valued. The result is accomplished and the human spirit is respected as well.

Such synergy is so important that it's usually best not to enter into an agreement if it can't be win/win. By keeping "no deal" as an option, we're freed from trying to make deals that won't work. We can afford to be open and understanding.

To keep open the option of "no-deal," it's valuable to know what our best alternative is to a negotiated agreement. This allows us a much better sense of what to accept in the negotiation. To vigorously clarify and develop what our best alternative would be is very freeing, because we don't feel that we have to make a deal if it can't benefit both parties.

The golden rule always aims for this balance in all our affairs—for all to be satisfied, including ourselves. By finding the creative solution that makes use of our differences, we can often build something together that's greater than what we could do separately.

Giving

*T*HE SIXTH AND last element of good relationships is to practice giving to others.

Giving means acts of caring that are unconditional, that is, where we love someone without asking anything in return. And we use the golden rule, tailor-making our gifts for each person so that the gifts are based on a knowledge of what they might actually need or want. If we want to be compassionate, we must meet others where they are.

Love is sometimes mistaken for a business transaction: "I'll do this for you if you'll do that for me." Quite often we don't verbalize this or even feel it; it's more often a hidden expectation. We find out that we have it because we feel upset when someone doesn't "reciprocate" in the way that we feel they ought to. But that isn't really love; that's accounting.

Love in its purest form means unconditional love, and that means unconditional giving. Unconditional love means to give of ourselves to another without keeping score and without concerning ourselves about what we're going to get in return. It enters into a realm where we release calculations of self-interest.

For most of us this issue arises most intensely in our intimate relationships, which bring out our most deep-seated needs. Let's examine, then, the area of romance: What does romance have to do with love? Can romance be made to last? How can we form a fruitful long-term relationship?

In looking at these questions, I would like to credit Harville Hendrix, who in turn builds upon the work of Freud, Perls, Ernst, Stuart and others. The ideas presented in the next two sections are mostly based on his very fine work.

The story of romantic love begins in small infancy. As discussed in chapter 5, we're born with natural spontaneity, creativity, intelligence, affection—our natural self. But in the course of childhood, all of us are traumatized in various ways by caretakers, peers, institutions, society.

So we put away our affection, or our creativity, or our anger or whatever. Parts of us feel unsafe, and those parts get repressed into the unconscious. But from then on, we feel incomplete, unconnected to our whole self.

Subconsciously, we long for the exuberant naturalness and delight in our whole being that we once felt so keenly. On a subconscious level, we want to redo it—we want to recreate the conditions of childhood, only this time with the totality of love and nurturing and support and affection that we wanted but didn't fully get. We want to be healed, to become whole once more.

Usually, our woundedness happened mostly around our caretakers, those people who took care of us when we were young. They were around us the most. Often this was our mother or father or both, but it can include anyone who had a significant influence on us.

Our caretakers had certain qualities, both positive and negative. Perhaps our mother was fun-loving but controlling, our father affectionate but critical, our brother or sister witty but treacherous. All of these traits are noted and filed away by our old brain, and the composite of them becomes our *imago*, the image of our caretakers—and therefore also our image of what we need in order to recreate childhood.

When we become adults and look for love, we unconsciously look for someone with the same traits as those in our imago-image. And when we find a potential romantic partner who's a good match for some of the more important traits, we feel that we've fallen in love. And to the extent that we match the other person's imago, they feel the same way.

On an unconscious level, our romantic partner is fused with our early caretakers, and we're back in childhood. To the old brain, the scene is recreated. Now we're going to get all the love and nurturing that we wanted but didn't get in childhood. This time it's going to go just right.

And indeed it does for a while. Our partner is loving and caring towards us. The sky seems bluer, the grass greener; the world feels like a wonderful place. We feel restored to wholeness and aliveness, because now we're finally getting the nurturing—from the right person—that we've sought for so long. To the old brain, our partner is "the one," the person who restores us to life.

But sooner or later, trouble enters into this romantic paradise. To understand what happens, we have to go back to infancy again. Our caretakers were ministering to our needs. But what happened if they missed something or didn't get to it soon enough? What did we do when we felt hungry or wet or cold? Basically, we opened our mouth and screamed.

In most cases this worked quite well. We were hungry and got fed, we were wet and got dry, we were cold and got warm. And our old brain noticed two important things:

First, that this complaining process, for the most part, worked like a charm. And second, that we didn't need to spell out what we needed. All we needed to do was complain, and our needs were magically taken care of. These two notions became deeply imprinted in our brains.

Now we're adults, and our romance has been going on for a while. And our old brain begins to notice a disturbing fact: That our partner—who is fused with our caretakers on an unconscious level—isn't taking care of our needs quite right. Our partner must know exactly what we need; after all, our caretakers did! Yet somehow they're just not coming through as much as we'd like.

Of course our partner can't come through exactly the way we'd like, because our needs have multiplied over and over since infancy, and because our partner isn't a mindreader the way our caretakers seemed to be. But our old brain doesn't care about any of that. All it cares about is that, from its point of view, our needs are not being met as well as they could be. The scenario is still not turning out quite right!

The solution the old brain comes up with is the one that worked in childhood. We open our mouths and start to complain. The adult version of our crying or screaming is a verbal complaint. We begin criticizing our partner, or withholding affection in some way. We indicate our distress, just as we did so successfully in infancy.

Unfortunately, our critical cry of distress has a much different effect on our partner than it did on our caretakers. When we criticize our partner, it tends to reactivate their old brain, to switch on its fight-or-flight mode, and most likely they criticize us back. A similar process has been going on with them, so perhaps they initiate the criticism.

Either way, a downward spiral is started. Criticism leads to counter-criticism. Can you imagine what this does to the relationship? We begin to wonder what we saw in the other person, and they're wondering the same about us.

At some point in this process our negative filters get turned on. Whereas before we denied negative qualities in the other, now we deny positive qualities in them. The emotional bank account is falling severely—now actions and words get interpreted more and more negatively.

Eventually we discover that we've migrated to a chillier climate, where affection and love are not so prevalent as they were before. We've arrived at "the power struggle." Now each partner is wounding the other in some of the same ways that their caretakers did.

From here, many couples break up. Most of the rest enter onto a "parallel togetherness," where, although they are more or less cordial to each other, the real juice has gone out of the relationship. And increasingly, each partner looks outside the relationship for gratification.

How can we reverse this downward spiral? How can the relationship help to heal us rather than re-wound us?

Giving II

$\mathcal{A}$NY RELATIONSHIP CAN benefit tremendously from elements discussed earlier—good listening, non-reactiveness, appreciation, and so on. But an intimate partnership needs more than that. It also needs to address the unconscious needs of the old brain. How do we do that?

We begin by just asking. Instead of trying to read the other person's mind, we directly ask them what they need and want. This begins what Harville Hendrix calls *reromancing* and Richard Stuart calls *caring days*. We ask the other person to write down some of the things they'd like us to do for them, and vice-versa. One way is like this:

Each partner writes down some sentences starting with these words: "I like it when you..." And answers might range from "...massage my back" to "...tell me you love me" to "...bring me breakfast in bed." Generally, these are things that our partner is already doing for us, at least to some extent.

Then a second group of sentences is begun with these words: "I used to like it when you...." Answers can range from "...wrote me love letters" to "...whispered sexy things in my ear." This recalls the past loving and caring behaviors of the romantic phase of the relationship.

Then a third type of sentence is completed: "I would like you to...." Answers can range from "go camping with me" to "sleep in the nude." Here we indulge our sense of what we'd really like in this romantic relationship.

The things we don't ask for include anything that's a source of conflict. (That's addressed further below.)

From the completions of these sentences, each partner writes down a list of what they would like from the other; then the lists are exchanged. Each item is then discussed using reflective listening, and ranked in terms of its difficulty. Using Curt Lewin's insight of graduated change, we begin with the easiest items on our partner's list and gift them to our partner, gradually working upward in difficulty.

But here's the kicker: Both of the lists are considered educational only. If we choose to stretch into new behaviors our partner's list gives us some direction, that's all. That is, on both sides these are *gifts only*. We are not obligated to fulfill any items on our partner's list and they are not obligated to fulfill anything on our list.

It has to be this way because of the way the old brain works. The old brain is not impressed by business gifts—"I'll do this for you if you'll do that for me." That doesn't generate feelings of love in the old brain. What it wants is gifts that are unconditional, the kind it used to receive from its caretakers when it was young.

Thus, those are the kinds of gifts we want to give. That is, we make the decision to offer these gifts to our partner regardless of whether our partner reciprocates or not. So we don't indulge in discussions of the type, "I gave this to you so why don't you give that to me?" Futile; that only leads back into the downward power struggle. Instead, we just stick to our process of giving, no matter what's happening.

When a couple does choose to unconditionally gift each other in this way, what happens is that they start recovering the feelings that they once felt for each other. The filters turn positive again. The partners start representing a source of life and pleasure to each other again.

It's helpful to use some randomness in this. If we give our partner flowers once a week, as requested, it will continue to provide pleasure, but less so as time goes on because of habituation (chapter 4). So we continue gifting the items in the request list, but also come up with some surprises—things that our partner wants but hasn't asked for.

How do we know they want them? Just by observation. If our partner mentions poetry, for instance, we might read her some or write one to her. Or a sweater that's remarked upon in a store might be given to our partner. To be effective, these surprises should be varied as to kind and timing. When such surprises are added to the other gifts on the request list, the positive effects can go on indefinitely.

Through this reromancing, the couple becomes much closer. Yet curiously, the same conflicts as before do arise once again. Why? Because reromancing doesn't affect deep-seated conflicts based on early conditioning any more than the original romancing did.

Since our partners were selected in part based on their unconscious resemblance to our caretakers, they will often let us down in many of the same ways that our caretakers did. So what we need the most can be precisely what our partner finds it hardest to give, and vice-versa.

If one of our caretakers wasn't affectionate, for example, then as the romantic phase wears off we may discover to our shock that our partner has that characteristic too. This is their area of woundedness as well as our own. Often, we and our partner were wounded in the same way but compensated in opposite directions.

For instance, we may have compensated for a lack of affection by always reaching out for it. Our partner may have compensated for the same thing by learning to look upon affection as a needless frivolity. So where we're neediest our partner may tend to be the most withholding. Conversely, we ourselves will often be withholding in our partner's areas of greatest need.

What can be done? We can look at precisely the areas that are most painful—our complaints about our partner and their complaints about us. Complaining normally drags down a relationship, but here it is used in the opposite direction, as a kind of magic wand.

This sublime idea starts by making a list of our chronic complaints against our partner. We complete, as many times as necessary, the sentence, "I don't like it when you...." And the answers can range from "...come home late" to "...criticize me in front of our friends."

Then we *isolate the desire hidden behind each complaint.* Within each complaint is something positive that we desire. "I would like more affection" or "I would like you to come home on time" or "I would like to be appreciated by you in front of our friends."

This is the essential transformation, but it's not finished yet. It's still too vague. Just how should our partner be more affectionate? How should our partner be more appreciative? The answers may seem obvious to us, but again, we can't expect our partner to be a mindreader, and they can't expect that of us either.

So we discuss each of these items of hidden desire so that it becomes clear just what is meant: "I would like at least a couple hugs a day." "Home for dinner means by six o'clock." "I would like a compliment from you in front of our friends periodically." We now draw up a new list with these requests on it, based on our desires but leaving out our complaints. We rank each item on this new list for its degree of importance to us. Then we exchange lists with our partner.

Next we go over our partner's list and rank each item by how difficult it would be for us to do. They do the same with our list. Then we discuss each other's list, once more using reflective listening. We listen and clarify so that a clearer understanding can emerge.

These requests to stretch into a new behavior are like the reromancing requests, except that they're more difficult since they involve areas of conflict. And like the reromancing list, our partner's requests here do not obligate us, nor do our requests obligate them.

So if we choose to fulfill these requests, we must purely gift them to our partner, with no strings, no conditions, no expectations of return. Unconditional love. Let's remember, that's the only kind that impresses the old brain.

Again starting with the easiest requests and working up in difficulty, we gift several of them to our partner each week. Whether we're optimistic or pessimistic, whether our partner is also making changes or not, we continue to give several of these behavioral gifts to our partner each week.

Now the interesting thing is, as we choose to heal our partner in this way, through unconditional gifts, we will also be healing ourselves. Here's how: Suppose our partner needs more affection. That may be hard for us, because it may be the very area where we were wounded in the opposite way. We may feel, coming from our own woundedness, that affection is overblown and not needed. We contracted in that area.

Thus when we choose to stretch into a new behavior, and for example, become more affectionate to our partner, we'll be recovering part of our own true and natural self that was repressed in order to survive. In being more affectionate, we'll be healing our own wound in that area even as we help to heal our partner.

Perhaps our partner feels we've been too critical and is asking us to be more validating. We don't have to agree that we've been too critical. All we have to do is begin granting the request—stretching our behavior by being more appreciative than we're used to.

In the process, we'll begin healing as well. We were not naturally critical as infants, so we'll be recovering some of our natural self. And as our partner grants some of our requests and helps us to heal, they'll be healing themselves also. Isn't that an interesting effect?

But the different lists are actually just training wheels. They help us get started, but what we really want to do is to focus in on our partner. How can we love them, appreciate them? What do they need? What's beautiful about them?

In sum, we love our partner in every conceivable way we can think of, and we just keep putting it out there without thinking about what we're getting in return. It's an amazing fact that if we do that well enough, over time our own needs will be met without our focusing unduly on them. To give is to receive. It may sound trite, but that's how it works.

There's another interesting factor: The old brain does not see or hear directly, but receives information only after heavy processing. It lives in a timeless place, somewhat cut off from the external world. There's evidence that the old brain, in this environment, interprets all energy as self-directed.

That is, if we express anger towards someone, the old brain experiences that as anger *directed towards itself.* If we're critical towards someone, the old brain feels that as criticism directed towards itself. Whatever energy we direct outside is experienced by the old brain as directed inward.

When we stretch into giving acts of unconditional love, the old brain experiences that as healing love *directed towards itself.* When we love others, we feel loved inside.

What we give out, we receive.

Jesus said it best: "Whatsoever ye do unto others, the same is done unto you."

Value Differences

I'D LIKE TO tell you a short true story. One day I had finished a chapter and was out on the town that night celebrating with a friend, Betsy. And we ran into Sally, whom I'd met briefly a few times. Sally asked me how I was, and I replied that I'd just finished a chapter. Sally leaned over to Betsy and said, "That's all he ever talks about, is his book."

I felt a little twinge of pain, and then watched my mind rapidly go through a range of scenarios:

My fight-or-flight old brain suggested the standard take-no-prisoners response of 30 years ago: "To hell with you, Sally. Where do you get off judging me?" Now of course that would have alienated Sally and me for a while.

Next up were various subtle ways of attacking Sally or putting her down. But none of it appealed to me any longer. Aside from the fact that they were not skillful, somewhere along the line I'd gotten clear that the world had enough hurt in it and that I didn't need to add any to it. It had to stop with me. So I watched those alternatives come and go.

Next was the idea from 15 years ago, from my second "spiritual" phase, to just stuff it and say nothing to Sally and pretend like everything was fine. That would have resulted in covert resentment, and Sally and I avoiding each other for a while. So I watched that one come and go.

Next was the idea to defend myself and say to Sally, "I talk about it because it's this glorious but heavy weight that's on me all the time, and besides I just finished a chapter." Well, a little better, but still not very skillful. It came and went.

Another alternative presented itself, to call Sally aside and perhaps say, "You know, your remark seemed unkind" or "You feel I'm talking about the book too much?" Those approaches at least gave an opening, but maybe there was something better.

A fifth alternative presented itself, and I chose to go with it. So I said something like, "Sally, I'm sorry if I've talked about the book too much. I'll try to be more present in the future."

Just bringing up the subject again let Sally know that I had been hurt a little—but hopefully in a gentle way, a way that might not turn on her own defenses, and that perhaps might leave the door open for something good between us.

What resulted? Sally pulled me aside and apologized. Then we went on to have a beautiful conversation for the next ten minutes, and ended up feeling much closer than before. My response to the situation had strongly affected the version of reality I would experience.

One alternative was beyond me at that moment: And that was to deliberately take the remark as humorous, and then give a reply in kind, perhaps a smile and something like, "God, I do, don't I?"

Even further beyond me at that moment was to see the real humor and information in her remark, and respond from my heart in that place, perhaps laughing with her and saying, "Thank you for listening, Sally!"

This example illustrates of course that our response to reality strongly influences the reality that we then experience. But it also sheds some light on something else, I believe: That in our attempts to love each other it really comes down to our little moment-to-moment interactions.

It's easy to say or feel that we "love humanity" or even that we "love existence," but it's much more difficult to love this person right in front of us—our family, our friend, our associate, our acquaintance, even our enemy—who may or may not be talking or acting as we would like. That's where it happens, right there.

It's not uncommon that our heart opens to the people in our group—tribal, spiritual, political, social, whatever—but not to others. We're intolerant of "them," "the others," "the outsiders," beings who we feel are different from us. But in my opinion, if our heart is opening here and not there, then we've still got work to do. In that sense, we've all got work to do in one way or another. We're all on the same journey.

And each of us is important. As Stephen Covey says, the key to everyone is the one. How we treat that one person—the difficult one, the one that tries our patience, the one who is different from us—suggests to others how we feel about them too. Because each of us is also a one.

He has a wonderful phrase: "Value the differences." We all appreciate the physical differences between men and women, and use them to create new life. We can also value and honor the other types of differences among us to create another kind of new life—a life of love among us.

397

We all want to love. It's worth saying again: We all want to love. Who among us has not thought of being more loving? But it often seems so impractical because we know we have to live in the real world.

It's easy to get inspired about the subject of love, but we know deep inside that what matters is how loving we can be with others in the day-to-day interactions of life. That love lives already inside of us. We don't have to create it or put it together since it's already there. And we can't force it.

But we can nurture it, water it, allow it—by being more still and aware inside, by doing our best to heal ourselves, by honoring and listening to and giving to others.

And we can see all beings as essentially like ourselves, partly wounded by life but beautiful just as we are. When people act hurtfully, we can look at that woundedness and have compassion. No condescension; no patronizing, no spiritual one-ups-manship.

Just a here-and-now empathy for people's pain, which sometimes comes out in aggressive or harmful ways. Just an appreciation for the great beauty and splendor of each person's natural self, which we can help to emerge. Just a willingness to be kind.

Though we may need to set up appropriate boundaries at times, still, we can potentially love everyone. We can notice the beauty in each person and appreciate it and say so. Then that beauty comes out more and more. And we don't need to be perfect at it. Just our best effort each day is plenty good enough, if we keep working at it.

As we do that in ordinary, practical ways, our own light can shine forth more and more. Just as the sun doesn't ask whether we're good or bad before shining on us, so our own gradually-emerging love can feel compassion for each part of existence. That's part of our journey.

When we patiently move in practical ways to be more conscious, appreciative, trustworthy, kind and so on, then—like the wake that must follow the boat—our love will follow and grow.

BOOK **7**
Inner Body
SIMPLICITY

Book 7, Inner Body, is about
discovering our natural physical
state of health and vitality, and
how to facilitate and encourage
that natural state.

Trust the Natural

$\mathcal{N}$ATURAL PROCESSES EVOLVED over countless eons of time. As such, they possess an innate wisdom that can be trusted. And in general, the older the process the more it can be trusted.

That's a primary difference between the body and the mind. The rational mind is a much more recent development than the body. It's like the new kid on the block, all sizzle and dazzle. And indeed, the mind has great powers which can be harnessed to our benefit. Nevertheless, it lacks the profound wisdom of the body because it doesn't have the maturity of the body. The thinking mind hasn't been around as long, it isn't as close to nature as the body is.

One time I paid a lot of money that I really couldn't afford to fly to a distant city and attend a two-week seminar. I left a failing business, but believed that the seminar might help; however, it proved to be unsuitable for that purpose, at least for me at that time. Then I wanted to leave, but felt that too much money and effort were already invested. Besides, maybe the seminar would get better.

What to do? Each day brought more indecision, more tension in my stomach and shoulders.

On the 5th day I woke up and wrote down my thoughts about staying and going. My mind gave me a number of good reasons for going, plus a number of equally good reasons for staying. I tried to sense my intuition, but couldn't seem to access it. A feeling of utter confusion enveloped me.

Then I had the presence of mind to ask my body if it would speak to me about the situation. I tore off a large new sheet and prepared to write its reply at length.

On the sheet one huge word formed: GO.

In that moment I made the decision to go and suddenly knew that I was doing the right thing. The tension in my stomach and shoulders disappeared. Harmony was restored.

The body always knows what to do to restore harmony because that is precisely its business. That is what it does all day long. I learned on that day that the body can be trusted. It doesn't prevaricate; it's not clever. Though the body is inconceivably complex, it expresses itself in a natural, organic simplicity. The body doesn't lie or sit on the fence.

As mentioned before, the body is so much wiser than the mind because it's so much older. It's been evolving for hundreds of millions of years longer than the mind. It has a flowingness about it, a balance. It's natural.

The mind, on the other hand, is a very beautiful child, but still young. It's still trying out its new powers: It can argue anything, take any side, justify anything. That's why it's said that the mind makes a wonderful servant, but a poor master—because it's smart, but not wise. It doesn't have the body's deep simplicity and wisdom.

404

Have you ever been in a situation you thought you liked, but your body felt rather uneasy? Have you ever liked somone instantly? Have you ever wanted to do something, but felt no energy towards it? The mind can get lost in its justifications and splitting of hairs, but the body has a simple, direct, and straightforward quality about it. Concerning any subject or situation at all, the body quickly knows whether it's "in-harmony" or "out-of-harmony."

Nature in general has a simple and organic wisdom that we do well to try to get in tune with. The days are gone when we fancied that we could use technology to lord it over nature. In areas from personal health to the ecology of the planet, we're finding out that we must let go of our arrogance and allow ourselves to learn from nature and align ourselves with its profound wisdom. To the extent we do, we go towards greater life. To the extent we don't, we swoon towards death.

This principle, like the others, applies in all dimensions. In this chapter let's explore its application to our personal body—our "inner" body:

The Real Healer

$\mathcal{O}$UR BODY HAS evolved powerful and elaborate systems for staying in balance. It's constantly regulating temperature, mineral levels, hormone levels, neural signals, sleep cycles, breathing, heart rate and thousands of other things in order to keep us stable and functioning.

If the body gets too hot, it sweats. If it gets too cold, it shivers. If we run fast, it pants to restore oxygen. If we cut our finger, the body heals it. It does these things and countless others automatically; it's a natural organism. We don't have to tell the body to stay in balance, because it's constantly striving to do just that.

Anything which lowers the body's overall harmony can be called a *stress*. In groundbreaking research earlier in this century, Hans Seyle proved that the body basically responds to all stresses in a similar way. That is, each stress that occurs to us not only causes its own unique response from the body, but also produces an energetic general response which is the same from one stress to the next—and which forces the body to lower, temporarily at first, its overall level of well-being.

The list of potential stresses is extremely broad and includes being too hot or too cold, being underfed or overfed, positive or negative feelings, exhaustion, food contamination, water or air pollution, vitamin/mineral/enzyme deficiencies or excesses, smoking, alcohol, drugs, radiation, burns, cuts, bacteria, viruses, parasites, lack of sleep, and so on.

Because such different stresses all affect the body in generalized ways, we can say that they affect the body's overall *life energy*, its overall harmony. When the body encounters stresses, its life energy lowers. If the stress is large the energy can lower rapidly, as in acute illness. Steady, chronic stress also lowers life energy over time, and manifests wherever the body is weakest.

However, the body is superbly prepared to deal with the average stresses of life. The damaged cells created by various toxins, for instance, are routinely identified, destroyed and carried away to be excreted. Bacteria and viruses are routinely neutralized; hormonal excesses caused by strong emotions are routinely rebalanced, and so forth.

Though it costs the body a certain amount of resources to deal with everyday stresses, the body is ready to pay the cost. As studies of long-lived peoples demonstrate, the body is normally prepared to generate abundant energy and balance for a century or more. It has evolved through eons of time in those ways which best allow it to do so.

When stresses become too large or persistent, however, the body's life energy goes down. On the other hand, when a stress is removed or lessened, the body automatically strives to rebuild a more optimal harmony. If we lower excess fats and proteins in our diet, for instance, the body will automatically switch to cleaner-burning metabolic pathways.

Because the body forever strives to achieve its natural potential, it will always attempt to raise its overall balance if given a chance to do so.

The thing to notice is that the body automatically does this. It will always make better choices if it can. This being so, often the most effective thing we can do in raising our life energy is to remove impediments to the body's own natural efforts in that direction.

The body itself, then, is the real healer when we're ill. Anything we do, anything anybody does, can only assist it in that process. Just as consciousness or love is not put together but rather uncovered, so also true health is not something that we fashion but rather something that we allow—by removing obstacles and stresses of various kinds.

Greatest Factor

*T*HE MOST SIGNIFICANT stresses on our body are self-imposed, that is to say, they come from our own lifestyle. Such stresses as overeating, drugs, alcohol, eating denatured foods, overwork and so on don't come from an external agent, or some malevolence somewhere, but from ourselves.

Of these self-imposed stresses, the most important is non-optimal nutrition. That is, the single greatest factor in our health is *our diet*.

Does that sound too strong? Well, let's look at some interesting evidence:

Several decades ago Robert McCarrison performed a series of fascinating studies. He began by dividing laboratory rats into three groups. The first group was given a typical British diet, the second a typical East Indian diet, and the third a Hunza diet—the Hunzas being usually considered the healthiest people on earth. But everything else about the three groups was kept exactly the same.

At the equivalent age of 50 years in a human being, the rats were killed and autopsied. What McCarrison found then was completely astonishing:

Each group of rats showed those diseases characteristic of the equivalent human society, *and in the same proportions* as found in that human society.

For instance, those rats fed a typical British diet developed diseases characteristic of British society. Approximately the same proportion of "British" rats developed heart disease, cancer, diabetes, etc. as is found among the British population itself. The other groups displayed a similar phenomenon.

This pioneer experiment, since replicated in a variety of ways, reveals the paramount importance of diet upon our health and well-being.

This notion, that our daily diet profoundly influences our health, is often disregarded in practice. Many of us don't —in practice—see a real connection between the diet we eat and the body's gradual loss of balance. Why is this?

Part of the reason, perhaps, is our views about our own diet. Historically, when I asked someone how their diet was, almost invariably their response was "pretty good." Yet when we actually looked into it, this rarely proved to be true. For many of us, perhaps the biggest obstacle to improving our diet is that we already think it's reasonably good.

A second important factor is the hidden power of long-term practices. What we eat at the next meal may not seem to matter all that much; and in one sense it doesn't because it's only one meal. Yet that meal and its cousins, multiplied many thousands of times over decades, have a *processional* effect; that is, the effect cumulates.

A third difficulty is the paradigm, seen in many other areas of life, that we're not responsible. It's so much easier if somebody can just do a quick-fix for us, if somebody else can be responsible for our health. Often we seem to look upon our body as a kind of car or washing machine, to be poked and prodded and fixed with new parts.

But in the chronic conditions so prevalent these days, we ourselves are mostly responsible; and such conditions often don't yield to a quick-fix very well if at all. A bodily problem that has developed over a long period of time may also take a period of time to reverse.

This way of looking at our body, as a whole self-healing organism, has the potential to be very effective. Once again, as Epictetus said, we reap as we sow. To be primarily responsible for our own health may feel like a burden at first, but in the end it liberates. It doesn't mean that we're guilty if we're ill, or all-powerful if we're not, but rather that we have much more influence over our health than we might imagine.

If we're primarily responsible for our own health, and if diet is a paramount consideration, how can we make the best use of this notion? How can we eat in a way that supports us? Unfortunately, in looking at this question, there are hundreds if not thousands of competing theories about what constitutes a good diet. How to choose?

When faced with such an environment, in my opinion the best approach is a very empirical one. First, let's just ask: Who are the healthiest and longest-lived peoples on earth? And second: What do *they* do?

Scientists are generally agreed that the longest-lived, healthiest peoples on earth are, first, the Hunzas of northern Pakistan; second, the Vilcambans of Ecuador; and third, the Abkasians of Georgian Russia. Dr. Alexander Leaf and many other researchers have studied these societies and noted a "striking similarity" in their diets.

The Hunzas are particularly notable, being universally considered to be the most robust people on the planet. Let's look at them now:

According to researchers, the Hunza's lifespan almost routinely exceeds 100 years and often 110 years, with a few even reaching beyond 120 or even 130. Particularly striking is the fact that not only do they live so long, but that they enjoy full, active lives even when elderly, and show no signs of the many degenerative diseases of "modern" cultures.

Now these are the same Hunzas considered in the McCarrison diet experiments. So we might want to inquire: When the "Hunza" rats were autopsied at an equivalent age of fifty years, what diseases and pathologies were found?

The answer is: None.

Incredible as it may seem, the scientists could find no evidence among the "Hunza" rats for heart disease, cancer, diabetes, stroke, osteoporosis, obesity, intestinal and kidney and liver diseases, and on and on. In fact, they couldn't find any pathology at all.

This is similar to the experience reported by physicians who have visited the Hunzas. They record their astonishment at finding that their services are unneeded except for minor things such as setting broken bones. They as well could find virtually no evidence of disease or pathology.

As the Hunzas receive increasing contact with modern cultures and their industrialized foods, this is becoming less true. But here's how it was a few decades ago, and to some extent, still is today:

The Hunzas resided in the valleys of the Himalayan mountains. Most worked tilling the fields. Indeed, it was not uncommon for a Hunzakut to work until the day of death. Because the elderly retained their mental faculties, wisdom accumulated and the elderly were revered. Men sired children into their 90's.

The diet was almost exclusively vegetarian. Fruit was either eaten raw, or dried and rehydrated. Vegetables were often eaten as a kind of salad. Harvesting and consumption of food frequently occured on the same day.

Often a vegetable stew was made. Every few weeks the stew might include a little meat, if available; usually it wasn't. An egg, or yogurt from unpasteurized milk, was consumed once or twice a month, if at all.

Every meal included a kind of bread called a *chapatti*, which was cooked on a grill like a pancake, though it had no milk or eggs. The flour for this chapatti was normally ground a short time before, and the cooked product was immediately consumed.

A little wine was made from apricots, and sometimes consumed on a festive night. Oil for cooking was made from apricot kernels, and used sparingly. In the spring the Hunzas sometimes ran out of food and went on a fast for a month or so until the new harvest came in.

Their diet was about 85% carbohydrates, measured by calories. It was about 7% fat, and about the same for protein. All animal food, including dairy, accounted for less than two percent of the calories consumed.

In sum, the diet of the Hunzas was almost exclusively fresh fruit, fresh vegetables, and fresh whole grains.

Now let's ask:

Was there any sort of common theme running through all aspects of their diet, something that might help guide us today in making good dietary choices?

I believe there was, and it can perhaps be best summed up in this simple way:

They ate very close to nature.

Our bodies evolved over tens of millions of years to be in harmony with the diet our ancient ancestors ate. So if we eat now about what we ate then, in about the same condition we ate it then, our bodies will automatically tend to resume the health and harmony of their natural state.

In other words, our body will automatically tend to rise to its peak harmony if we give it only those foods, in those forms, that it optimized for over so many millions of years.

Let's examine this principle by looking at the different aspects of it as embodied by the Hunzas. Let's ask:

What exactly are the characteristics of the diet of the healthiest people on earth?

Vegetarian

*F*IRST, THE DIET of the Hunzas is *vegetarian*. Their diet is almost exclusively from the plant kingdom. All animal foods, including dairy products, are negligible. And though it doesn't suffice by itself, this may be the single most valuable choice we can make in maintaining or restoring our natural well-being.

Why is being a vegetarian close to nature?...close to our nature? Consider these clues:

A carnivore's intestines are three times the length of its trunk. It's a short, straight tunnel designed for rapid transit and expulsion of putrefying flesh. In contrast, our intestines are twelve times the length of our trunks. They're long and winding, with complex passageways and puckered bowel walls designed for maximum extraction of nutrients from plants. It's the intestine of an herbivore.

Carnivores have long, sharp, pointed teeth for tearing flesh. Their jaws move only up and down, for the purpose of biting and tearing. Their saliva is acid, geared to the digestion of animal protein.

Our primary teeth are molars, designed for crushing plants. Our jaws move side-to-side to help the molars grind plant food. Our saliva is alkaline, like that of all herbivores, and promotes the digestion of plant carbohydrates. It contains ptyalin for the digestion of starch, like all other herbivores. No carnivore can produce ptyalin.

A carnivore's stomach secretes about ten times more hydrochloric acid than ours, so that it can quickly sterilize and break down animal flesh before it putrefies. And a carnivore's urine is acid; an herbivore's is alkaline. Ours is alkaline.

The digestion of animal protein creates huge quantities of a toxic chemical, uric acid. Carnivores can neutralize ten times more uric acid than our bodies can. Carnivores use an enzyme, uricase, to break down the uric acid before it can harm them. All carnivores have this enzyme, and no herbivore does. We humans don't have it.

All these differences exist because the carnivore's body is geared to the special requirements of eating animal flesh. A piece of meat, poultry or fish rapidly putrefies, particularly in the higher temperature of a body. Therefore the carnivore's system is designed to quickly digest and expel its foods before the putrefying process can set in.

Our digestive system, however, is designed for the long transit times needed to extract nutrients from plant foods. This longer transit-time means that animal foods putrefy in our bodies, creating enormous quantities of bacteria, gas, and toxins. Thus, anyone who eats animal foods will have some degree of toxemia, since our bodies are not organized for the optimal handling of such foods.

Another difference is psychological, as pointed out by Harvey and Marilyn Diamond: Imagine coming across a dead dog. Does your mouth water at the prospect? It would if we were true carnivores. It's only by tenderizing and/or cooking the dead flesh that we make it palatable to ourselves.

Other clues come from empirical studies, as superbly documented by John Robbins:

In 1968 a team of Danish scientists fed a group of men three different diets, then tested them on a stationary bicycle for strength and endurance. Here's what happened:

—When given a diet including meat and dairy, the average time that the men could pedal before muscle failure was *57 minutes*.

—When the animal foods were reduced and grains and vegetables increased, then the average time to muscle failure increased to *114 minutes*.

—When the men were put on a purely vegan diet of fruits, vegetables and grains, the average time to failure then increased to *167 minutes*.

Isn't that revealing?

A study of 24,000 people at Loma Linda University in California found that lacto-ovo-vegetarians—vegetarians who eat dairy and eggs—had a *third* the rate of heart disease as meat-eaters. Very impressive. But wait. Vegans, who eat only plant foods, had *one-tenth* the rate of meat-eaters.

In the U.S., studies show that vegetarians have kidney stones at only half the rate of the general population. Pretty good—but vegans have a rate close to zero.

Researches on colon cancer have shown that all high meat-eating countries, without exception, have high rates of colon cancer. And conversely, all countries with low rates of meat consumption, without exception, have very low rates of colon cancer.

A study of 122,000 women in Tokyo found that the risk of breast cancer was *twice as great* for women who ate dairy products daily, and *four times as great* for women who ate meat daily, as compared to those who ate only plant foods.

Numerous studies, on everything from heart disease to strokes to high blood pressure to cancer, have shown that mortality rates display the following striking pattern:

-Meat-eaters, the highest rate of mortality;

-Ovo-lacto-vegetarians, the 2nd highest;

-Vegans (pure vegetarians), the lowest rate.

Considered from a number of different angles, eating a vegetarian diet is a fundamental step towards improving and maintaining our physical well-being.

Living Foods

*S*ECOND, THE DIET of the Hunzas contains a large amount of *living foods*. "Living" is another word for "raw" or "uncooked," but it's perhaps a better one because the word "raw" connotes something incomplete. But living foods are already fully completed by nature.

It's worth noting that except for ourselves, and domesticated animals who have no choice, no animal on earth eats cooked food.

The Hunzas eat a lot of living fruits and vegetables, in addition to cooked vegetables and grain. This makes sense because raw food is closer to nature. For example, we see raw cherries in nature. But we don't see cherry pies, cherry sodas, or maraschino cherries, all of which are further away from what nature produced, and thus further away from being an ideal food for our bodies.

The desirability of living foods is strongly corroborated by various clues:

For example, Francis Pottenger conducted a series of classic experiments on cats. Some ate cooked meat or milk. Others ate only raw meat or milk. Those cats fed only cooked food developed various degenerative diseases in time, and in addition the severity of these illnesses increased with each succeeding generation. In contrast, those cats fed an identical but raw diet stayed healthy and continued to produce healthy offspring generation after generation.

The results of this experiment have been very widely confirmed. In every species of animal studied, without exception, researchers have found much greater health and well-being on a diet of living foods.

For another clue, let's consider Norman Walker of Arizona. Mr. Walker wrote about health, which isn't so unusual. What's unusual is that he died at 109 years old, and stayed mentally and physically active, continuing to write books and tend his vegetable garden, until quite shortly before his death. Good credentials.

His diet consisted of fresh fruit, fresh raw vegetables as salad, fresh raw vegetable juices, and some raw seeds and nuts. Notice that this diet, which contributed to such a vital and long life, consisted exclusively of living foods.

Living foods contain living enzymes. For example, a peach contains about 600. But all enzymes are destroyed above 129 degrees F. Thus whenever we cook food, all of the enzymes are rendered useless. In addition the vitamins and minerals of the food are reduced and made less accessible. The same is true when milk or juice is pasteurized.

But we needn't know about enzymes, the importance of which was only recently discovered. Intuitively, we know that living foods are closer to nature than cooked ones. By using this principle of eating closer to nature, we'll tend towards raw foods when we want to lift the life-energy of our bodies. And we don't need to be a scientist, or know specifically about enzymes, vitamins, minerals or anything else in order to do it. Our own innate knowledge can inform us.

Let's apply our test right away:

Which do you think will be healthier for you, raw food or raw food that's been irradiated to "preserve" it? Which will be healthier, cooked dried corn or fresh raw corn? We can just keep asking which is closer to nature, and rely on our inner knowing.

This doesn't mean that we should never eat cooked corn, for example. What it does mean is that the more living foods we have in our diet, the greater the contribution to our well-being.

Consider Ann Wigmore, who helped countless people regain health through nutritional means, often from cancer and other serious diseases. She advocated a diet of primarily fruits, raw vegetables, and cereal grass—an exclusively living-food diet.

Knowing the great benefit of living foods, we're free to incorporate them into our diet as much as seems appropriate. If our life energy is lower than we would wish, we may want to increase the amount of living food in our diet, or even move to an exclusively living-food diet for a while.

Unprocessed

*T*HIRD, THE HUNZA diet is *unprocessed.* This lack of processing shows up in two ways. Their food is, for the most part, not processed by the passage of time; and it's also not processed by distant factories.

Oxygen and bacteria create changes in foods with time. Carbohydrates ferment, protein putrefies, and fats become rancid. All of these processes become progressively toxic to the body. Thus fresh food, which is closer to the way nature produced it, is highly desirable.

In Hunza, fruits are often eaten right from the tree. Fruits and vegetables are often consumed the very same day they're harvested. Since they don't spend long periods of time in storage or transportation, the foods are at their peak.

Thus, the tomato plucked from our garden this afternoon is going to do us more good than one traveling for a week to reach the supermarket. A freshly prepared meal is better for us than one that's been sitting on a steam table for hours. A freshly-juiced carrot is more nutritious now than an hour from now.

Also in accord with this notion, the Hunzas grind their grain and use the resulting flour quite quickly in making chapattis. Their flour undergoes no further processing or storage. Contrast that with our own modern flours, which are highly processed in factories, then stored for weeks or months before being used.

The moment a grain is ground into flour, oxygen begins to destroy the enzymes in it, as well as vitamins E, A and others. The oil from the germ of the grain begins to grow rancid, as oxygen is added to its carbon atoms.

To counter that process, white flour was developed. By stripping out the bran and germ of the grain, it was discovered, the flour would store well for months. In doing so, however, 30 to 40 nutrients as well as fiber are severely reduced. Adding back a few synthetic vitamins and calling the resulting flour "enriched" is a poor substitute for the real thing.

It's helpful to know that when a food label says "flour" or "wheat flour" that means white, denatured flour. Better is if it says "whole wheat flour," but such flour is ground in high-speed steel mills which get very hot and cause the oils in the flour to become rancid. (Hence the development of white flour which, being stripped, has nothing to go rancid with, so that the mills can run very fast and the shelf life is long.)

Better yet is if the flour says "stone-ground 100% whole wheat flour." Why stone-ground? Because stones stay cool relative to steel. In practice, such flour is also usually ground in steel mills, but they are run much slower (so that the steel doesn't get hot), thus increasing the expense. Best of all is 100% stone-ground whole wheat flour where the label says that the flour is ground fresh daily.

As soon as a grain is opened, whether by grinding, cutting or whatever, the oils in it start to oxidize and go rancid. Hence ideally, grain should be ground into flour just before it will be used. Rancidity is important because fats are vital in building all the walls of our cells. Cells made with rancid oils are much more permeable, thus making it much more difficult for the cell to keep out toxins and microbial intruders.

Other grains undergo a similar process. For instance, whole rice is stripped of its outer bran, which is extremely rich in nutrients, and refined into white rice which has far fewer micro-nutrients. "Organic brown rice" is the real thing.

Refined sugar, corn syrup, jams and jellies, white flour, white rice, etc. are all examples of products whose nutritional value has been largely refined away. Foods made with such refined foods will impose extra burdens on the body.

"Empty calories" describes foods that have been refined to the point where they are largely nutrient-free. Such foods don't give the body all the raw materials it needs, and displace foods that do. Moreover, since the body must call upon its own limited reserves of vitamins and minerals to digest these foods, they have the net effect of actually reducing valuable nutrients in the body.

In the early decades of this century, Dr. Weston Price travelled worldwide to study the differences between primitive and modern peoples. He found striking differences in health between native and modern tribes living just a few miles apart. Why this difference?

The crucial factor, Price found, was that the "modern" tribes had introduced refined commercial foods into their diet, whereas the native tribes, who were much healthier, had not. He found strong correlations between the introduction of refined foods and the appearance of chronic diseases.

But we needn't know about that, or the intricacies of modern flour milling, in order to improve our well-being. By applying the principle of eating closer to nature, we automatically gravitate towards unrefined foods and their benefits.

Thus we can choose products made from whole-wheat flour instead of refined flour. We can refrigerate flour, use it fairly quickly, or even grind our own with a personal mill just before using it. We can choose whole-grain rice over white rice. We can eat fresh fruit instead of refined sweets. We can prefer fresh vegetables to frozen, frozen to canned (which are heat processed), fresh fruit to dried, fresh-squeezed juice to pasteurized juice, and so on.

In general, the more a food is processed the less useful and benign it's going to be in our bodies. A banana will be better for us than a home-made banana cream pie with whole-wheat crust. That, in turn, is better than commercial banana cream pie with a white-flour crust and synthetic banana filling from chemicals.

In each case we can be guided in the right direction, without detailed knowledge, by seeking what is fresher, less processed, less refined—closer to nature.

Unadulterated

Fourth, the diet of the Hunzas is *unadulterated*. It's virtually free of chemical additives and toxic contaminants of metals and pesticides. Not having such noxious components, their food is much closer to the natural state and therefore more beneficial to them.

In the course of its functioning, our body manufactures approximately 100,000 different chemicals every day, and performs countless chemical and electrical operations. To do that, it needs 50 or so raw materials each day. Equally important, the body needs to avoid receiving substances that are toxic to its delicate, complex and balanced operations.

Pesticides are among the most toxic chemicals known to science, designed to kill living creatures. Along with other industrial metals and toxins, they run off into our lakes, rivers and oceans, polluting both water supplies and marine animals.

These toxins become more concentrated as they move up the food chain. From phytoplankton to zooplankton to small fish to larger fish, the metals and chemicals concentrate as they move up. That's why a large fish like tuna has more mercury, for instance, than a smaller fish like cod; tuna is further up the food chain.

In addition, shellfish filter large quantities of water for sustenance. Thus shellfish can reach chemical concentrations in their bodies many thousands of times the surrounding water. Because they're close to shorelines, which are compromised all over the world, shellfish are particularly susceptible to contamination.

Livestock animals also concentrate, in their flesh and fat, toxic chemicals in their food. Since pollutants are in all food now, this concentration is occurring ubiquitously. In addition, virtually all livestock now receive heavy doses of antibiotics to counter the diseased conditions associated with tight confinement on factory farms.

This toxic concentration as we move up the food chain is confirmed in tests. In a study from 1964 to 1968, for instance, it was found that, compared to the average pesticide residues found in plant foods:

—dairy foods had about three times as much;

—meat, fish & poultry had about six times as much.

Eating lower on the food chain, then, is especially helpful in lowering our ingestion of harmful toxins. The closer we come to being the vegans that we were in nature for most of our evolution, the fewer harmful metals and chemicals we take in.

We can also choose organic foods when available. This is a loose term currently, but generally means fruits and vegetables grown without pesticides or herbicides. Sometimes it means, in addition, produce grown with compost or other organic fertilizer (returning trace minerals to the soil) rather than with inorganic chemical fertilizers.

Another choice is to read labels on boxes, cans and bottles carefully and so choose foods that have few or no chemical additives. This often brings about greater energy. And it stands to reason. Our bodies evolved over roughly a hundred million years to process the nutrients in fruits and vegetables. Nothing prepared our bodies (though they try valiantly) to adequately deal with the thousands of chemical additives and pesticides which now contaminate our foods.

Every time the body must devote resources to the attempt to detoxify and expel these toxins, energy is taken away from other and better uses. Sometimes the body simply doesn't have the time or resources to deal with them (more are coming at the next meal) and so stores them away in the fat or the muscles.

A good guideline is that if we find it difficult to pronounce one or more ingredients on a label, it's probably best to pass that food by. Even better is to avoid packaged foods altogether when possible, and eat meals prepared from fresh ingredients.

In this connection it's worth noting that salt itself, when over-consumed, is a toxic chemical. Our raw vegan diet of five million years ago provided much more potassium than sodium, and the two need to be balanced, so the body had evolved to conserve sodium. But now, when our refined diets contain much more sodium than potassium, the damage to our overburdened kidneys can be severe.

Sodium from our salt shakers, as well as the salt added to processed foods, is also an important contributor to high blood pressure, heart disease and strokes. The Japanese, who have the highest salt consumption in the world, also have the highest death rate from strokes.

Sodium consumption can come in unexpected ways. For instance, we can banish the salt shaker from the table only to restore it by the back door by using soy sauce, which is 20% salt. Excess sodium can also come from artificial products such as sodium saccharine, monosodium glutamate, etc.

Other toxins that can be reduced or eliminated are, of course, alcohol, nicotine and caffeine. The evidence linking them to degeneration of the body is so compelling and such common knowledge as to need no elaboration here.

Yet life surely has a place for its little pleasures, too. The Hunzas have a glass of wine now and then. My mother, an energetic 77 at this writing, has had a cup of coffee every morning for 60 years. There's a world of difference between the first glass of wine and the fifth, the first cup of coffee and the fifth. That old cliche, moderation, can be so valuable. Everything depends upon degree.

And avoiding a fanatical or rigid state of mind—which the subject of diet sometimes seems to foster—is probably more important than a rigidly perfect diet. To the extent possible, staying easy and tolerant about whatever we're doing can be as valuable a contribution as the thing itself.

We can learn this from Francis of Assisi, a vegetarian and lover of animals if there ever was one. Yet when he was served meat by a host one time and his companions asked what to do, Francis said they should gratefully eat what was offered to them. He was very much a vegetarian, yes, but he was not fanatical; he was easy and graceful about it.

Low-fat

$\mathscr{F}$IFTH, THE DIET of the Hunzas is *low in fat.*

These next two sections are largely based on ideas from the admirable work of John Robbins. A number of people have spoken out eloquently about the subjects discussed next, but his work has an unusual clarity:

The story starts by noticing that heart attacks are the leading cause of death in the U.S.; strokes are third. Together, they account for 50% of all deaths. Yet research has demonstrated that they arise from the same thing:

Atherosclerosis is a process in which our arteries slowly accumulate waxy and fatty plaque deposits on their inner walls. As the plaque deposits build up, the arteries progressively narrow.

When these deposits progress far enough, their fatty contents can rupture from the arterial wall and form a blood clot, which can block the narrowed artery. If this occurs in one of the arteries supplying the heart, we call it a heart attack. If it happens in one of the arteries supplying the brain, we call it a stroke. But it's really the same disease.

Where does it come from? Let's look at two very interesting studies:

From 1963 to 1965 the International Atherosclerotic Project examined the arteries of over 20,000 autopsied bodies around the world, and a clear correlation was found: People in parts of the world with high consumption of saturated fat and cholesterol also had high rates of atherosclerosis. The reverse was also true.

Another study at UC Berkeley examined men of Japanese descent who lived in various areas of the world and ate the local diet. The results showed an almost exact statistical correlation between deaths from coronary heart disease and the consumption of saturated fat and cholesterol.

And where do saturated fat and cholesterol come from? Almost exclusively from animal foods.

Dietary cholesterol is found only in animal foods. Plants do not manufacture it. For instance, per hundred grams the cholesterol in beef is 70 mg; in ice cream, 45; chicken, 60; oysters, 200; an egg, 550. Yet the cholesterol content of all grains, all vegetables, all fruits, seeds, nuts, legumes and vegetable oils is zero.

Saturated fat comes mostly from animals, although it can also be manufactured, as in margarine. It's a fat that's solid at room temperature because of the many hydrogen atoms linked to its carbon chains. Meat, dairy products and eggs all tend to be high in it.

Conversely, most plant foods contain an insignificant amount of saturated fat. The exceptions are chocolate, nuts, seeds, tropical oils such as coconut and palm, and margarine (where the hydrogen atoms are added in a factory).

The diet of the Hunzas, consisting of fruits, vegetables and grains, is extremely low in saturated fat. And if a vegan adds a few raw seeds and nuts, as Norman Walker did, total saturated fat is still low and cholesterol is still zero.

It's now known that the process of atherosclerosis is reversible. At the University of Iowa, monkeys fed diets rich in saturated fat and cholesterol rapidly developed atherosclerosis. When arteries were half closed the monkeys were then put on a diet very low in these substances—18 months later their atherosclerosis had declined by two-thirds.

In 1990, this process was confirmed in humans. In a study by Dean Ornish at UC San Francisco it was found that a near-vegan low-fat diet, combined with moderate exercise and stress-reduction, produced an increasing reversal of human atherosclerosis.

Dietary fat is also strongly implicated in cancer. It's instructive to compare dietary fat patterns and rates of cancer by country. For instance, populations who consume 140 grams of fat or more per day have prostate cancer rates ten times those of populations consuming 40 grams or less per day. Colon cancer, ten times as much. Breast cancer, five times.

A chart showing dietary fat by country versus the general rate of cancer by country is very illuminating. On the chart, each dot represents a country, plotted by fat consumption vs. cancer rate. The dots are tightly clustered in a form similar to a straight line, showing a strong linear correlation— the more fat, the more cancer.

Dietary fat is also implicated in other diseases:

Arthritis. At Wayne State University, rheumatoid arthritis patients were put on a fat-free diet. In seven weeks, all symptoms disappeared. Then dietary fats were reintroduced. In three days, symptoms had reappeared.

Multiple sclerosis. The nine nations with the greatest incidence of MS have per-capita fat intakes of 105 to 151 grams per day. The nine nations with the lowest incidence of MS have per-capita fat intakes of 24 to 60 grams per day.

Diabetes. In Lancet, a study was published of 80 diabetic patients who were put on diets with very low amounts of fat and sugar. In six weeks, over 60% of the patients no longer needed insulin. Eventually the figure rose to 70%, and those that still needed insulin needed much smaller amounts.

It's often thought that diabetes is a disease concerning only carbohydrate metabolism. Yet diabetes is routinely produced in laboratory animals not through a high-sugar diet but rather through a high-fat diet.

Much discussion has occurred about whether the real issue in fat is HDL's, LDL's, cholesterol, saturates, polyunsaturates, and so on. Saturated fat is strongly linked to heart disease; unsaturated fat to cancer. But a consensus is emerging that the real problem is just plain too much fat, of any kind.

Our bodies are just not designed to deal with a lot of dietary fat. The short intestine of a carnivore eliminates fat quickly, before it can go rancid. Its liver can neutralize almost unlimited amounts of cholesterol. Our liver has a very limited capacity to do so.

Finally, fats cause a loss of energy. Fats cause our blood cells to clump together, which restricts their access to many of the body's tiny capillaries and causes a shortage of oxygen to the cells including the brain. That's why after a big high-fat meal, like the usual holiday one, everybody feels like going to sleep. A lesser effect occurs from any high-fat meal.

The diets of the healthiest peoples on earth average 7 to 8% fat by calories. Compare that with the typical modern diet, which gets 40% or so of its calories from fat. Eating that much fat, whether it's animal or vegetable, saturated or unsaturated, creates monumental problems for the body.

Sometimes we switch to a vegetarian diet but still eat cheese, milk, eggs and products made from them. Or we start using high quantities of vegetable oil. Since these are still high-fat foods, we can still suffer the deleterious long-term effects of a high-fat diet.

Or we can be a vegan, but still load up on french fries, chips, crackers, pastries, and so on. If so, our bodies will labor under a great disadvantage even if we're eating only plant foods. Even the no-fat desserts now appearing on the market are best used only as special treats. They're not natural foods, and so cannot promote our well-being very well.

It's easy to eat a high-fat diet and believe we're eating a low-fat one. As Nathan Pritikin pointed out, this happens because of two different ways of measuring fat. If we measure fat by weight, it often seems low. For instance, whole milk is a little over 3% fat by weight. Yet if we measure it by calories—the way the body measures it—the same milk is 49% fat. An enormous difference.

Measured by calories, "low-fat" milk labeled as 2% fat is actually 31% fat. An egg is 70% fat; so is cheese. A burger is 55% fat, a lean steak 70%. Chicken is about 30%; turkey is more. Fish can be low or high, but average about 35%.

Switching from red meat to chicken and fish doesn't really help us all that much. We're still eating animal foods, with all the problems they present to the body. In addition, chicken and fish have just as much cholesterol as red meat. They're still too low in fiber (having none) and too high in protein (see below). And they're still much too high in fat.

Compare that to the average grain. Measured by calories, it's about 7 to 8% fat. The average bean or pea is lower. The average fruit is 3 to 4%. The average vegetable is about 6%, though it ranges from 1% to about 11%. Exceptions are nuts, avocados and olives (all of which are 80% or more), soybeans at 37%, and tofu at 54%.

Thus in creating a diet low in fat, John McDougall and others recommend a diet centered around starches. Whereas sugars are short chains of carbohydrate, starches are long chains of them. They are foods such as rice, potatoes, breads, pastas, cereals, winter squash, and so on.

By adding vegetables and fruits to our whole starch, and a small amount of spices and condiments, a nutritious and tasty diet can be created which is vegetarian and below 10% fat by calories. Many good cookbooks can now be found for such a diet.

The diets that reverse heart disease, arthritis, diabetes and many other diseases in both humans and animals get less than 10% of their calories from fat. Our diet in nature was below that figure. The healthiest populations on earth are below it now. We can be too.

Low-protein

$\mathcal{S}$IXTH, THE DIET of the Hunzas is *low in protein.*

Many of us, when contemplating a vegetarian diet, wonder if we'll get enough protein. In fact, well over 20% of the calories of a modern diet come from protein, versus roughly 7% among the healthiest peoples on earth.

This excess carries severe costs, as documented by many people but perhaps best of all by John Robbins and Harvey and Marilyn Diamond:

One cost of excess protein is *negative mineral balance.* The body is constantly regulating the PH of the blood to keep it neutral to slightly alkaline. Blood that becomes too acidic can cause death, so the body does whatever is necessary to prevent that from happening.

All meat, fish, eggs and dairy products are acid-forming foods. Eggs, for instance, create 19.7 mg acid residue per 100 grams. Cheddar cheese, 5.4. Beefsteak, 23.5, and so forth. In contrast, almost all plant foods form alkali residues. Tomatoes, for example, -5.6; carrots, -9.0, etc.

If the diet contains too much protein, then excess uric acid is formed, which must be neutralized in the bloodstream. In order to do this, the body pulls alkaline minerals such as iron, zinc, and magnesium from body structures.

Because calcium in the bones and teeth is the largest mineral supply available to the body, the body relies upon this storehouse extensively when faced with too much acid. As high-protein foods are digested, the body pulls minute but significant amounts of calcium out of the bones in order to neutralize the blood's PH.

Over a period of decades this calcium drain causes severe loss of bone density, which is called osteoporosis. It leads to such problems as chronic back pain, spinal problems, fractures, decreased height, bent-over posture, etc. These are considered normal signs of aging in the U.S. and other high protein-consuming countries.

Lacto-ovo-vegetarians (who eat dairy and eggs) show a much lower bone loss. In the U.S., by the age of 65 the average female vegetarian has lost only half the bone-mass that the average female meat-eater has. And female vegans show almost no bone loss whatever.

Studies on African Bantu women, who eat a low-protein vegan diet, show that they take in only 350 mg of calcium per day. That's all. Yet they show no signs of demineralization or osteoporosis, even while bearing and nursing an average of nine children.

Negative calcium balance has also been implicated in the physical and emotional pain of PMS, because blood calcium dips especially low just before menstruation.

Many in our culture consume milk or other dairy products in order to get more calcium. But research has shown that on a high-protein diet we will go into negative calcium balance regardless of how much supplemental calcium we take.

In one study, women on typical high-protein diets were divided into groups and given supplemental calcium in amounts ranging from zero to 2,000 mg per day. At the end of two years, there was no difference in the bone demineralization of the various groups. In other words, calcium supplements won't keep our bones healthy long-term; only a low-protein diet can do that.

Dairy products, because of their high protein content, actually contribute to the process of demineralization even though they contain calcium. World health statistics show that those countries where the consumption of dairy products is highest, including the U.S., Finland and Sweden, also have the highest rates of osteoporosis.

A diet without dairy products is closer to nature. No animal in the wild consumes milk or dairy products past the period of nursing. Neither did humans until very recently. We apparently began with the domestication of livestock about 10,000 years ago, a mere moment compared to the tens of millions of years during which our herbivore bodies evolved.

The idea that extra protein builds strength or endurance is commonly advanced in some quarters. Yet the strongest animals on earth, including elephants and bulls, eat only plant foods. Their bones are strong and do not demineralize.

Strength? The world record in weight bench-pressing has been held by a vegetarian. Endurance? The world-record holders of both the triathlon and the 24-hour triathlon have been vegetarians. So has the world's premier long-distance runner, holding nine Olympic medals.

Consider, as Pritikin did, the Tarahumara Indians of Mexico, who consume a vegan diet of corn, squash, beans, and other native vegetables and fruits. Though their diet is less than 10% protein, they can carry a 100-pound pack for 110 miles in 70 hours.

Mounting evidence shows that, ideally, our bodies need about 5% to 10% of their calories from protein. This is what the Hunzas, Abkhasians, and Vilcambans get, who remain in superb condition all their life.

This need is amply supplied by plant foods: Measured by calories, wheat is 13% protein; cabbages are 13%, potatoes are 8%, oranges are 7%. The average vegetable is over 10% protein; the average fruit over 5%. The lowest-protein grain, brown rice, is 7%. The average legume is over 20%.

Because beans and peas (legumes) are quite high in protein, they are best eaten sparingly. The Hunzas don't use them. An overabundance of legumes in our diet can create the same high-protein problems as animal foods do—though it does avoid the problems of excess fat. On the other hand, if we're under unusual stress our need for protein increases; and legumes can easily supply such extra protein.

Earlier in this century it was thought that animal foods supplied superior protein to plant foods because experiments showed that animals grew faster and larger on animal-protein diets. But later research demonstrated that those same animals also had more diseases and much shorter life spans.

It's also been advocated that animal proteins are needed for vitamin B-12, since this vitamin is not provided by plant foods. But the obvious question is, where do the other herbivores get it?

No animal in the wild takes B-12 pills. So where does it come from for them?

It turns out that the intestine of a healthy herbivore contains certain favorable bacteria which manufacture this vitamin. This healthy intestinal climate is greatly damaged by putrefactive bacteria associated with eating animal proteins. However, a vegan diet will gradually re-establish this desirable intestinal flora.

In addition, vitamin B-12 has recently been detected in plant foods by more sophisticated tests than were used formerly. Moreover, it's now estimated that the requirement of B-12 needed per day is an order of magnitude lower than previously thought. This accords with the common-sense observation that some of the healthiest peoples on earth are vegans; yet neither they, nor healthy herbivorous animals in the wild, consume B-12 supplements with their meals.

Another once-popular idea was that grains needed to be combined with legumes or dairy at a meal to form complete proteins. This idea has now been abandoned. Studies have shown that a diet of whole grains, fresh vegetables and fruits will supply more than adequate protein.

A 1984 study, for instance, found that vegan diets supplied more than twice the requirement for each *amino acid* (the building blocks of protein). And indeed, the healthiest people on earth, the Hunzas, normally eat their grains without adding legumes or dairy.

Other potential problems associated with excess protein intake are:

Anemia. People with large amounts of dairy products in their diet, for instance, can become anemic because dairy products contain almost no iron, yet crowd out foods that do. It takes almost 50 gallons of milk to supply the iron in a single bowl of spinach.

Kidney problems. The more high-protein foods eaten, the harder the kidneys must work to excrete high levels of uric acid and calcium in the blood. The former can severely damage the kidneys over time; the latter can precipitate into kidney stones.

Vegans, studies show, are virtually free of the above conditions. This is congruent with many other studies from around the world, including the huge China Project headed by T. Colin Campbell, which demonstrate the excellent overall health of peoples on low-protein diets.

Generally, it is not possible to obtain a true low-protein diet while eating animal foods, since they are uniformly high in protein. Only on a plant-food diet will we generally be able to get our protein below 10% by calories—and join the ranks of the healthiest peoples on earth.

High-fiber

$\mathcal{S}$EVENTH, THE DIET of the Hunzas is *high in fiber.*

In modern industrialized societies, and in particular among the elderly, serious problems of the intestinal tract are widespread, including diverticulosis, hemorrhoids, spastic colon, and so on. And a high proportion of the population has constipation.

A high-fiber diet ensures that the *bolus*—the food mass being digested in the body—is mostly fiber. Since fiber retains and absorbs water, the bolus remains soft and thus moves easily through the intestines. A high-fiber bolus eventually turns into a high-fiber stool, which retains a high water-content and continues to move easily through the colon.

When the diet is low in fiber, however, a different story emerges. Without adequate fiber the bolus becomes dry and difficult to move along. Pockets of hard, dry matter, called "diverticuli," can form in the intestines, causing inflammation, blockage and pain. A partial blockage of the appendix can produce appendicitis.

Since the colon is designed to absorb moisture, when a low-fiber bolus enters the colon its dryness and hardness now increase. Its reduced bulk causes less peristaltic action, longer transit time, and thus even more dryness, compounding the problem. The increased transit-time also facilitates bacterial putrefaction of the bolus, producing gas, toxins, and a state of *auto-toxemia*—low-level but chronic poisoning.

Hemorrhoids can result from straining to expel hard and dry stools. Diverticulitis, constipation, spastic colon and other problems, considered almost normal now as one ages, can all result from eating a diet low in fiber.

Sometimes it's thought that we can eat a high animal-product, low-fiber diet and then add bran or other fiber to minimize the effects. But problems remain. Putrefaction still occurs. And saturated animal fat, even with added fiber, clogs the intestines as grease clogs a drain. Experiments have shown that diets with supplemental fiber are not nearly as successful as diets that are naturally high in fiber.

Where do we find natural fiber? Since it's so important, let's inquire: How much fiber is found in animal products? How much in meat, fish, eggs and dairy products?

None.

Because fiber is found *only* in plants. All plants contain it. It's in all fruits, vegetables, grains, legumes, and so on. A diet of plant foods is therefore naturally high in fiber, and needs no additional fiber.

To me, one of the most intriguing things about the diet of the Hunzas is that it doesn't contain any magic bullets. It has no miracle foods or magic ingredients or supplements. Rather, their diet just gives the body the nutrients it needs while avoiding the toxins and empty calories it doesn't need. The body itself takes care of the rest.

Moreover, the Hunzas don't know anything about fiber or low-fat diets, excess protein or the food chain. The importance of these things and others wasn't recognized until relatively recently, yet the Hunzas didn't need to know about them and still don't. They just eat a diet that is close to nature, and nature takes care of the rest.

Because fiber holds water, high-fiber foods tend to be *hydrated*, that is, to contain a high content of water. This, of course, describes fresh fruit and vegetables. But even when high-fiber foods are dry, such as pasta, the fiber in them tends to attract water in the intestines and thus to hydrate in the body.

The contrast to this is a *concentrated* or low-fiber food. Examples are a steak, an egg, a piece of fish or poultry, or a sweet dessert. Concentrated foods contain more calories, fat and protein for a given bulk of food.

Concentrated substances of any kind tend to have an addictive quality. Coca leaf is not addictive to peasants in the Andes, but when concentrated a hundredfold as cocaine it becomes addictive. When concentrated additionally as crack it becomes super-addictive.

Though not nearly to the same extent, concentrated foods seem to also have an addictive quality. Most binges are not about celery or apples, after all, but usually involve foods with high concentrations of fat, protein, salt or sugar. A diet naturally high in fiber, and thus low in concentrated foods, can, I believe, gradually remove this subtle tendency towards being addicted to certain types of food.

Moreover, by focusing on low-concentration, high-fiber foods such as fresh fruits, vegetables and whole grains (refined grains lose much of their fiber), we help ourselves to easily control the total amount of calories consumed as well. This is important because any diet, no matter how good it may be, can be made into a life-shortening one by the simple act of eating too much of it.

A fascinating experiment has been repeated many times: Animals are divided into two groups. The first group is fed a nutritious and varied diet, and is allowed to eat as much of it as it wants. The second group is fed the exact same diet, except the quantity is cut in half. In some studies the second group is given 60-65% of the food eaten by the first group.

What happens? The animals live 35% to 50% longer. Isn't that astounding? And yet no other changes of diet or lifestyle were involved.

Experiments at the University of Texas show that calorie-restricted diets eliminate excess glucose. It's been proven recently that free-floating glucose from excess calories leads to cross-proteinization in our cells, a prime suspect in aging. Moreover, studies indicate that animals on food-restricted diets also have far less damage to cell membranes from free-radical oxygen.

In nature, before our comparatively recent role as omnivores, we followed a vegan—exclusively plant foods—diet for tens of millions of years. On such a diet, overeating is not a problem. Yet in modern cultures, obesity and weight-control are prominent concerns.

Animals are not fat when living in nature. And obesity is not a problem today among the Hunzas, the Abkasians, the Vilcambans, the Tarahumaras. On a natural diet of fresh fruits, fresh vegetables and whole grains, the body tends to automatically gravitate toward its ideal weight. It's not something that we normally have to focus upon, because it tends to happen naturally and gradually.

Just the opposite happens when we eat foods that are refined and concentrated. In the brain is a small nerve-center called the *appestat*, whose purpose is to regulate our hunger. When we eat foods concentrated in protein or refined calories such as fish, chicken, white-flour pizza, sweet concoctions and so on, the appestat tells us to go on eating and eating. Why? Because the body is still starving for the micro-nutrients and phyto-chemicals found in unrefined plants.

When we eat a high-fat food such as a hamburger the same thing happens. Protein and carbohydrates are about 4 calories per gram, but fat is 9 calories per gram, sometimes more. Thus in a high-fat food a large number of calories can be contained in a small package with little bulk.

Concentrated foods have a high calorie-to-bulk ratio. Imagine how much easier it is to eat 1.5 ounces of potato chips than to eat 12 ounces of baked potato. Yet they contain the same number of calories. When we eat concentrated foods we're getting far less bulk for the same number of calories. Thus we still feel hungry and tend to eat more.

This is the main reason why diets don't work. If we eat concentrated foods such as meat, fish, dairy, sweets, etc. and then try to cut down on calories, we feel hungry most of the time because of the low bulk. Sooner or later we go off such a diet and binge, gaining the weight back.

446

Thus if we're overweight it's valuable, instead of struggling with it directly, to focus on changing to a healthy dietary lifestyle instead, and eat a plant-based high-fiber diet. Then the body will tend to slowly and naturally bring itself to its ideal weight, just as it restores other forms of balance.

By focusing on optimal well-being, weight problems tend to get handled as a side-effect. And the change can last, since a natural lifestyle can be maintained and enjoyed for a lifetime.

To those of us who have never tried it, a plant-based diet probably sounds quite dull and drab. It certainly did to me for many years. I can remember a time when I couldn't imagine giving up meat. Then poultry and fish. Even when I'd given up meat, poultry and fish, and found how delightful that could be, I couldn't imagine giving up dairy. But eventually I did, and gladly, because of the benefits to well-being.

It probably has to be experienced to be believed, but a plant-based diet can be unbelievably tasty and delicious. Our taste preferences actually seem to change with time, given new choices. There are a number of good plant-based cookbooks on the market now, and you may find that they well repay an investment of time and energy looking into them.

Evolutionarily Old

$\mathcal{E}$IGHTH, THE HUNZA diet is *evolutionarily old*.

Consider the work of Alan Walker of John Hopkins University. By studying striation markings on teeth through an electron microscope, he developed a way of distinguishing between the types of foods that an animal or a human had eaten in its lifetime. He then applied this criterion to a wide range of hominid fossils in order to answer the question: What exactly did our ancestors eat?

The answer is quite surprising. Over the period examined, the entire twelve million years leading up to homo erectus, every tooth showed clear evidence that its owner was a fruitarian, or fruit-eater. Specifically, the diet of every hominid examined was fruit, leaves and nuts. No exceptions whatever were found until homo erectus around 1.5 million years ago.

Apparently, our early human ancestors were all fruitarians. Their diet was fruits, leafy greens and nuts. (Nuts, growing on trees, are botanically classified as a form of fruit.) This may seem an unusual notion, but actually it makes good sense. Let's see why:

It took about one hundred million years or so for the development from mammals to primates, the family of monkeys, apes and humans. There is strong evidence that during this time we were *arboreans*—tree-dwellers. In East Africa we lived in the trees of the dense jungles in order to avoid the deadly predators roaming below.

In such an environment the food most available to us was the fruit and tree leaves provided by the trees themselves. Since that is what we ate, our bodies evolved over this roughly hundred million year period to completely optimize this diet. It's the diet that the body became ideally suited to.

Then, beginning about 1.5 million years ago, we became *omnivores*—eaters of anything. It seems probable that we first added stalk and root vegetables, then wild grasses (grains), and then meat. But evidence shows that animal food was never more than a small percentage of this omnivorous diet—until recently.

As we came down out of the trees and made our living on the prairies, 80% or more of our calories were still coming from plants. This stayed true even during the Agricultural Revolution about 10,000 years ago, when our diet became predominantly cereal grains.

In fact, it's only been in the last 100 to 150 years that the affluence associated with the Industrial Revolution has caused animal foods to become available at every meal, and to become the main staple of modern industrialized diets.

As these radical changes in diet have occurred over the last million-and-a-half years or so, our bodies have done their best to evolve to be able to handle them. They do the best they can, and it's a valiant effort. But what our body is really optimized for is the eating of raw fruits, greens, nuts and seeds, the food that we ate for roughly a hundred million years. The body had a long time to adjust to that diet, and seems to do the very best on it.

But can an animal really live on such a diet? Consider gorillas, perhaps our closest animal relatives. We share 99.6% of our DNA with these primates. Anthropologists report that in the wild they thrive as *fruitarians* and *folivors* (leaf eaters). For instance, it's reported that gorillas will eat exclusively fruit or tree leaves so long as that is available. Only if that supply runs out will they turn to other foods in desperation.

This knowledge becomes important when we desire, for any reason, the utmost potential for well-being. Perhaps we desire it for its own sake, or perhaps because our health is compromised. If that is the case we may want to move more in the direction of a fruitarian diet in order to give our body perhaps the maximum potential to rebuild, detoxify, and rebalance itself.

Does fruit supply enough protein for growth? Well, consider that mother's milk, which is supplied to us during the period of our most rapid growth, is 5% protein. That 5% is about the same percentage of protein as the average fruit has. High water content? Fruits have the highest water-content of any food, usually exceeding 80%.

Calcium? Strong bones? Consider that the gorilla is about 2 times heavier than us but 30 times stronger. And in the wild, osteoporosis is absolutely unknown.

Fiber? All fruits and greens are loaded with fiber, so long as they are unprocessed. Low-fat? All fruits and greens are low-fat. Vitamins, minerals, enzymes? Fruits and greens are loaded with all of them. And nuts, if not overdone, are excellent sources of high-grade fat and protein.

To be of value to us, fruit must be eaten raw. Once fruit is cooked—or juice is pasteurized, as almost all bottled juices are now—then it loses its enzymes, and some of its vitamins, and becomes just another refined and processed food that the body must deal with somehow. In addition, cooked fruit rapidly ferments in the body.

The feeling of well-being, clarity and lightness that one experiences on a true fruitarian diet is quite striking, and is one of those things that must be experienced to be believed. I'm not currently a fruitarian myself, though—I like hot meals too much, especially while writing this book.

So currently I eat a low-fat, low-protein, low-sodium, low-sugar diet of basically whole grains and fresh produce, a good deal of it lightly steamed; and I enjoy that diet very much and recommend it highly. But if there is a need for the maximum degree of health potential, then it is probably wise to move further in the raw fruitarian/folivorian direction—that is, farther back in time.

Natural Choices

*T*HESE ARE THE eight elements of the diet of the Hunzas. They all have the common factor that they are much closer to the way our diet was in ancient times.

Basically, we increase wellbeing by getting closer to our nature. What this means, in effect, is that we travel back along our evolutionary path to an earlier diet to the extent desirable or necessary. The farther back in time our diet goes, the more optimized our body is to it.

The unhealthiest diet is the one that has appeared in modern industrial societies during the last 150 years or so. It's high in animal flesh, high in dairy, high in protein, high in fat, cholesterol, salt, sugar, toxins, additives, refinement and processing. It's low in natural carbohydrates, low in enzymes, low in fiber, minerals, vitamins and phyto-chemicals. It is poorly digested and creates auto-toxemia.

If we want or need a healthier diet than that, we can return back to the diet created by the Agricultural Revolution. That's the diet that we have primarily eaten for the last 10,000 years or so, since the discovery of agriculture. This diet—a starch-centered, low-fat, plant-based diet—most of us can do extremely well on, and thoroughly enjoy as well.

If we desire even more potential well-being, we can go back a million years, before the discovery of fire, and eat mostly or exclusively raw living foods. And if we desire the utmost in supporting our body, then we can go back to our arboreal life millions of years ago and eat a fruitarian—and organic—diet that includes leafy greens and nuts.

Let's remember, we're all responsible for ourselves. So it's wise to consult a trusted health professional, one who can be aware of our personal situation, before starting any new or different regimen. But personally, I find that as I go farther back on the time scale my well-being improves dramatically. You may find this true as well.

At any point in our life, whatever our current diet, we can begin going in a direction of greater vitality by moving towards a diet that is closer to nature—by, in effect, trusting nature more. From that paradigm, we can easily make better choices without having to be nutritional experts.

A peach pie, for instance, is several steps away from a natural peach. It's cooked, it's sugared, it's got added fat, etc. We don't need to know the technical details; we can simply recognize that a peach pie is several steps further away from nature than a peach is, and thus further away from being ideal for us and our diet.

We know that canned vegetables are further away than fresh ones, that white bread is further away than whole-grain bread. We know that a porkchop is further away than a pear, that pasteurized juice is further away than raw, that cake is further away than pita bread, that processed food is further away than unprocessed, and so on.

Concerning virtually any food, in whatever form, we can intuitively know, without learning a great deal of specialized knowledge, how close that food is to nature and thus its value for us. We're always free to choose. We know that we can choose to have the peach pie instead of the peach this time, but we know too that if we choose it often its processional effect will be to slowly lower our life energy.

Thus we can greatly increase our chances to live longer, feel better, have more energy, and reduce suffering by moving towards a more natural diet—by being more natural. We can move towards more raw, unprocessed, and earlier foods.

As we go back on the scale, violence also decreases. A flesh diet is obviously more violent than a lacto-vegetarian one, which still enslaves some animals. That in turn is more violent than a vegan diet. And finally, the least violent of all is the fruitarian diet, because trees literally offer their fruit.

I find it fascinating that the more we tend towards diets that involve the greatest well-being for our fellow animals, the more we tend towards producing the greatest well-being for ourselves. Isn't that an interesting "coincidence"?

Getting Well

$\mathcal{W}$E'VE LOOKED AT diet as the primary element favoring increased physical well-being. But what other elements are there? And in particular, how can they be used in helping to heal ourselves when necessary?

The basic principle in getting well, taken from Shelton and other pioneers of Natural Hygiene, is that *the things that best maintain health are the same things that best restore it.*

If a toxic drug doesn't help us to maintain superb health it's unlikely to restore it either, long-term. Suppression of symptoms and healing of causes are two different things.

There is large and increasing evidence that our chronic diseases are caused by our lifestyle—particularly our diet. In my opinion only the body itself can truly reverse, over time, the causes of such chronic diseases, when that is still possible. We give it the best chance to do so when we adopt a lifestyle that supports the body's efforts rather than hindering them.

The focus is on moving towards a natural, sustainable lifestyle, so that our life can potentially reveal the beauty, harmony, and health of its natural state. This sense of moving towards something beautiful, of allowing ourselves to be attracted towards something rather than fighting something, is, I believe, a primary modality of restoring and maintaining health, physical or otherwise.

To explore other aspects of a physically healing lifestyle, let's look at someone else's experience.

Though a few details have been altered to reflect more recent knowledge, the following story is essentially true:

A friend's daughter, Rini, 21 years old, was diagnosed with terminal cancer. She had exploratory surgery because of some pain and paralysis; tumors were found in her spine, kidneys and ovaries. Her father was informed that she had about six weeks to live.

Rini mapped out a program for herself similar to the one below. That was 19 years ago, and she was still enjoying it years later when I lost touch with her. She was lucky, yes; but whatever the outcome had been, the important thing is that she was sailing her boat in the right direction each day, doing what she could to reveal her truest, most vital self.

As a foundation, Rini shifted to a more natural diet, similar to that discussed above. Like the Hunzas, she emphasized fresh, whole fruits and vegetables, whole grains, and very little else. She ate a fair amount of it uncooked.

For breakfast she might have some fresh-squeezed fruit juice, some fruit, and a dish of brown rice with cinnamon and soy milk. For lunch she might have a vegetable sandwich or a vegetable tamale and a bowl of soup. For dinner, a large salad, some grilled or steamed vegetables, and perhaps a potato dish or brown rice curry, for example.

She'd use herbs, spices (except salt) and small amounts of condiments to flavor the food. She'd often have a glass of fresh-squeezed vegetable juice before lunch or dinner, and if desired, a piece of fruit for dessert. She made use of some of the wonderful vegan cookbooks available.

In other words, she took primary responsibility for her own health. She supported the body's natural tendency to heal itself, and trusted that as the body in general got more healthy it might be able to clear up the specific areas of weakness. She trusted her own nature more.

Along with the shift in her diet, Rini carried out other additional lifestyle measures, which we'll look at next.

Let's remember, before making any lifestyle changes, to take care of ourselves as self-responsible beings by consulting a trusted health professional, someone who can consider our particular situation.

But here is what Rini did:

Fasting

*F*IRST, SHE WENT on a series of *fasts*.

Fasting is something that's been used for millennia. The dean of the Natural Hygiene movement in the U.S., Herbert Shelton, supervised thousands of fasts in his lifetime and helped people overcome ailments ranging from arthritis to heart disease, from ulcers to damaged kidneys.

The Hunzas used to go on a month-long fast every year, when food ran out. And when animals in the wild are ill, they usually fast as well. Fasting is a natural thing, perhaps the most natural thing we can do since it involves doing nothing at all and letting the natural body work totally unimpeded.

Fasting has a very significant healing potential, in part because our greatest consumption of energy is for digestion. When there's no food to digest, the body can turn its energy and resources to another purpose. What it does, in effect, is undertake a spring housecleaning.

In a fast, the body starts feeding on itself, decomposing its own cells for nutrients. But the body reveals again its innate wisdom, because in this process it first consumes old, dead, fat and diseased cells. For as long as possible it consumes only those cells that are the least helpful to its harmonious functioning.

In this process we glimpse again the body's automatic movement towards a higher balance whenever given the conditions to do so.

Thus a clear distinction can be made between fasting and starvation. Fasting is the stage of housecleaning, usually the first 30 days or so, when inessential cells are broken down and removed. After that time the body must begin using vital cells for nutrients, and that's when the process of starvation begins. Continued, death will normally come around the 90th day, though that can vary widely.

The line between fasting and starvation is quite clearly marked; here's how: After the first two or three days of a fast we don't ordinarily feel actual physical hunger. Psychological hunger may continue for a while, but we sense that there's no real need for food. The body turns off the appetite because it wants to work on itself without having to digest food.

This quiescent sensation continues for weeks, as the body continues its housecleaning. It's surprising, but a fasting person does not go around feeling hungry. Then one day, often somewhere in the fifth week or so, we suddenly feel a desire for food again. That's the body's sign that the line separating benefit from harm is being crossed, and that the time has come to eat again.

Often it's not practical or desirable to do a long fast. Because Rini was quite weak, for instance, she did a series of shorter, six-day fasts interspersed with six days of a natural diet. She kept alternating like this for four months and then ended the series of fasts, their cleansing work having been accomplished.

After that, about once a season she would do a week-long fast, if it felt right, to allow the body any further cleansing it wanted. Such periodic fasts have been recommended by a number of health advocates, including Paul Bragg, a man of remarkable vigor who died while surfing the big waves off Hawaii at the age of 95.

When fasting, it's normal to sometimes undergo what are known as *healing crises*. The degree of these will depend on how toxic our body is. They can range from headaches to asthma to joint pains. The symptoms of any illness we had in the past will probably show up briefly again. As toxins are pulled out of storage, they first circulate in the blood stream and can make us feel poorly. (Here is where a health advisor experienced in fasting can monitor us and help us decide to keep going or to stop.)

At first it will often seem as if things are getting worse. The tongue becomes brown and coated, the breath becomes foul, energy can lessen. Yet as the fast progresses the tongue eventually becomes pink, the breath becomes sweet; energy returns more than ever.

The purest fasts are conducted with just water. These are the most uncomfortable, especially at first, because the body is conducting the highest rate of cleasing. If we want to slow down the rate of cleansing, we can do so by doing a fast of fresh-squeezed juices.

Note that the juices themselves do not cleanse, because only the body has the natural intelligence to do that. But they give the body some calories and micro-nutrients to work with, and so the cleansing process tends to be more comfortable, though somewhat slower.

There are advocates for both types of fasts, and I have tried both, up to 30 and 40 days. The water fast seems to go deeper, but we have far less energy during the fast. Ideally we should be resting during a fast, but if we must keep working then a juice fast is better since we'll have more energy.

A juice fast can be as simple as a glass of fresh-squeezed fruit juice in the morning (diluted with water), and several glasses of fresh-squeezed vegetable juices during the rest of the day. Juices provide an abundance of nutrients, but are still one step away from nature. Thus, because of their concentration, they can sometimes provide too much natural sugar.

So on a juice fast, or whenever using juices, it's good to dilute them with water and be moderate in our intake, no more three or four glasses each day. As with anything else, too much of a good thing can turn it into a bad thing.

Good water is important on a fast, and indeed, at all times. Tap water is not usually acceptable because of added chlorine and fluorine and the presence of toxic metals. Probably the best water to drink in these increasingly contaminated times is distilled water, because it's often the only truly pure water. If it's pure enough, spring water is good.

Because the digestion of protein requires a lot of water, people on high-protein diets sometimes believe that eight or more glasses of water must be drunk every day. But if we're eating a natural low-protein diet, we can rely upon the body's own natural mechanism and just drink when thirsty. As we come more into alignment with nature, life gets simpler.

Supplements

$\mathcal{S}$ECOND, RINI TOOK some *supplements*.

On a healthy plant-based diet, supplements might seem unnecessary and unnatural. Hunzas don't take supplements, and animals in the wild don't. Why should we?

There's a good deal of truth in that sentiment, I believe. If we can live the elements of a healthy lifestyle, including a diet of fresh organic whole fruits, greens and grains, then I think it's especially true.

However, many of our foods do not have the same natural nutrients they once did, and we cannot always obtain fresh local *organic foods* (foods grown with natural fertilizers and without pesticides or herbicides). Moreover, the stresses on our bodies, particularly from pollutants, may be increasing. Under such circumstances, it may be prudent to add a small degree of supplementation.

Most widely-available foods are not as nutritious as they used to be. As an example, it's estimated that a commercial apple now contains less than a quarter of the vitamins and minerals of an apple 50 years ago; and this is representative of other foods as well. Why?

First, because intensive farming methods are depleting the topsoil worldwide. As the topsoil diminishes, so does the quality of the food. In the U.S., for instance, 200 years ago most croplands had 21 inches or more of topsoil; today that's down to about 6 inches. (It's worth noting that a vegetarian makes only one-tenth the demand on the soil that the meat-eater does; 70% of US grain is fed to livestock.)

Secondly, modern intensive farming practices strip the soil of many trace minerals while adding back only a few artificial chemicals. (This is similar to refining whole grains to white, severely depleting natural nutrients in the process, and then adding back a few synthetic vitamins.)

The soil becomes depleted from this practice, resulting in plants that may look the same but are deficient in nutrients. Widely-used pesticides can also partially block a plant's uptake of minerals. Thus our foods tend to contain less nourishment than before, unless grown organically.

And in modern life, our bodies must deal with increased stresses, including metal and chemical contamination of air, water and food. Such stresses place extra demands on the body while depleting nutrients. For these reasons, I believe it may be best to take limited supplements, especially if ill, while remembering that they are not a true substitute for the benefits of a natural diet and an organic planet.

Let's begin. The most valuable supplement, I believe, is *vitamin C*, by a wide margin. There are compelling reasons for placing this vitamin in a unique category:

For one thing, vitamin C is apparently so important that every mammal except ourselves and the other primates manufactures it internally. For instance, a hundred-pound dog will manufacture and use about 10,000 mg of C per day. But wait, that's puzzling: If it's so important, then why don't our bodies manufacture it?

An interesting question. Apparently our fruitarian and folivorian diet, eaten for so many tens of millions of years, provided such massive quantities of vitamin C that we lost the ability to make it because the body was getting all it needed from diet alone. It's estimated that when we lived in the trees we got about 16,000 mg of vitamin C daily in our diet. That's hefty. So we lost the ability to make it.

We still need it as much as ever, though, as all mammals do. Every animal tested has manufactured vitamin C at a daily rate of about 100 mg per pound of body weight. If we eat only fresh, mostly raw, organic plant foods, we probably get all the C we need. But otherwise, to supplement with a few thousand mg per day seems prudent.

It is known that vitamin C is involved in hundreds of vital processes in the body. This is particularly true for the various parts of the immune system, the structure of cells, and the production of stress hormones. Linus Pauling, the noted biochemist, recommends an intake of 6,000 mg or more of C per day, especially if under the stress of illness.

Each morning upon arising, Rini took a rounded teaspoon of powdered mixed mineral ascorbates (about 4500 mg of vitamin C) in a large glass of water, usually followed by a glass of fresh-squeezed orange-juice. (She rinsed her mouth afterward to prevent dental cavities from acidity long term.) She then waited half an hour or so, so that the vitamin C could leave the stomach, before eating breakfast.

Many people I know, including myself, have benefited a great deal from adding this little routine to their daily lifestyle.

It can have a profound effect on energy levels, colds, flus, allergies, infections, and all sorts of things. If we're not ill and getting closer to a living vegan diet, perhaps 2,000 mg or so might be sufficient.

If we're ill and choose to take larger amounts, there's an approximate way to tell if we're getting the right amount of vitamin C; it's called the bowel tolerance limit. If the body gets more vitamin C than it can use, diarrhea results. This is normal for the first few days of increased C intake, but if it occurs after that then the amount of C is gradually lowered until that reaction disappears.

As a general rule, the lower our life energy balance the higher the amount the body can and will use. Persons with severe illness such as cancer, HIV, etc. have been known to absorb as much as 20 grams and even more per day.

When increased intake occurs, a number of beneficial enzyme systems depending on C gear up in the body. If we then skip a day or more, those enzyme systems grab whatever C is available, leaving little or none for the immune system. This temporarily increases our risk of colds, flus, infections, etc. Thus it's important to be consistent in our intake of C, and to raise or lower daily levels in a gradual way.

The next most important supplement is *vitamin E*. Like other *anti-oxidants* such as C and A, vitamin E helps to protect against dangerous *free radicals*. Greater amounts of free radicals are promoted by high-fat and high-protein diets, toxic metals and chemicals, and other bodily insults. Rini took 400 units of E per day, later reduced to 200 units.

As a very potent anti-oxidant, vitamin E helps to protect against rancidity of both fatty acids and vitamin A in the body. Vitamin E has been shown to retard and ameliorate the progression of arteriosclerosis. It is also extremely effective with burns. Its direct application on a burn, by reducing the burned cells' need for oxygen, often dramatically relieves suffering and improves healing.

Another key anti-oxidant is *beta-carotene,* which can become vitamin A in the body. Animals given the equivalent of 25,000 units of A a day have shown significantly greater health and longevity. Rini took 25,000 units of beta carotene daily, and later reduced it to 5,000 units a day.

Next most important, perhaps, is a group of vitamins called the *B-complex.* These are vital in all sorts of systems from the nerves to digestion to the skin. Because the B vitamins works best together, foods containing the full complex are desirable. Whole grains, and particularly brown rice, are considered excellent sources of the whole B-complex.

Since members of the B-complex act synergistically, it's usually unwise to emphasize any one or several of them over others too much. Thus multi-vitamins that give too-high amounts may actually help to create deficiencies in B's that are under-represented. I believe, if we use supplements at all, that it's best to be moderate in our consumption of them.

The need for a number of B-vitamins goes up during periods of stress. The most important of these is *pantothenic acid.* If we're under stress—including the stress of disease iself—it may be wise to supplement pantothenic acid.

466

Rini took 100 mg of pantothenic acid after each meal, which was later reduced to 100 mg a day, and a low-dosage multi-vitamin capsule which included the B-complex.

Vitamin D supplements could become increasingly significant if exposure to sunlight must be reduced because of gaps in the ozone layer. Rini took 400 units a day.

Trace minerals from seaweeds can also be beneficial, perhaps, if available fruits and vegetables are nutrient-poor. Fresh-squeezed fruit and vegetable juices are an excellent source of extra nutrients in a fairly natural form, especially if our bodies are below par.

Supplements are not a substitute for a living diet. Too much of them, like too much of anything, can turn them into contaminants or stimulants that the body must deal with. And as concentrated substances, they may perhaps be somewhat addictive. Moderation is almost always a good idea.

But when properly used, supplements may have great potential value for us, particularly as part of a restorative diet and lifestyle. I have personally seen a number of encouraging examples.

Exercise

*T*HIRD, RINI GOT some daily *aerobic exercise.*

There are basically two types of exercise—muscular and aerobic.

Muscular exercise, such as weight-lifting, is designed to build strength or appearance. It can have value to someone trying to lose weight since muscle cells burn more calories than fat cells do, and increasing muscle cells thus raises our basic metabolic rate.

Aerobic exercise is somewhat more valuable, since it directly affects the health of the circulatory, pulmonary and lymphatic systems throughout the body. "Aerobic" is a word meaning "oxygenated." Simply, it's an exercise that causes us to huff and puff a bit for a continuous period of time.

What exactly does aerobic exercise do for us?

To answer, I've partly drawn on ideas in the pioneering work of Nathan Pritikin:

First, it *relaxes us.* Muscles that are inactive build up strong electrical potentials, which can make us feel anxious. Exercise discharges these voltages, as tranquilizers do, but more naturally and without polluting the body. Among other benefits, this greatly helps our sleep at night.

Second, exercise *invigorates us.* It does this primarily by increasing the blood's oxygen-carrying capacity. As our cells get more oxygen, and get it more efficiently and rapidly, they display greater vitality and energy.

This new efficiency greatly benefits the circulatory system. It lowers the blood pressure and heart rate, allowing the heart to work less. It reduces blood-clotting time, making arterial clots less likely. And the process of atherosclerosis is slowed; though, as the deaths of several prominent athletes attest, exercise cannot substitute for a low-fat diet.

Third, aerobic exercise tends to *increase our general level of health*. We have less illness, and faster recovery when illness does occur. A study of freshman coeds found that those who didn't exercise had many complaints ranging from headaches to backaches to colds to allergies, while those who exercised had far fewer complaints.

Fourth, exercise *beautifies us*. It increases circulation to the facial arteries, thus improving our complexion. It gives us better posture. It helps us reach a trim weight. It removes fat from hips, thighs and buttocks, while simultaneously bringing tone and definition to the muscles.

And finally, aerobic exercise *improves our emotional health*. A study at Purdue University found that such exercise greatly improved self-confidence, emotional stability, and even imagination. A study at the University of Virginia found that moderate exercise triggers the release of mood-elevating hormones.

In sum, aerobic exercise reduces tension, lowers blood pressure, improves mood, tones muscles including the heart, improves oxygen availability and raises cellular efficiency—all while slimming and shaping us. We feel younger, live longer, improve our health and energy, and brighten our outlook.

As Pritikin said, what do you suppose we'd be willing to pay for a wonder drug that did all that?

As in other areas, benefits come with consistency. An occasional ski trip, or vigorous tennis on the weekends, won't help nearly as much as consistent, moderate exercise throughout the week. Naturally, it's wise to start slowly and build up gradually in any exercise program.

On a practical level, anything that keeps us just slightly out-of-breath for 20 or 30 minutes several times a week will provide aerobic benefit. Many exercises can fit the bill, from swimming to jogging to rebounding, according to preference. But research has shown that stop-and-go exercises are not as beneficial as more constant exercises like skating or cycling.

An exercise often singled out for praise is *walking*. Rini took a walk each day. It can be done anywhere, at any time, by young or old, requires no equipment, and almost never injures. For these reasons, it's very conducive to exercising consistently over a lifetime. Walking is also a natural exercise, paralleling what we did so much of in the natural state.

Another type of exercise is *stretching* to develop greater flexibility. The oldest and most classic form of this is *yoga*, which includes stretching but goes beyond it. Part of what we're doing in *hatha yoga* (the physical form of yoga) is not just the position itself, but our state of mind while we're engaged in it.

Yoga can be very valuable in learning to release blockages at a deep level, as can a number of more modern forms of bodywork.

The last part of this section is the other side of exercise, that is, getting a good night's sleep. Exercise uses motion, sleep uses lack of motion, to help the body to accomplish the same goal of harmonious function.

An interesting study was done in a nursing home. The residents, almost all of whom had various ailments, were mostly sleeping four to five hours a night. The researchers asked them to do just one thing: to sleep eight hours each night, and if they woke up early to rest in bed until the eighth hour was up. Dramatic improvement in many ailments was reported from this one change.

Brain-wave research has confirmed that elements of a simple and natural lifestyle are the prime facilitators of good sleep. By becoming aware of our natural rhythms and falling into harmony with them, we fulfill the body's appreciation of daily routine.

Thus it helps to go to sleep each night at the same time, and if possible, in the same bed and the same room. Positive conditioning such as this tends to foster good sleep as a habit. Also helpful is sleeping in a quiet, dark place, and avoiding near bedtime any substances (caffeine, alcohol, food, etc.) or activities (exercise, emotional books or films, etc.) that, in stimulating the body, cause the release of adrenalin.

When we have insomnia, the problem is sometimes emotional rather than physical. It can be extremely helpful to get up and write down our thoughts and feelings—whatever it is that is occupying our mind. Chances are good that sleep will be immediate and deep afterwards.

Also helpful is any regimen that relaxes and tones the organism. In addition to stretching, such things as meditation and massage can be invaluable. So can other approaches such as t'ai chi or rebalancing.

Any exercise undertaken at least a few hours earlier in the day is particularly conducive to sleep. Sleep and exercise, the two ends of the scale of activity, support each other very well in harmonizing the body.

Finally, a warm bath taken before bedtime is especially relaxing. After that: "Good night."

Natural Self

*F*OURTH, RINI PUT her attention on bringing out her *natural self* in all dimensions of her life.

One thing she did was to sit silently for a period each day. The purpose of this silence was to slow down, relax, let go of the burden that she had to get somewhere or be somebody or solve some kind of problem before she could appreciate this moment.

She also attempted to be more mindful in daily life. Even in something as simple as brushing her teeth, she began to observe that she could rush through it automatically and mechanically, driving towards breakfast, or she could allow herself to slow down and become aware of it.

She looked carefully at the mind's driving impulse to "get through" everything and onto the next thing; and that very awareness helped to return her to the present moment and to better enjoy whatever she was doing.

Before she went to sleep each night, she also thought of all the things that she could be grateful for, all the little and not-so-little things in her life that contributed to it so much. She let herself surrender, and sent her love and appreciation to every part of existence.

Another thing that Rini did was to use visualization. Every day she visualized being happy and well, balanced and at peace. She visualized what it would be like to be healthy and enjoying life.

Rather than battling against something negative, she created a positive image as a focus for her energies.

She asked herself what an *ideal day* would be like, and visualized it. Not an extraordinary day or vacation day, but an average day as she would really like to live it. By visualizing her ideal day, she was able to blend her different goals into one integrated vision, a life-vision of how she wanted to live and use her time, regardless of the outcome.

She did her best to heal her heart. She knew that holding on to old resentments would only hurt her, that keeping up emotional barriers to others would only take away energy needed for healing. So she worked to heal old relationships that had gone bad.

She apologized and forgave. She let herself release self-righteousness and tune in to the other person. She let herself see that others had acted out of ignorance and conditioning, just as she had. She began to really forgive in her heart, to let that pain go. And for wrongs she had done, she apologized and did her best to make restitution.

And in her current relationships she did her best to act skillfully, to respond to various situations in a balanced and understanding way so that they added to the nourishment and love in her life, so that her heart could be more open.

This affected not only her relationships but her state of mind and body as well. All dimensions affect each other; all dimensions are, in the end, the same thing.

Finally, Rini spent some time each day just being with the beauty of nature.

By taking her daily walk out in nature, she compounded the benefits of it. But at other times she would just sit and look at the sky, or at her garden, or at her animals. And this, too, was healing.

To be with nature usually gets us out into fresh air and light, of course, but it's more than that. Tuning in to nature, with its profound beauty and harmony, can help us gain perspective, feel more peaceful, let go. Nature's sublimity can help to open us, soften us, bring us new insight.

Nature is especially helpful when we're feeling troubled, because it helps us feel again the mystery and awe of existence, to recapture that sense of timeless beauty that we once felt as children. As we spend time in nature, feeling its stillness and silence, its harmony and serenity, these qualities suffuse into us as well. We begin to reflect nature, becoming more serene and silent ourselves, more in touch with our own nature.

In early 1982 I was depressed by a sea of troubles and couldn't imagine what to do, so I began walking in the woods each day for an hour or two. It was tremendously healing. Walking up and down those paths, crossing those streams, my sense of harmony and awe gradually returned. Once more I became able to move in the world and trust it. The sublimity of nature is very restorative.

In all these ways, we can help our physical body to heal. When we know that the body itself is the real healer, we seek to align ourselves with nature, to trust the vast natural wisdom the body has accumulated over so many eons of time.

Knowing that there are no guarantees in life, yet we still can trust nature—that is, more natural choices—to maximize our potential for that harmony and vitality of body that nature meant for us to enjoy.

BOOK **8**
Outer Body
COMPASSION

Book 8, Outer Body, is about
the purpose of pain, our heroic
journey to our truest being, and
how to honor that journey in
the midst of ordinary life.

Love This Too

𝒫ERHAPS THE MOST salient feature of the physical world is the existence of pain and suffering. Not that it can't exist at other levels, but at the physical level pain can't be ignored; it strongly grabs our attention. When armies collide, people die. When physical pain is there it can be agonizing. Even our emotions seem to be grounded in the body.

So Body is the dimension where pain and death stare us in the face. It's the dimension of joy too, of course, but we don't worry about that. When our environment presents us with positive energy, we tend to just enjoy it. We don't ask why it's there; we don't analyze it. We just respond happily.

It's when the environment presents us with negative energy—pain, suffering, loss, defeat, anger, fear, illness, and so on—the whole litany of negativity—that our challenges begin. Now we must come up with some more resourceful way of dealing with this energy, because it hurts.

To me, pain and suffering may be the biggest mystery of all. I can remember as a child thinking, "If God is totally loving and all powerful, then why do pain and suffering exist?" Somehow, if God could allow pain and suffering to exist, the universe felt a little unsafe. Maybe more than a little.

So pain and negativity are, in a sense, the cutting edge. How to deal with them?

It might be fruitful to ask in the first place what we mean by "negativity." What does it mean when we say that something is bad or wrong, or that it's negative?

Basically, we seem to experience something as negative when it imperils the existence or aliveness of ourselves or something that we're strongly identified with. So anything that imperils our personal image, our body, our family, our country, our team, our tribe, our group, our ideas, territory and so on, can be seen as negative.

Something negative has another quality too: It's already stuck around long enough to have caught our attention more than once; it's a problem. When we can easily or quickly handle something, we don't think of it as negative or a problem; it's just a part of life. So negativity is a problem that's persisting; it's causing us some perplexity.

For instance, if we keep driving our car it will sooner or later run out of gas and be unable to run; that's a problem. But the problem is normally solved so easily and routinely—by pulling into the nearest gas station—that we don't ordinarily think of it as a problem, something negative. So "negativity" means that our initial or routine approach to a problem has not made it go away. What now?

In my opinion, the essence of dealing with something negative, that is, something imperiling what we're identified with, and which can't be routinely handled, is to *transcend the system in which the problem has occurred.*

480

Einstein said that the problems that really plague us can't be solved at the level at which they're posed. In other words, if something is a problem in our normal paradigm, that paradigm is probably not the most enlightening lens through which to look at the problem.

Thus any problem that's persistent in troubling us will probably not be readily or easily solved at the level at which it came into being. To "jump out of the system," in Ron Kurtz' memorable phrase, means to come out of our ordinary system for looking at or dealing with this kind of problem.

An example is Rini, discussed in chapter 7. Basically, she solved her problem by jumping out of the paradigm she was in. By considering the problem through a new system, as one involving the balance and vitality of her whole body rather than the illness of specific organs within it, she was able to give herself a much better chance to successfully meet the challenge.

In doing so, she had to grow. She had to perceive things in a different way. That is usually the primary characteristic of a successful response to any kind of persistent negativity.

A very radical transcendence of any system we're in is to increase the wholeness of the system itself by reframing or incorporating those parts of it that are rejected, condemned, or considered worthless. In practical terms, that comes down to the question, "Can we love this too?" Can we really have compassion for this part of existence too?

The Heroic Journey

*I*T CAME AS a great surprise to me to realize one day that pain and suffering were going to be a part of my life for as long as I lived. Up until then I had always thought that if I could just learn enough or become skillful enough, that somehow I could effectively shut pain out of my life.

But I can't; none of us can. For as long as we live, we're going to win some and lose some. Sometimes things will go our way and sometimes they won't. Sometimes we'll feel good and sometimes we won't. And inevitably, we're going to lose some people and situations that we love; tragedies and stupid things can happen. All of that is inevitable; it's part of the very fabric of things, and has to be.

In other words, no matter how well we create our lives, no matter how fulfilled we become, no matter how well we reveal the intrinsic beauty of our lives, we'll still face periodic pain, negativity, suffering—whatever word we'd like to use.

Thus, the future of our life is predictable. It's going to look kind of like this: Pleasure-pain-pleasure-pain-pleasure-pain, ad infinitum. In fact, the notion that we can somehow experience only the "ups" of this great process is in itself a source of suffering.

So no matter what deep transformations or conversions we may go through, we'll still encounter pain and suffering. To think that we'll be the one person who will avoid suffering is already to be living in a contracted state.

Yet—how we treat that suffering, how we relate to the pain and negativities in our life, has a very great deal to do with our happiness.

One way of looking at this is that the inevitable pains of life are the dragons we encounter on our heroic journey to discover the treasure of our truest self.

Heroic? Yes, each of us can be thought of as a hero or heroine on a journey. It's a journey towards the light, towards our natural wholeness and beauty, a journey to our natural and authentic being—a journey, strangely enough, to ourself.

In order to relate a version of the mythological story, I've drawn on the work of Carl Jung, Joseph Campbell and others who've worked in the field of archetypes. Of those, my personal favorite is Carol Pearson, whose insight and acumen are inspiring. I've partly drawn on the ideas in her splendid work to tell this version of our human story:

In this metaphor, we start out as *innocents*. Innocence is our original nature. We can see it in the eyes of a baby. Its look is unclouded by categories, beliefs, or condemnations. Its trust is total. It is pristine, pure, still relatively unwounded. It has no attitudes, no agendas to push, nothing at all. Because it does not draw distinctions, it is united with all of life.

Needless to say, this state of pristine bliss does not last long. Just in the nature of things, we leave Eden, fall from grace—that is, become wounded by life in various ways. Not the least of these woundings is that we learn how to think and thus to make judgments. We become an *orphan*, we feel cast out and adrift. It's a necessary but painful step.

The metaphor of the orphan represents our encounter with suffering and disillusionment. We learn that life can have discomfort and pain. We learn that we can stumble and fall. We begin to suspect that God may be dead or uncaring.

Our caretakers, society, our young peers, etc. hurt us in countless ways. Much of it is unintended, but it happens. We learn that the government is not always good, that people can lie, have hidden motives and act in hurtful ways. We learn that "love" is often conditional on how we behave. We learn that we can be hurt and feel pain, that the universe isn't safe.

The orphan feels powerless, fearful, resentful, grief-stricken to a large extent. Innocence and idealism have been disappointed or crushed. The negative side of life has been encountered, and it doesn't feel good.

As orphans, we often deal with our encounter with pain by denying it, repressing it, or numbing out in some way. We want to be saved from it, to be rescued by someone or something. We may dull our pain through drugs, overwork, rituals, shopping, fanaticism—almost anything can be used.

But whether acknowledged or not, now we're in pain. Though we can distract ourselves from it, at some level life feels disjointed, fragmented, off-center somehow. And that's where the heroic journey begins. We begin to look for a more promising way to deal with the inevitable dragons of life.

The Wanderer

*W*E DON'T NECESSARILY take on heroic archtypes in any particular order, but do tend to cycle through them again and again, learning their lessons at deeper levels.

Yet *the wanderer* is often the first heroic archtype of our journey. The wanderer arises when the pain of being an orphan becomes too great, and we feel that we must set out on a journey to find some answers. So in one way or another, the wanderer leaves the safe confines of normal life, or the normal way of doing things.

As a wanderer, we're looking for something different, a new answer. So we set out on a new course, away from our normal consolations, on a path into the unknown.

An enduring theme in art and mythology is the story of someone on a journey. The traveler, the knight, the cowboy, the prince or princess seeking something—the treasure, the goal, the holy grail that will lend meaning or fulfillment to life and remove its sense of disjointedness.

The journey may be inner or outer, of course, and it may not look dramatic. It can be something as simple as trying out a new style of doing something, or something as profound as beginning a spiritual path. Since it doesn't necessarily look a particular way, our external circumstances may or may not stay the same when we begin our journey.

Often, the wanderer's story begins in captivity. In fairy tales this is often a literal captivity in cave or castle, perhaps imprisoned by a dark force or a spell or a dragon. Closer to home, we may just feel that our life is confining in some way. Our relationships, our society, our job, even life itself may come to seem oppressive.

The wanderer breaks free in some way, attempting to find something that feels more life-affirming, more authentic, more real and alive.

The journeys of both the Buddha and Francis of Assisi began this way. In both cases they possessed "everything"—status, money, kinship, pleasure, etc.—and yet in the midst of this plenty felt that something was still missing. So Francis renounced all his possessions, and the future Buddha left a kingdom and a family and rode off at night into the forest and an unknown fate.

But our journey need not necessarily involve a change in our circumstances. Sometimes we begin our journey while still fulfilling our customary roles in life, as a spouse or parent or worker or whatever. Or maybe not—nobody can say except for us. But one way or another, we've begun searching.

This in itself already alters our relationship to pain and suffering. For by taking on the archetype of the wanderer, we've declared that life is not fundamentally pain, but rather, an adventure.

The danger of the wanderer archetype is the loss of community, of being self-absorbed and thus missing the joys of love and giving and relationship. But what we can learn from it is to trust ourselves, to trust our inner knowingness, our sense of what is right for us.

One quintessential form of the wanderer archetype is the spiritual search. There isn't any way to have somebody else go inward for us, not even a master. For even when it's done with a group of like-minded people, the journey inward is still always a solitary one, always unknown, always to some extent uncharted. Like all journeys of the wanderer.

Above all, the journey of every wanderer takes courage and a measure of trust in existence. And so those are the first things that it teaches.

The Warrior

*T*HE *warrior* IS SOMEONE trying a different response to the dragon— to stay and fight, to hold one's ground, to take a stand instead of escaping.

This is the premiere archetype of the hero in human culture so far. The dragon may be represented as a villain, as a class or country, as disease or injustice. But whatever it is, it's to be conquered, destroyed, defeated.

This is *us-versus-them thinking,* the root cause of the violence in human history against ourselves, against animals, against the planet. Whenever we decide that something or somebody belongs to the outside, to "them," and not to "us," we devalue it or them accordingly.

"Naming," discussed in chapter 5, can be used in a life-affirming or life-denying way. During times of tension or confrontation, the other side is often given names or slang terms that make them seem contemptible or worthless, and so more worthy of being treated poorly.

This has happened at various times to immigrants and natives, blacks and whites, easterners and westerners, hippies and police, capitalists and communists, men and women, workers and environmentalists—on and on. There is no end, apparently, to the capacity of the mind to create categories and then judge one of them to be wrong or deficient.

The danger of warrioring, then, is to live in a world of absolutes. You're on our side or you're not. You're one of us or one of them. The cause, the idea, the organization, the tribe, the position, etc. is right, and anything not allied with "us" is therefore wrong and deserves to get what it gets.

In this prevalent form of warrioring, the warrior lives in a hierarchical world of conquering and conquered, victors and vanquished. It's a world of duality. It's either right or wrong, good or bad. You are either superior or inferior. This is the world of struggle, since struggle is always *against* something— against the opponent, against the barrier, against the problem, against the dragon.

That same struggle is pursued against one's own "bad" qualities. Duality is again applied: Inappropriate feelings or parts of our psyche are to be repressed, defeated, ignored or minimized. In doing so, we wall off and deny our inherent wholeness, the natural being that we once were.

So the warrior's life can come to feel like the struggle that it is. It can wear the warrior down because of the need to stay tough-minded, to avoid too much large-heartedness. Thus "facts" are focused on, logic is emphasized, and the world can lose much of its richness and depth.

A more mature form of warrioring might properly be called *building*. In this form, we don't attempt to conquer or slay darkness, but instead, do what we can to turn on a light. We're trying to achieve a result by creating something new, perhaps a new kind of alternative or a new way of seeing things, rather than defeating something else.

And as Robert Bly pointed out, every time we carry something through to completion or persevere in the face of difficulties, we're using our warrior energy. Every time that we appreciate what's good in someone or something instead of just condemning what's bad, we're turning on a light and helping to nurture the world. Because it is less dramatic and romantic, such mature warrioring takes more patience and skill and courage.

Not that it's always inappropriate to fight an opponent; sometimes it is. And the ability to do so should be part of our palette, one of the options available to us. But mature warriors find less need to fight opponents, being aware that often the real battle is to find a light-source so compelling that the old dualistic polarities can be healed in its warmth.

It's good to be careful in choosing our battles, because we only have so much time and attention and energy. There are many potential battles that we could fight, many potential projects that we could take on. But if we try to fight them all, take them all on, our effectiveness will be nil.

To be effective, we need to concentrate our energy in one or a few important areas, and work diligently on those to see if we can make a difference. We can't afford to squander our warrior energy on petty squabbles, vendettas, unimportant issues or too many things. Sometimes we have to pass up what seem like good worthy battles in order to focus on something more important.

What the warrior archetype teaches is to have courage, to be able to stand up for ourselves, others or a principle when that's appropriate. We learn that we can affect our world when we have the courage to follow our path or our inner light.

We learn that we have a right to be here and a right to attempt to make a difference.

Perhaps most importantly, we learn to act in the face of risks, obstacles and setbacks with steadfastness and courage and creative problem-solving.

The Lover

*T*HE *lover* IS LEARNING the lesson of compassion. As lovers, we're learning about continuing to care, of maintaining our love for others and for life in the face of hardships. Now we're not escaping or battling the dragon, but learning to understand it and relate to it from that understanding.

At one end of the scale, this can look like appeasement of the dragon or sacrifice to it. If our compassion feels too much like sacrifice, we become martyrs. Like orphans, martyrs agree that a way must be found to be saved, and martyrs believe that this comes from sacrifice—for God, for the cause, for the family, the organization or whatever.

As Carol Pearson says, in the process martyrs will often give up parts of themselves that don't seem to please others. The danger is that the service of martyrdom can become a way to avoid continuing our journey, to avoid taking a stand or finding out who we are.

Sacrifice can be transformative. Countless people labor each day in obscure or difficult ways to nurture the world, and I want to honor every one. Yet it's also good to ensure that our sacrifice is not caused by fear of stepping out into life.

When we're true lovers, we send love as a gift, a gift given fearlessly, freely, with nothing held back and nothing expected. It's done not to be saved, not from sacrifice, but just for the sheer joy of giving. As lovers, we give whatever we can just for the sake of the giving, just for the sake of life itself.

And our gifts are very important, because they reflect the unique contribution that only we can make. Though on the vast scale of things we're like grains of sand on an endless shore, yet our lives can make a difference in our little corner of the world.

And that difference can really be a difference. Haven't there been people in your life who really made a difference just by giving the gift of their life, their caring, their example? Would your life have been the same without them?

As lovers, we give fearlessly because we have great trust in existence. We trust that our gift will be the right one, that our gift will be needed by the universe, by others, by ourselves. And it doesn't matter whether the gift is great or small, because the gift of each of us is needed. What matters is just that we do what we can to give it.

Our gift may not meet our models of how it all should be, or the models of others either, but if we make the attempt to authentically give, then the very attempt is our gift.

The Magician

$\mathcal{T}$HE *magician* IS THE archetype of someone learning to work with negativity by attempting to use its energy in a constructive way.

A good model is an aikido master, who does not oppose an opponent's energy, but rather aligns with the energy and then skillfully makes use of it.

Essentially, that's what magicians do. They find a way to align with the energy somehow, perhaps even take it further, and in the process be creative enough to find a way to use the energy constructively.

A good example is how the Grateful Dead dealt with the problem of unauthorized tapings at their concerts. Instead of opposing the idea, the band created a new special section, optimally placed, at a higher price, where anyone could tape the show in peace. That's using energy magically.

Breathwork is another example. We all have wounded places inside, which we usually keep minimized and sealed off in the unconscious. But in breathwork these holding areas for pain are deliberately amplified. They're brought to the surface, welcomed, and integrated into consciousness, enriching our wholeness and aliveness.

Once, when the master Osho was a schoolboy, he was punished by his father by being locked in the bathroom. What the boy did was *use the situation as an opportunity*. He just started meditating. Hours went by, and no sound came out.

Finally the father became worried and opened the door—only to find the boy enjoying himself in meditation. The "punishment" was not repeated.

The approach of a magician is to consider all energy, all situations, as potentially fruitful and positive. Then, to search for what that positivity might be and express or nurture it in some way. It begins by being willing to see all situations with a certain equanimity. When we just want to reject or eradicate something, that aversive energy clouds our mind and prevents the most effective or resourceful solutions.

Another example: I vividly recall driving down a street in Paris one freezing night in late 1983 and seeing prostitutes on the streetcorners huddled in the cold. The next day I was in Amsterdam, where the temperature was equally frigid, and saw prostitutes sitting behind shopwindows—comfortable, relaxed, listening to music. And nice and warm. It made quite an impression on me.

City officials must have said to themselves something like this: "Look, prostitution is going to go on here just like everyplace else whether we outlaw it or not. Meanwhile, it's freezing outside. So let's bring it inside, license it, and through regular check-ups, help keep everyone more free of sexually-transmitted diseases as well."

To me, it was an enlightened recognition of reality, and a constructive use of it. A similar thing was done with drugs such as marijuana, which were decriminalized but regulated. The result? Amsterdam has the lowest crime statistics of any major city in Europe.

Jesus of course was a great magician.

Here are two of his statements about the magical way of looking at life:

"If someone compels you to go a mile with them, go an extra mile as well." "If someone wants your shirt, let them have your coat also."

I'm reminded of the true story of the thief who stole into an Hasidic monastery and stole 3 out of 4 precious scrolls held since antiquity. When the master returned a short time later, he went after the thief and gave him the 4th scroll as well, explaining that they were a set and the first 3 would be of less value without the 4th.

What happened? An outcome not normally expected. The thief returned a short time later and begged the master to take him on as a disciple.

What often happens when we accept energy and even take it further is that there's a tendency—not a certainty—for the "negativity" to wake up in some way. For negativity is the result of unconsciousness in the first place. Accepting it and going further with it is a puzzling and mysterious response which sometimes will arouse consciousness.

The magical way of looking at things is the source of the famous healing injunction:

Prescribe the symptom.

It's also the source of the famous advice to actors:

Use the difficulty.

These sayings are alternate descriptions of aligning with the energy and extending it, finding a way to use it.

Say you have the hiccups and can't get them to stop. Then try going the other way—try hiccuping as much as you can and see what happens. When Milton Erickson advised an overweight client to *gain* exactly 11 pounds in the next few weeks, he was helping her achieve control of a process. If she could learn how to take it one way, she would know how to take it the other way.

Sometimes reframing a problem allows us to understand it as a strength. For instance, when we begin to witness our inner process we'll notice *more,* not less, frantic activity in the mind. But actually, we're simply becoming more aware of what is already there. It's a constructive process.

Prescribing the symptom occurs when we exaggerate a pain in order to integrate it. For example, once I was covered with poison ivy and feeling a great deal of very uncomfortable itching. I got into a warm shower and the itching seemed to get even worse for a short time. Then, miraculously, it greatly lessened for awhile.

If you're feeling angry, try getting even more angry—but don't act it out on others, just do it privately. Shout and scream and kick and punch a bag or pillow to your heart's content. You'll soon find that the anger has dissipated and left just a sense of aliveness in your body. You're using magic.

I love a good Lincoln story, and here's a good one: Once the President issued a military order. Soon after an aide came into his office and said that Stanton, the Secretary of War, had privately called the President an idiot for promulgating such an ignorant order.

Let's pause a moment. What would *we* do? Reprove Stanton, call him arrogant, fire him, defend the intelligence of the order? Not Lincoln. He was too mature and truly humble. And he liked to use magic, too.

"Stanton said that?" Lincoln said. "Well, Mr. Stanton is a very intelligent man, so if he said that we'd better go on over to his office and see if this order is correct."

Large-minded, open-ended, humorous.

Magical.

The Healer

*A*s BEAUTIFUL AS magic can be, the notable thing is that magical responses are not necessarily healing. Magic can be used simply to get a result, as in this example:

In the movie The Lover, the Chinese man has taken his lover and her mother and brothers out to dinner. At one point the hostile and drunken older brother breaks a glass and challenges him to a fight, saying: "It would take two of you to defeat me."

The protagonist replies: "Oh no. It would take at least four of me to defeat you. You have no idea how weak I really am." The reply is magical and does indeed defuse the situation for the moment, but it's not a healing reply.

Compare that example to a truly healing response. This is a true story, told by Robert Bly about George Docsi:

When the latter was a boy in Hungary, a pogrom had begun in Russia and many Jews were fleeing across the border. The boy's grandfather went to the train station and brought many of them home, where they crowded into the living and dining rooms. With so many to feed, supper was late.

The boy waited and waited, and then finally threw a fit: "I want my supper! I want my supper!" The maid offered him a piece of bread. He threw it on the floor and screamed again, "I want my supper!" At that moment his grandfather entered the room. He picked up the bread from the floor, gently kissed it, and then handed it to the boy—who ate it.

A gesture of magic, but also of great healing. There's no scolding or anger at the boy, no guilty reminders that others are starving, none of that. Just a gesture of pure beauty and healing, which the boy remembered for a lifetime.

Who we are as a being and what state of mind we're in is always the real message we're sending.

If grandfather had been angry, no matter how justified it might have been, that would have been the real message the boy received. Instead grandfather, through being who he was, sent a healing message with an unforgettable impact.

Another example of a healing response, told me by my sister Jeanne. One time she was visiting Grandma Grace and grandma gave her some coins to play with. Jeanne stole about ten of the coins, and when grandma discovered the theft she sat down with Jeanne and told her that if she stole again her parents would have to be told.

When our parents came home Jeanne was scared stiff that grandma would tell them. When they asked how Jeanne had been, grandma said, "She's been the most perfect child." Then grandma looked over at Jeanne and winked. Jeanne said that at that moment a stab of love for grandma went through her heart—and she never stole again.

The healer is a name that we might give to an archetype that has learned some of the lessons of the other archetypes— wanderer, warrior, lover, magician—and so can call upon them. The idea is not to have a set solution to any problem or challenge, but rather, to be flexible enough to have a wide range of options.

We could call such an archetype a "wise fool" perhaps or something like that, but I've come to prefer the term "healer" because it addresses what it seems that we'd all really like to do—heal ourselves, and in some way, the world.

Imagine that you and I succeeded in transforming the world somehow, but that it still wasn't healed yet. Wasn't warm yet, wasn't loving yet. Would we have accomplished anything, really? Without love, all other achievements seem empty. Healing love gives life.

The two words "healing" and "wholeness" come from the same root. And they have much in common. To become healed is to become whole. Healing means that parts that were previously warring, whether within us or outside in the world, have come into communication and formed a relationship together. Conflicts and divisions have harmonized.

As many people have pointed out, *healing* and *curing* aren't the same thing. We can be cured but not healed, as when we use drugs to suppress the symptoms of some disease but leave the cause unaddressed. And conversely, we can heal without being cured, as when a disease progresses to death but we are healed from a lifetime of bitterness in the meantime. It's possible to have a healing death.

In the realm of healing, a distinction is usually drawn between *pain* and *suffering*. Pain is the actual sensation felt in the body. Suffering, however, is the *resistance* that we feel towards the pain, physical or emotional—our condemnation of it, our aversion to it. The suffering caused by our resistance is frequently much greater than the pain itself.

Usually when we have a pain our first response to it is to feel revulsion: "Go away!" If we accidentally hit our finger with a hammer, for instance, our immediate response may be to curse the finger. We send out aversive energy, in this case to a part of ourselves.

The resistance to pain has a fascinating effect—it's the great magnifier of it. Aversive energy of any kind—anger, fear, rejection, etc.—amplifies the sense of suffering.

So if suffering has arisen, instead of sending aversion to our pain we can send love and compassion to it instead, as Stephen Levine and many others have recommended.

By surrendering our resistance, something can let go inside and healing can arise even if the pain is still there. And often, the pain does indeed diminish or vanish.

But either way, the pain is incorporated and included, so that our relationship to it changes, our experience of it can shift to a different realm.

A last example:

One time Jorge Luis Borges was suffering greatly in an unusually bad prison, condemning his miserable life and fate. Why had life done this to him? Why was there so much evil and suffering? He hated his jailers and condemned his rotten cell and this rotten world.

But one day he had an extraordinary insight and he did something completely different instead—*he blessed it all.*

He blessed the cement cell, the bitter cold, his own "wasted" life, his poor emaciated body, even the cockroaches.

Yes, and even the jailers.

He blessed his whole grim and absurd situation, and absurdly, felt great compassion for everyone and everything in this universe, including himself and all the life in his barren surroundings.

Suddenly, to his surprise, he entered a wholly different realm. A sweetness and warmth and happiness spread through him such as he had never known before, and he had a true glimpse of the inclusiveness of divine love.

Nothing had changed in his grim circumstances, there was no "cure" of his situation. But he was sublimely healed.

The Healer II

*H*EALERS DEAL WITH dragons in a radical way, by recognizing that the dragons are really a part of ourselves— that they represent the ugly, unwanted, or threatening parts, the ones excluded from our ideal world or ideal self-image.

Healers recognize that the treasure of our truest selves cannot be approached without incorporating our dragons, for they are us. Our external dragons are, mostly, projections of our internal dragons. In general, that's why we encounter the particular dragons that we do.

As Jung and Bly and others have pointed out, we drag a long bag behind us, and we stuff into the bag everything that doesn't fit into the self-image we're constructing. Very early on we're usually taught that anger, for instance, is unacceptable; that goes into the bag. Our spontaneity goes into the bag. Our sexuality or wildness might go into the bag.

Little boys' vulnerability and little girls' toughness often go into the bag. Anything that doesn't please our peers goes into it. The world-view of our tribe, our nation, our group can cause many other things to be unacceptable and go into the bag. By the time we're twenty, only a small slice is left of our original 360-degree radiance. We spend the rest of our life trying to get it back.

The bag can be called the *shadow*, because it represents the shadow side of us, the parts of us that we reject or deny. All of us have this shadow side that is mostly out of our awareness and that we do not love. Many ways of working on ourselves can be considered ways of trying to surface shadow material and deal more effectively with it.

But there is an additional way to pierce the veil of our shadow, one that can be used any time. And that is to simply notice what *hooks* us—what gets us angry, fearful, upset; who or what we become obsessive about. That indicates a part of ourselves that is repressed in the shadow, something we don't want to see in ourselves.

If self-righteous people hook us, for instance, we may be repressing our own self-righteous side—or emphasizing it. If we dislike people who are weak, we may be feeling weak inside ourselves. If people who are freely sexual irritate us, we may be repressing some of our own sexuality, and so on.

Whatever we find irritating, hateful, disgusting, stupid, etc. is giving us a clue. It's telling us that this may be part of us also; otherwise it wouldn't hook us so much. If it's not part of our own shadow, we may find a particular quality in others interesting, but it won't unduly disturb us; we won't obsess about it. In general, we're disturbed by the things that are too close to home in ourselves.

For example, once I found myself disliking someone because he seemed consumed by greed for money, and willing to sacrifice almost anything for it. And I would think, "How immature, how blind." Later on, I found the same greediness in myself. Not greediness for money or power, but greediness for knowledge, greediness for answers. The object differed, but the grasping was the same. That's why it hooked me.

Often in my life I accused people of being over-reactive or judgmental. Those qualities irritated and hooked me when I saw them in others. Of course that was a side of myself that I was denying, put away in the bag to service a self-image as a "good man," or later, a "spiritual person."

Thus a vital function of our external dragons is to act as signals to us—to show us the parts of ourselves, our society, our group, our paradigm that are still unacceptable, denied, shut-out.

An illustration is a story Stephen Levine tells about a cancer patient in great pain. Because of her bitter complaints and generally negative attitude, the hospital staff and even her family were avoiding her. Indeed, she had been avoided most of her life for much the same reason.

One night her pain grew so terrible that she could no longer contain it. Something inside let go and surrendered. Suddenly images flashed before her eyes of other people in the world in pain at that moment; and suddenly it was not "her" pain any more, but "the" pain, the pain of the world.

Her heart broke open, and a gentleness and compassion came over her. She saw that her condemnation of the world arose not from the nature of the world, but from the nature of what she was sending out into it.

In the weeks before her death, she transformed and healed her world. She showered love upon that world now, she healed every relationship she possibly could. And when she died she was grieved by everyone she had touched. Notice that pain—the dragon—led her towards that healing.

As healers, we claim the universe as our home again, the way we once did as innocents. We see the world once more as inviting, friendly, shimmering, new. And though we now have some harsh experience of it, yet we can see again in the world the transcendent beauty that our innocence once saw.

Wounded Healer

$\mathscr{A}$s a less inspired though perhaps also worthwhile example, I could offer the writing of this book. In 1987 my world basically fell apart. I'd stopped visualizing long before. After all, I was so lucky, what did I need to visualize for? In any event, I lost my fiancée, business, money, houses on the ocean—it seemed like I'd lost everything.

Did I contribute to this? Yes. My own woundedness contributed a great deal to it. My basic reactive conditioning and failure programming took over. Despite years of work on myself, I just wasn't skillful enough to deal with the situation that arose. Everything seemed lost.

I was quite devastated. I couldn't figure out why to get out of bed in the morning, or why to do anything at all except maybe to survive. Life seemed meaningless and a dumb idea. "Why does this stupid universe exist, anyway?" I would say. "Why do I exist? What's the point?"

I did one smart thing—I let myself grieve. I let myself feel the grief a lot, I didn't fight it. The grief wanted to overwhelm me, so I let it. I would just sit there and feel it.

Using the magician's principle, we know that feeling a grief or any feeling completely will gradually lead to some true lightening of it—whereas otherwise it hangs on like a low-level hangover. So after awhile a question arose, and I began hanging out with it. The question was: "How can I turn this experience into something positive?"

At first there didn't seem to be an answer, or rather, the answer was: There's no way. But I kept hanging out with the question anyway.

After another while the question became more positive, and changed to: "Are there any notions that would tend to make life happier and more fulfilled?" And later on: "What are the notions that would tend in that direction?"

In spite of all the things I'd done to try to grow as a human being, I had to start from scratch. What did I really know? At that point it became abundantly clear to me that I knew nothing at all about how to be happy.

So I started playing around with things, drawing upon experiences both "good" and "bad." What really works? I'd write out answers on a whiteboard, and smile at my naivete. Yet after a long time something did start assembling—a desire to write something down, and in the process perhaps learn or relearn some things. That process became this book.

It wasn't going to be written right away, because first I needed to be practical and make some money. But grief had affected my health, and though I had nothing overtly wrong I found myself wondering how long I would live. One day I asked myself: What would I work on if I had only six months to live? And it became clear that this book was what I would work on. Trusting as much as I could, I just started in.

It was clear that I wasn't qualified. I had no money. My health was mediocre at best. I was grieving a good deal of the time. And based on recent experience, I didn't know much if anything about how to be happy and fulfilled.

If ever there's been a wounded healer, I'm it. I've given and taken offense easily most of my life. I've had suicidal depressions, thunderous rages, paralyzing fears, lots of sexual fantasies—you name it. Lots of people over the years have concluded I wasn't worth it and ended our relationship. I've been thoughtless or hurtful countless times. Not to mention insensitive, self-righteous, reactive, a good victim—name it, I've been there—many times!

Centered? Walking my talk? The other night I was in the supermarket at 2 am, after working 14 hours and capping a series of seven-day weeks getting this book ready for the press. I remember catching a glimpse of myself in one of the display case windows, and noticing how bedraggled I looked, how like a dishrag. I felt fragile, irritable, anything but joyful. This is the "balanced" author whose book you are reading!

In other words, I had gotten lost in my role of "writing this book and getting it to press." It took me awhile to realize that I had gotten caught, and to unhook a bit. In the process of awakening, it's not like we're going to wake up forever next Tuesday. Rather, we'll probably be waking up for the rest of our lives—and that's okay. In fact, it's perfect. Part of our great human nature.

Healing? Some years ago I had a verbal fight with an elderly lady friend, Paj. And boy, did I know I was right. A few months later, being way more advanced than I, she called up and said she wanted to heal our relationship. In my self-righteous arrogance I said, "There's nothing to heal," and got off the phone. After that, we lost track of each other.

As Paj found out, it's not always possible to heal something externally right away. Sometimes we can, sometimes we can't at this moment. Sometimes we're just not skillful enough or lucky enough. Sometimes the things we do to make things better make them worse instead. That's all part of being here. Our job, as always, is just to do the best we can.

Superhuman notions can be the source of a lot of pain, I believe. The idea that if we were only advanced enough.... we'd be able to heal everything right away, control all of the circumstances in life, or get everybody to appreciate us.

Well, let me tell you a story about selling my BMW. One time I owned this BMW that had been a little damaged, and I put an ad in the paper to sell it. About a dozen people came by to see it, and the price was firm, so it was just about whether they liked the car or not. And I noticed that each person went right away into one of two groups:

The first group liked the car very much. They'd notice features that they liked, and we'd get excited together. I'd look at my car as if for the first time and think, "God, that's been a great car." But the second group didn't like the car much. They'd tell me all sorts of things about what was wrong with it; this and that. They hated it and told me 17 reasons why it was a terrible car and no good.

What struck me was that it was the very same car they were talking about. Even people such as Gandhi and Lincoln were intensely disliked by some. And we think it's reasonable to believe that if we could just get advanced enough nobody would ever dislike us?

Another superhuman notion is that we create everything that happens to us. Sometimes sick people use such a notion to make themselves feel guilty if they don't get better. But if a massive meteor slams into the earth today, we needn't wonder how we created it. Bad fortune can happen.

As healers, it's hubris to think we're going to be able to heal every situation that comes our way. To think that we could heal everything would be to deny our basic humanity, which is always imperfect.

But that said, it's also true that we have great influence on our own lives and the lives of others. So we can do various things to try to bring harmony to any situation, often with surprisingly good results.

But we have a much greater influence on our *experience* of what happens than what happens. So we can seek to heal situations on an inner level, even if we can't heal them on an outer level yet. That's very important because the outside will tend to follow the inside anyway. And it's empowering to feel that we can do something in any situation—and we can.

But even on an inner level, to try to force ourselves to forgive, for instance, would be to miss the point of forgiveness. Forgiveness arises as a joy, as something we want to do, not as an obligation. So if we can do it, great; if we can't, that's okay too. Maybe someday we will.

We need not put the burden of being superhuman on ourselves, as healers or anything else. Because every archetype is a two-sided coin; it can't have just one side. As George Ohsawa says, for every front there's a back.

For example, the healer archetype is actually the healer-wounded archetype. That is, every healer without exception is wounded; and every wounded person is a potential healer—indeed, our greatest wound often leads to the discovery of our life's calling. A good teacher must be a perpetual student, and every student also has something to teach. Even the greatest master will stumble now and then, and the merest beginner is capable of mastery on occasion.

Thus we'll always be wounded healers; that's the nature of life. We'll always cast a shadow when we try to stand in the sun. But that's okay. Our simple humanity is enough. Whatever we can do today is enough.

Wounded Healer II

I'VE MADE COUNTLESS mistakes in my life, and I'll make countless more if I live long enough. We've all made countless mistakes, and we'll all make more. Hopefully, we'll grow from them. If not, we'll make some more mistakes and grow from *them*. Deep down, it's all okay.

On that basis, I decided to go forward with this book. Even though it was clear that I wasn't qualified, I decided to just do the best I could do each day, and leave it at that. Then existence could take care of the outcome—whether the book is helpful or unhelpful, a success or a failure.

Further, if the book has any merit it's because of the "negative" things I went through. It simply wouldn't exist if I hadn't gone through them. The biggest disaster of my life led to the greatest privilege of my life. We peer into the darkness to find the light.

Within every negative, there's a gift. It's our challenge to find it and use it. In doing so, we just sail our boat as best we can each day, and let go of the outcome.

A beautiful Muslim Sufi story: Once a boy went away from home and his father. When neighbors commiserated with the father for his misfortune, he just said, "We'll see."

Then the boy came back, riding a beautiful horse, and the neighbors congratulated the farmer. "We'll see," he said. Then while riding the horse the boy broke his leg. "Too bad," said the neighbors. "We'll see," said the farmer.

Then troops came by conscripting young men into the military, and left the boy behind because of his broken leg. Again the neighbors congratulated the father, and again he just said, "We'll see."

Do we know the ultimate outcome of anything? Highly doubtful. To accept the ambiguity of the universe, its tragedy, its imperfection, its humor, its mystery—is to love it. That love is our only real job. To find compassion for all things, inner and outer, is our only real occupation.

As Gerald Jampolsky stresses, peace of mind should be our primary goal. Not peace of mind at some point in the future, but peace of mind right now, while we're doing what we're doing. Forgiving all things goes a long way towards that goal. Forgiveness is joy.

A very effective daily practice for opening our hearts was suggested by the Buddha and mentioned earlier. Here it's adapted in a somewhat different form:

We bring to mind some person or situation that feels unhealed to us; and we engage in an inner dialogue with that person or situation. Then we do our best to forgive ourselves for any wrong we did to that person or in that situation, and also to forgive them or the situation for any wrong that was done to us.

Next we do the best we can to forgive ourselves for any wrong we have ever committed in thought, word, or deed to anyone or anything, innocently or otherwise; and conversely, to forgive anyone or anything that has ever wronged us or those we love.

Then we send out love, first to everyone and everything that we like and love, next to those we dislike. Finally, we send loving-kindness to all corners of the universe, to all beings wherever they may be. We wish every part of existence—with nothing left out—peace and happiness.

Can we learn to love every part of the existence with nothing left out? It's precisely whomever or whatever that we can't love yet that's our greatest opportunity—the hidden gift in the darkness.

The great Chinese master Lao-Tzu said:

Rejoice in the way things are.

I love that phrase. Lao-Tzu didn't say to tolerate or learn to grudgingly like the way things are. No...

Rejoice in the way things are.

Choose it all to be the way it is.

From that point of non-resistance, our *compassionate presence* can shine through us, can be alive in our heart, and will know what best to do.

Innocence

To LOOK FURTHER into the subject of healing, we go again now to that master healer, Jesus. I'm not referring to the miracles here, but to the much deeper healing that Jesus was attempting to do with anyone who could hear him.

Some of Jesus' feelings about healing, in modern-day language, might be put approximately this way:

If we're good only to those who are good to us, what credit is that to us? That's what everybody does. If we love only those who love us, what have we accomplished? Anybody can do that. Where our hearts really open is in learning to love the other part, the unlovable and unacceptable in life.

In order to do this, we have to begin to let go of our mind's tendency to judge and condemn and put certain things and people out of our heart. Jesus emphasized this under-standing in a number of different ways:

"Judge not, that ye be not judged."
"Remove the log from your own eye before noticing the splinter in your brother's eye."
"The measure by which you give is the measure by which you receive."
"Let he who is without sin cast the first stone."

Jesus is pointing out to us that we all have a shadow side, that we're all human; that there are no exceptions. We have all been hurt and wounded, we have all done things we're not proud of, we're all both saint and sinner. Thus we can see each other with the heart of compassion, because we're all in the same boat.

Jesus' emphasis is on opening our hearts to parts of the world that we want to reject, the "unlovable," the "worthless," the "unforgivable." Not open in a way that says, "They're contemptible, but I'll forgive them anyway." Rather, in a way that sees everyone as essentially innocent.

We've all had our hearts broken, over and over in different ways. The better I've gotten to know people the more I've understood that nobody escapes without a broken heart. And we've all acted out our hidden pain and woundedness from time to time in hurtful ways.

Even so, we're all essentially innocent in our essence. We didn't ask to be wounded, we didn't ask to have our hearts broken. It's just part of living and growing up, just part of the cost of doing business down here that we're going to pick up some pain—and sometimes express it in inappropriate ways.

As Gerald Jampolsky says, does that mean we have to let everybody out of prison? Does it mean we have to take our old job back? Does it mean we have to remarry our ex-spouse? Does it mean that boundaries can never be set? No.

We're responsible for what we do. For instance, we're responsible to gravity to act appropriately towards it. If we jump off a building we're going to go splat, regardless of how innocent we might be. If we make a mess, the environment or the law or whatever may exact a penalty on us. If we hurt another, they'll feel hurt. We tend to receive what we send out. All these are examples of ways in which we're responsible to ourselves and to existence.

So opening our hearts doesn't necessarily mean that we absolve someone of all responsibility. Human beings are capable of acting in thoughtless, venal and even ruthless ways. So we still may need to leave someone; we still may need to set an appropriate boundary; we still may need to be a warrior. It simply means that we don't throw anyone or anything out of our heart. We try to act from a pure heart.

To the best of our ability at each moment, we see everyone and everything with compassion, and then act from that inner place. It's impossible to predict what the actions are that will come out of that, but they'll have a tendency towards greater understanding and harmony for all concerned.

We may have to set a boundary, but if so, we try to do so in a loving way. Or our compassion may create a different reality where we don't have to set a boundary. We can't say ahead of time. If our heart is in the right place, we can trust that our actions each moment will arise appropriately from that moment. Rules and guidelines are simply ways of trying to codify what's already there if the heart is there.

Each of us, though we're responsible, is also blameless because of our essential innocence. As Harvey Jackins has said, at every moment of our life, considering our background and experiences, we did the very best we knew how to do.

It may not have been good enough, it may have been a mess, but it was the best we could do at the time. If we could have been more conscious, we would have been. If we could have been more skillful, we would have been. At all times we're doing the very best that we know how to do.

So, as said before, we can forgive ourselves. We can forgive ourselves for stuffing parts of ourselves away in the bag. We can forgive ourselves for creating our shadow—it was our way of surviving. We can forgive ourselves for the times when our shadow has acted out in some unconscious way.

By the same token, we can forgive the world. Every part of the world is responsible; causes have effects. But it's also blameless. Every part of the world is also doing the best it knows how to do. I'm being the best Jimmy that I know how to be, you're being the best you that you know how to be—every moment. Everyone else is too.

Even though there is grievous hurtfulness in the world, you and I and every part of the world are completely innocent at the core. This is the true basis of forgiveness. It's not based on some rationale, but rather on seeing the innocence at the core of things.

Every being is like us, wanting to survive, to make a difference somehow, to love and be loved, trying to stumble towards the light as best it knows how. Seeing this reflection of ourselves, forgiveness lets go of judgment.

Phyllis McGinley expresses this well: "The wonderful thing about saints is that they were human. They lost their tempers, scolded God, were egotistical or testy or impatient in their turns, made mistakes and regretted them. Still they went on doggedly blundering toward heaven."

Forgiveness sees that the world is perfectly imperfect; that its very imperfection is its perfection. Forgiveness sees that the world cannot be any different than the way it is at this moment. Next moment it may be different, but right now it has to be this way. Forgiveness sees this essential innocence in all things.

Jesus is looking at this innocence at the core of all things when he says:

"Love your enemies; do good to them that hate you; pray for those that mistreat you."

Nothing and nobody is left out. Everything, everybody is included. That's why love is divine. Because it expresses the divine love of existence itself, which, as Jesus reminds us—

...makes its sun to rise on the good and the bad, and sends its rain to saint and sinner alike.

Light and Darkness

*T*HE MIND LIKES to separate light and dark, and then see them in opposition to each other. But light and darkness actually always go together—they're a package deal.

When the sun shines on anything, a shadow is created at the same time. Where there's light, there's always a shadow too. And the brighter the light, the deeper the shadow.

Conversely, where there is shadow there is light also. The darker the shadow, the brighter the light that is shining just nearby. If that light can be discovered, uncovered, brought out in some way—O, what a great light it will be.

So let's never give up on anybody, including ourselves. "Love your enemies," Jesus says. Let's open our hearts to all of existence, just exactly as it is—in all of its splendidly perfect imperfection.

Lao-Tzu says, in the Stephen Mitchell translation:

The Master is available to all people
and doesn't reject anyone.

The master knows that everyone is wounded, but also sees the essential innocence and potential healing power in everyone. All of it can be viewed with compassion:

The Master views the parts with compassion,
because he understands the whole.

The whole is completely undifferentiated. From undifferentiated wholeness, opposites spring into existence at the same time: Up and down. Hot and cold. Beautiful and ugly. Good and bad.

As soon as we create the concept of "up," the concept of "down" also comes into existence simultaneously—because the idea of "up" has no meaning without the idea of "down." The idea of "beauty" has no meaning without the idea of "ugliness." As soon as we create the concept of anything, the concept of its direct opposite also begins to exist. Opposites exist together.

Summer and winter are two parts of one thing. Night must follow day; they are not in opposition, but faces of the same thing. You can't have mountains without valleys. A tree is both the leaves playing in the light and the roots digging in the dark earth. Both are necessary; both are one plant, one thing. Light and shadow are one phenomenon.

Someone once asked Robert Bly if it were possible for someone not to have a shadow. He replied, "Have you ever seen anyone walk in the sun and yet the shadow was missing?" To be human means to be imperfect. To exist means to be imperfect.

Long ago I got used to the idea that all my heroes have feet of clay. If they didn't they wouldn't be here; because we can't exist in this reality without partaking of duality. To acknowledge that essential imperfection and duality in all beings, including ourselves and even our heroes, is to recognize reality but also to celebrate it.

Because after awhile, we come to view the very imperfection of the world as the essence of its beauty. For example, in formal Zen-inspired gardens imperfections are deliberately introduced—because otherwise they wouldn't be as beautiful. And in my opinion, our heroes are more beautiful when we can acknowledge their humanness.

As healers, our true power comes from the recognition and acceptance of our own imperfection and the world's. It means that we no longer seal off and reject our own shadow material. On the contrary, we welcome it. Lao-Tzu says:

> Darkness within darkness.
> The gateway to all understanding.

When we mindfully meditate, for instance, we are looking further and further into darkness, further and further into our sealed-off pain, because that is where the light is found. When we shine the light of love on our shadow, we are in that very process revealing that light. "Compassionate presence," in Stephen Schwartz's term, is found within deep silence and stillness and darkness.

Indeed, the general principle of dealing with negativity might be said to look deeply enough into it to find the light, the seed, the gift that it bears.

All negativity, whether in the world or in ourselves, is a message bearing a gift. To take a simple example, when our shoe doesn't fit right we feel pain. That pain is simply a signal telling us to do something about our shoe.

ssage, signalling to us that
nd that a change needs to
n is pressure to change in

nging in order to stay in
wise, life and its environ-
is the mechanism causing
ey fit together.
colder, for example, those
v temperature will survive
to speak. Because of that
ll pain among life. Pain,
leading to less pain.
ts great enough, we turn
first step in dealing with
tead *turn our gaze upon it.*
not seeing it yet. What
gaze of acceptance, a letting it.
age might be. Why is this
nat is the gift it's trying to
g----. in the case of the tight shoe, for instance, the pain is
trying to tell us that something needs to be done. Once we get
the message, we act on it as best we can. Maybe we go home
and change shoes if possible. If not, maybe we learn about
focusing in on pain with compassion.

Third, *we redirect our attention back to a positive focus,*
incorporating the lesson of the negativity. Perhaps we make a

mental note to be more careful about the size the next time we buy shoes; in this way our life tends toward greater harmony. If that message got through, for instance, we're more likely to have well-fitting shoes for the rest of our life.

Negativity's gift can be different in different situations. To one cancer patient it might come as a call to a new type of diet and lifestyle; to another it might come as a message to let go of lifelong bitterness and heal old wounds. But we'll know the message if we earnestly look for it.

There are lots of ways to do this. We might consult our inner guidance, the intuitive message of our wisdom-heart. Or we might close our eyes and ask for an animal or other inner figure to appear and deliver the message. We can pay attention to our dreams, which contain rich and symbolic messages normally blocked from our waking mind.

We can use focusing, breathwork, mindfulness, drawings, story-telling, inner dialogues and many other things to let that gift reveal itself. The method doesn't matter as much as the intention to discover the gift and open up to it.

Thus, within the negative, we find a positive seed and water it. Within the darkness, we find the light that's nearby and that is always there and must be there, and then do what we can to reveal it, uncover it, nourish it.

If we dislike someone, for instance, we can use that as a way of observing our shadow. What trait have we sealed off in ourselves that we notice only in the other? *What hooks us?* Can we forgive them? Can we look for the good in that person, and water that with appreciation?

If we look, every problem bears a gift. And the larger the problem, the larger the gift. The deeper the shadow, the greater the light. But this gift is potential only. It's residing within the suffering, the negativity, the problem. It's up to us to find that gift, allow it, develop it, bring it out.

A beautiful children's story called *Jerome The Frog*, by Philip Ressner, illustrates this. In the story a playful witch tells Jerome that she's turned him into a prince. He still looks like a frog, but just in case he might really be a prince the town begins sending him on quests, with some success. So finally Jerome is given the quest of slaying the dragon who's been terrorizing the area by breathing fire and burning villages.

Jerome locates the dragon, then pulls out his sword and prepares to try to slay him. But the dragon asks why. He points out that it's his nature to breathe fire and burn things. Jerome ponders this fact; then they have a discussion. Finally a solution agreeable to everyone is reached: The dragon will burn the town garbage on Tuesdays and Thursdays.

Rather than trying to defeat the dragon, Jerome incorporates him. He helps the town by helping the dragon be more truly who he is, since dragons not only like to breathe fire and burn things, but also—like everything else in the universe—to be appreciated and valued.

This kind of victimless problem-solving involves opening to our shadows and seeing what they're about. It involves understanding their nature, seeing them as part of the whole. Our challenge is to incorporate our dragons, whether external or internal, into a greater wholeness.

Beauty & the Beast

There's a BEAUTIFUL parable about this. Remember Beauty and the Beast? By learning to open her heart beyond the usual, by learning to love something previously unlovable, Beauty heals her own spirit. Let's retell the story...

Because of a series of unfortunate incidents, Beauty has to go live with the Beast in his castle. And every night the Beast comes to dinner. At first Beauty is terrified of the Beast because he appears so horrible, yet as she gets to know him she calms down and begins to tolerate his presence.

As time goes on Beauty begins to notice that the Beast has a soul, that behind his horribleness is a being like her. She begins to like the Beast, yet still holds back. The Beast knows that she can transform him, but only when she completely accepts him. And only she can do it. Only she can choose to really see his true nature. He can't make that choice for her.

Beauty goes away at one point and rejoins her family. She forgets about the Beast and that strange, beautiful nightmare that she had had. Of course the Beast languishes. He had been noticed by Beauty, somewhat loved and appreciated by her, and now he's forgotten, unnoticed, repressed. It looks as if the Beast will die as a Beast.

But Beauty has a dream in which she observes the Beast dying, and this remembrance that the Beast can be lost allows her at last to fully see the soul in him. She returns to the Beast and accepts him, completely and without reservation. Doing this allows the Beast to reveal his true nature. Once again he becomes a prince.

Beauty and the Beast are married; the two become one. The happy ending occurs when Beauty unites with her Beast, reclaims that rejected part of her world. Beauty could not have reached her fullest expression of life without the Beast. By denying the Beast she was denying herself as well. When she accepts the Beast she accepts a higher, truer self.

Love transforms.

The power of love—a much greater power than "power over" things or people—is precisely the power to accept existence exactly as it is, including ourselves and others. In the transformative fire of that pure acceptance, the prince behind the Beast emerges. The dragon first transforms into a dancing partner and then becomes part of ourselves, a richer, truer, more joyful self.

All of this is made possible by openness. Beauty could have kept herself and her heart closed off from the Beast. Then, of course, he would always have remained a Beast to her. The greater possibilities would have remained dormant.

Our suffering, our pain, our difficulties, our obstacles, our death, our dragons, are in some ways the greatest gifts to us from existence. In each case, they're a message from the universe, an invitation to us to re-integrate at a higher, purer, more beautiful level.

About our dragons, we can ask: What are we denying? What are we resisting? What is it, in ourselves or in the world, that we're not willing to experience? To love?

A friend used to remark in his seminars, "If you want change in your life, stop resisting." So long as we resist seeing the soul in the Beast, resist seeing it as part of us, so long will it stay a Beast.

Again, this doesn't mean being incapable of defending ourselves or our boundaries. Healers have learned the lessons of the warrior. They can set boundaries or do battle when that's an appropriate action. But they also know that almost always something deeper is happening.

Evil, suffering, pain, dragons all have messages for us. But we can only receive those messages when we soften and open, when we risk being vulnerable, when we look deeply enough into the dragon to see that it's part of us.

When Rini found out that she had tumors, it was evil, awful, threatening. And yet that dragon carried a message— her unnatural lifestyle was killing her. In effect, those tumors were her body's last-ditch effort to get her attention. When she incorporated the message of that terrible dragon, when her lifestyle became more natural in various ways, she found greater aliveness.

Our dragons point the way to increased life.

We humans are currently struggling to become conscious enough to become the heart and mind of the planet. The death of species, the loss of topsoil, the sickness of our confined livestock, global warming, holes in the ozone layer and many other evils are actually messages to us.

These dragons are trying to get our attention before it's too late. Can we see our environment, our planetary body, not as something to use but as something to live within, be a part of? Can we be part of the self-sustaining, self-renewing cycles of the earth? Can we open up to the messages from these fearsome dragons? Can we be conscious enough?

If not, we'll surely perish.

But if so, we'll be reborn as a planetary consciousness, transformed into a planetary heart. Our earth "body" will be respected, appreciated, treated as part of us. No longer will nature or the planet seem like something other than us, to be exploited.

Instead, the whole planet will value itself, will value its preciousness, including us as a valuable part of it. We'll see ourselves as part of a larger, truer self.

Death and Suffering

THE GIFT WITHIN each dragon can be the secret key to unlocking more of our truest, most conscious self. This is especially true of our most terrible dragons. Let's look now at the most fearsome of them all—*death* and *suffering*.

Let's consider death first, and ask: What would happen if this evil called death did not exist?

For one thing, very soon we'd run out of room. There'd be no space for anything or anybody new; there'd be less and less change. Mental calcification would begin to occur, since the young are often willing to entertain ideas and approaches foreign to the elderly. Stagnation in general would set in.

In our own lives, death makes surprise, adventure, risk, excitement possible. Precisely because we're conscious of the limits of life, we're compelled to bring out whatever is in us. When we choose not to hold back, we do so because we see that this time is our chance to make a contribution, to express our unique being. The knowledge that death is awaiting us compels us to attempt whatever we're going to attempt.

Death is also the greatest contributor to our sense of the preciousness and beauty of life. When we see a bird in flight or look into the eyes of a loved one, we're aware at some level that we may never see that beautiful sight again, so we give it more value.

When we remember death and that it can happen at any moment, everything comes into perspective. Suddenly the surrender happens to us—because this may be our last moment, our last act on earth, our last day, our last time with this person, our last chance to appreciate.

If we knew we were dying soon, wouldn't we appreciate everything around us with a tremendous sense of love—that flower, that animal, that person, that sky? If we were with someone we love and knew that it would be the last time, wouldn't we let them know how much we appreciate them?

Imagine that we only had a few moments left. Wouldn't we tremendously appreciate this existence, and our chance to be here? That is death's gift. If we knew we were dying in a week, wouldn't we write letters and make visits and get on the phone to let people know that we love them, especially those that aren't sure we do? That is death's gift.

The prospect of death transforms, lends preciousness to life. Otherwise we could too easily get caught up in our games and defenses. Again, the imminence of death puts things in perspective. There's no more time for games and barriers, or for holding back. There's only a desire to express love.

That love arises as we comprehend that time is limited. If we knew that we were dying soon, love would become the predominant theme of our life, wouldn't it? But actually, we may very well be dying soon; we don't know. We can let our hearts surrender now to the beauty and majesty of existence. We can let our gratitude arise now; we can let our affirmation of life and our love for all parts of it be expressed now.

The Yaqui sorcerer Don Juan used to tell Carlos Castaneda that death was always over his left shoulder, as a way of reminding him of what was true and important. Life's sense of fragility, that it can be lost, allows us to experience the precious value of our life. Each moment of our life can potentially take on a transcendent beauty if we remember that it may be the last one, if we surrender into it.

As Brian Swimme points out, it's the knowledge of our mortality that allows this. Unlike other animals, we bear the burden of knowing that we'll die. But that very dragon is what allows us to appreciate existence.

When we see a horse in a meadow or the trees ablaze in autumn or a salmon jumping upstream, we can appreciate their fragile beauty as they themselves cannot. They are spared the anguish of the knowledge of their approaching death, yet because of that they cannot appreciate their own beauty.

That is our greatest human gift to the world, that we can appreciate the preciousness of life. Sentient beings are the universe's way of appreciating itself, of loving itself. And that is made possible by the existence of death, by our knowledge of death's approach. When we don't deny the dragon of death, when we allow ourselves to sense our limited time, our love naturally blossoms. Death's supreme gift.

What is so about death is also so about our other great dragon, suffering. Our pains and losses and disillusionments bear gifts for us. To sense this is to perceive that, in this moment, everything is as it should be. Everything plays its part. Everything is necessary. In this moment, things couldn't be any different. They may be different tomorrow, but they have to be this way right now.

Like our physical bodies, the planet we're on is an organism which automatically strives to achieve the highest harmony possible. And so too with the universe. The present state of the universe represents the highest, greatest and most harmonious balance that these organisms can achieve at this moment.

Within this balance there are things perceived by us as dragons, areas which we perceive as dark. But like the dark areas in a painting, they're necessary too, and also contribute to the whole.

That includes all the dark areas in our own life, all the things which we find so unlovable and so unacceptable. Those unacceptable beasts are the very magic wand that we've been looking for. The very imperfection, the very thing we don't want to look at, is waiting for the healer to transform it.

And like Beauty, only we can do it. The beasts cannot transform themselves; they wait upon us.

And what do we need to do it? The two wings of love, *appreciation* and *compassion*. If death brings the first, suffering brings the second. Compassion is suffering's gift. It's because of our pain that we can feel the pain of others.

It's because of our pain that we can allow ourselves to let go of the judging for a little bit and just feel another's heart. Our pain allows us to see that the other being is like us, hurts like us. It's our suffering that grows our heart. It's in our pain that we learn to empathize with others, to walk in their shoes for a moment and feel what it's like to see life through their feelings and paradigms.

In other words, the very negativities and obstacles and dragons in our life are what allow us to see where our heart is still incomplete, where our opportunities exist for becoming more unified and larger in consciousness. Thus:

The barriers to the treasure are also the bridges to it.

That is, everything that's in our life right now is either contributing directly to our fulfillment *or teaching us where we're stuck* on the journey towards it. On the journey to our truest selves it's all pulling in the same direction—if we let it. And even when we don't, it still all pulls that way; it just takes a little longer. Everything is a message about waking up.

Light and Darkness II

$\mathscr{B}$EAUTY DID NOT have to love the Beast. She could have avoided him, avoided seeing into his nature. Similarly, we can use the pain in our life to become bitter, to feel angry and negative and justified about it. We have that choice. But again, when we resist any kind of pain, it gets amplified.

When we can open to the pain, soften to it, look into it, it transforms. Not that we change anything, but that it transforms by itself. Our very acceptance transforms it.

That applies to any kind of pain. Whether our pain is physical or emotional or otherwise, we want to pull away from it, make it go away, not notice it. That denial adds suffering to the pain itself. Our unwillingness to face the unpleasant, to acknowledge it, to see into its nature, is the energy that creates the dragon as a dragon.

That is why healers don't spend a lot of time waging external battles. They'll battle if it's appropriate to do so, but they know that the real battles are usually internal, and aren't even battles. They know that *the world changes as we change,* that our real contribution to the world is waking up, seeing our own co-creation of our situations.

When we can acknowledge the pain and just allow ourselves to gaze upon it, neither condemning it nor sacrificing to it, neither pushing it away nor clinging to it, it softens. The acceptance of it changes how we experience it, indeed, how it experiences itself.

When our consciousness and our pain come together, the dragon disappears. The prodigal son returns home.

Stephen Levine tells about being in a meditation retreat and one day seeing a huge depression coming on. A sense of great dread overtook him. But even so, he just let it come on, watched it, danced with it, let it do its thing—and it lasted 90 seconds!

When we take the time to be mindful, to sit and watch, all these fantastic dragons from the unconscious bubble up. And when they do, the temptation is to try to control them in some way, because they look so overwhelming, so fearsome, so painful. And God knows, we don't want to feel any more pain, because we've felt enough already.

So the temptation is to fight them, control them, put them out of mind. But with such an approach the pain never really goes away. It stays in the unconscious, controlling our behavior from there. And periodically it erupts, as thoughts and feelings internally or as acting-out externally. It wants to be noticed and appreciated, just like us.

Thus mindfulness partakes of paradox, because in the very process by which we experience greater serenity we also experience for a time greater pain. As we move deeper into our loneliness, sadness, fear, etc. it can seem overwhelming because, in that spaciousness, more of it comes up. There's tremendously more pain inside than we imagined.

But even that sense of overwhelm can be watched in mindfulness. With practice, even our most terrible fear and rage and despair can be watched with softness and love.

And as we do, a sense of equanimity slowly begins to become more of a factor in our lives, a sense of harmony and peace and balance that tends to depend less and less upon the contents of our mind or the external status of our world.

Once again we glimpse the wholeness of light and dark. Witnessing the darkness is at the very same time turning on the light, awakening from our sleep of dark dreams. We can't turn on the light if we don't recognize that the room is dark. Only by accepting our own darkness, loving and accepting its presence and messages, can we begin to turn on the light.

That internal silence, peace, equanimity is a small flame at first, and there will be many setbacks. But it slowly grows as we accept more dragons into consciousness, as we accept our own imperfections more, as we apply the power of our acceptance, our love, our compassion for all things.

Like a physical flame, that internal flame converts all sorts of different fuels into its light. We have all sorts of different hurts and losses and buried pains, and in opening and softening to them we get to grieve over all of them, to really feel the pain that we have. But our openness to that pain is the very thing that takes us to the treasure of our truest selves, is the very thing that brings light to our darkness.

Our dragons supply the fuel for the journey across the dark night of the soul towards the light—the light that goes beyond both light and darkness, and includes both.

Playing Our Part

$\mathscr{A}$s our inner balance and light grow, we become more flexible, more appropriate. Our response to situations tends to become more spontaneous, less programmed by the unconscious. We can more appropriately respond to this moment because we're more open to whatever it is. We can let it in, accept it, feel it.

Simultaneously our sense of surrender grows too. As we grow more tolerant of the imperfections of life, we begin to see again and yet again that the very imperfection of life is its perfection. We can begin to love life as it is. No longer do we need to try to force ourselves, others, or the world to live up to some model about how it all should be.

Healers act as rainmakers. Rainmakers create rain not by forcing it, but by allowing it, attracting it. The very power of our openness allows things to become as they need to be. We increase the light in the world by increasing our own light, by opening up our hearts to the unwanted.

Then we play our role, make our contribution as best we can, but without being attached to the outcome. We become more playful; we play our role more lightly. We trust in the process more and more, knowing that our journey must contain both suffering and gladness, joy and sorrow, knowing that it must be perfectly imperfect.

Opening to our deepest pain—our desperate hunger for life, love, happiness—allows us to merge with our dragons, marry our prince, reveal that love in the least likely place, our very own self.

Eventually our love can become like the light from the sun, recklessly shining on saint and sinner alike, on low and high alike, on the beautiful and ugly alike—knowing that all of it, even us, is beautiful, precious, and necessary.

To accept the beauty of this moment—just as it is, in all its ordinariness—allows us to dance with existence without turning away, without holding on, holding our burden lightly and playfully, with a grateful smile for the privilege of playing our part.

There's a Chinese Taoist story...

A monk meditated for many years, and tried very hard to reach full awakening, but without success. The true treasure seemed always to recede from him, remaining mysterious and ungraspable.

Finally, in complete exhaustion, his life unfulfilled, the monk left his monastery and went up into the mountains to die. But as he was climbing up the road away from the village, there appeared before him an old man coming down the road with a great big bundle on his back.

Something about the old man caught the monk's attention. Was it the bliss in his eyes? Was it the sense of peace and harmony? He seemed like just an innocent fool, and yet...

On a hunch, the monk greeted the quiet old man and then asked his lifelong question: "Do you by chance know anything about this thing called enlightenment?"

As the monk finished speaking, the old man simply let go of his burden and it dropped to the ground.

The monk understood. And he, too, let go of it all. He surrendered his whole life, all the judgments and divisions, drowned into the gorgeous mystery, became drunk on the beauty of life. Died as a little self, was reborn as an ocean of spaciousness.

Enraptured in liberation, the monk laughed from his belly and cried out, "Just this!"

"Oh, I forgot, one more thing," the old man said.

With that he once again shouldered his burden, faced gently towards the village, smiled a great big smile of love, and walked off down the road.

Afterword

TRUE STORY:

A monk went to visit his zen master one night. When they were finished, the master offered a lantern for the walk home, which the monk gratefully accepted. But just as the monk was leaving, the master blew out the lantern.

A very strange act. Whatever can it mean?

Perhaps the master was saying that we can't really make our journey with borrowed light—that we need to uncover our own light.

Here's to the beautiful light within you...

Jimmy Sloman

Reading List

If someone is mentioned
in the text they will normally be listed here,
unless they're so famous
as to need no listing.

Recommended Reading

*T*HIS LIST, UNFORTUNATELY, must leave out many wonderful authors. For each person listed here there are other, countless giants whose contribution to us all is immense and yet who must go unnamed. Many of the authors below have also written other works, not listed here, of equal value.

Allen, James; *As a Man Thinketh.*

Anonymous; *A Course In Miracles.*

Bandler, Richard & Grinder, John; *Frogs Into Princes.*

Bly, Robert; *A Little Book on the Human Shadow.* Yes, a little book that's very large in wisdom and insight.

Bradshaw, John; *Homecoming.*

Bry, Adelaide; *Visualization.*

Capra, Fritjof; *The Turning Point.* Contains a good discussion of general systems theory.

Carnegie, Dale; *How to Stop Worrying and Start Living.* A sincere desire to help is very evident.

Castaneda, Carlos; *Journey to Ixtlan.* A great story.

Castillejo, Irene de; *Knowing Woman.* Contains a very good description of rainmaker-magicians.

Coit, Lee; *Listening.* Simple, clear, recommended.

Colegrave, Sukie; *By Way of Pain.* This book does an excellent job of describing the journey of growth.

Connelly, Dianne; *All Sickness is Home Sickness.* Mature and insightful.

Covey, Stephen; *Seven Habits of Highly Effective People.* A remarkable book by a remarkable person. Dr. Covey lets his beautiful insights come from his heart. It would be difficult to imagine a literate human being who would not benefit from this sublime book.

Crum, Thomas; *The Magic of Conflict.*

Csikszentmihalyi, Mihaly; *Flow.* An excellent discussion of the feeling of alignment.

Davis, Adelle; *Let's Get Well.* A pioneer in nutrition who worked hard to help others.

Dawood, N.J., translator; *The Koran.*

Diamond, Harvey and Marilyn; *Fit for Life.* A very good exposition of natural hygiene.

Dossey, Larry; *Beyond Illness.* A brilliant author who ventures beyond medicine.

Erhard, Werner; *The Forum* (workshop). A courageous pioneer who has contributed greatly to the lives of many.

Fay, Allen; *PQR.*

Fisher, Roger and Ury, William; *Getting To Yes.* A real treasure about the difficult subject of negotiation. Brilliant.

Francis of Assisi; *The Little Flowers.*

Frankl, Victor; *Man's Search for Meaning.*

Gangaji; *You are That!* A wonderful soul; brilliant but grounded in awakening.

Gawain, Shakti; *Creative Visualization.* A clear and good book. Infectious.

Gendlin, Eugene; *Focusing.* A very useful book for anyone seeking to grow.

550

Goddard, Dwight, editor; *A Buddhist Bible.* A great compilation.

Goldstein, Joseph & Kornfield, Jack; *Seeking the Heart of Wisdom.* Two people who have quietly put a lot of light into the world. Highly recommended.

Goleman, Daniel; *Varieties of the Meditative Experience.* A very clear and insightful observer.

Grof, Christina; *The Thirst for Wholeness.*

Hendrix, Harville; *Getting The Love You Want.* Chapter 10 alone is worth the price of admission.

Hubbard, L. Ron; *Dianetics.*

Huxley, Laura; *You Are Not the Target.*

Hyatt,Carole&Gottlieb,Linda; *When Smart People Fail.*

Jackins, Harvey; *The Human Side Of Human Beings.* A very lucid presentation of distress and its removal.

Jampolsky, Gerald; *Teach Only Love.* A very forthright and impressive person. Ideal for virtually anyone.

St. John of the Cross; *The Dark Night of the Soul.*

Jones, Susan Smith; *The Main Ingredients of Health and Happiness.* Someone whose heart is really in the right place. Recommended.

Kabat-Zinn, Jon; *Full Catastrophe Living.* A mature and thorough discussion of mindfulness and everyday life. Impressive and recommended.

Katie, Byron; *What To Do When Nothing Works.* A great awakened being. It doesn't get any better than Byron Katie.

Kapleau, Philip, editor; *The Three Pillars of Zen.* A true classic, and deservedly so.

Keen, Sam & Valley-Fox, Anne; *Your Mythic Journey.* Wonderfully expansive and open-ended.

Keyes, Ken, Jr; *Handbook to Higher Consciousness.* Heartful, helpful, insightful.

Kriedman, Ellen; *Light Her Fire.* A genuine master of validation.

Krishnamurti, J.; *The First and Last Freedom.* A deep and fully-enlightened person.

Kurtz, Ron; *Body-Centered Psychotherapy.* A discussion of hakomi by its founder. Great.

Lao-Tzu; *Tao Te Ching,* translated by Stephen Mitchell. A sublime translation of Lao-Tzu's transcendent masterpiece. Recommended for a lifetime.

LeBoeuf, Michael; *GMP.* A very good discussion of the subject of reinforcement.

Leonard, Jim; *The Skill of Happiness.* A great discussion of breathwork and self-observation.

Lerner, Eric; *Journey of Insight Meditation.*

Levine, Stephen; *A Gradual Awakening.* Very clear and balanced, lucid and loving. A real treasure.

Maltz, Maxwell; *Psycho-Cybernetics.*

Mandel, Bob; *Open Heart Therapy.* Great.

Marks, Linda; *Living with Vision.*

Mascaro, Juan, translator; *The Bhagavad Gita.*

Mascaro, Juan, translator; *The Upanishads.*

McDougall, John; *The McDougall Plan.* A thoughtful and impressive book about diet and nutrition. Beneficial.

Merton, Thomas, editor; *The Way of Chuang Tzu.*

Miller, Alice; *The Drama Of The Gifted Child.* A cornerstone of the codependence movement.

Miller, Emmett; *Software for the Mind.* Very lucid about how we adapt to pain and pleasure.

Miller, Jeanne & Laut, Phil; *Love, Sex and Communication.* Very helpful.

Mitchell, Stephen; *The Gospel According to Jesus.* Great translation, compilation, and commentary on Jesus. A mature perspective.

Moore, Robert & Gillette, Douglas; *King, Warrior, Magician, Lover.*

Moore, Thomas; *Care of the Soul.* A penetrating and mature discussion of everyday life. A great book.

Naranjo, Claudio and Ornstein, Robert; *On The Psychology Of Meditation.* Very lucid.

NY Intl Bible Society, *The New International Bible.*

Ornish, Dean; *Program For Reversing Heart Disease.*

Osho; *Only One Sky.* This great master was deep and simple at the same time. My life has benefitted very much from his. To me, a beautiful and courageous being.

Pauling, Linus; *How to Live Longer and Feel Better.* A pioneering and helpful scientist.

Pearson, Carol; *The Hero Within.* Of the writings inspired by the work of Carl Jung, I find this the most helpful and insightful. She expresses as a woman while completely including men as well. A wonderful book.

Phillips, Michael; *The Seven Laws Of Money.*

Pritikin, Nathan; *Pritikin Program For Diet & Exercise.*

Ram Dass; *Journey of Awakening.* He has contributed so much just through his vulnerability, honesty, and complete acceptance of being human. A great man.

Ray, Sondra; *Loving Relationships.* A good general book on the subject.

Robbins, Anthony; *Awaken The Giant Within.* Combines knowledge, enthusiasm, and going-for-it. Inspiring.

Robbins, John; *Diet for a New America.* An important book about how our lifestyle affects ourselves, animals, and the planet. A tremendous contribution.

Roman, Sanaya and Packer, Duane; *Creating Money.* Very good indeed, and about much more than the title.

Russianoff, Penelope; *When Am I Going to be Happy?* Insightful and very practical.

Scheid, Robert; *Beyond the Love Game.*

Schwartz, Stephen; *The Compassionate Presence.* Illuminating and heartful at the same time.

Seligman, Martin; *Learned Optimism.* Useful and well-researched.

Shelton, Herbert; *Fasting Can Save Your Life.*

Sher, Barbara; *Wishcraft.* A very loving but thoroughly practical manual for discovering our role in life and living it. Very encouraging.

Siegel, Bernie; *Love, Medicine & Miracles.* A very candid and warm book. Inspiring.

Simon, Sidney and Suzanne; *Forgiveness.*

Smalley, Gary and Trent, John; *The Gift Of Honor.*

Sole-Leris, Amadeo; *Tranquility & Insight.*

Sosan; *Verses on Faith Mind.* A transcendent masterpiece by the third patriarch of Zen.

Strange de Jim; *Visioning.* A playful gem.

Swimme, Brian; *The Universe Is A Green Dragon.* This physicist shows his love for life on every page.

Teresa of Avila: *The Interior Castle.* A great soul.

Van der Kloot, William; *Behavior.*

Walker, N. W.; *Fresh Vegetable Juices.*

Ward, Milton; *The Brilliant Function Of Pain.*

Wellwood, John; *Journey Of The Heart.*

Whitfield, Charles; *Healing The Child Within.*

Wigmore, Ann; *The Hippocrates Diet.* Courageous and ahead of her time.

Zenrin-kushu. A collection of early Chinese Ch'an writings which equals in depth and beauty the writings of Sosan and Lao-Tzu, and the sayings of Jesus.

If you or someone you know
would like to order this book,
either singly or in bulk,
please call

800-852-4890

James Sloman is an investigative writer whose subject is the human condition. He has sought understanding from a range of teachers past and present, famous and obscure, and traditions ranging from India to the kitchen table.

He draws from experience in an eclectic career which has included a bachelor's degree in philosophy (Princeton), a copywriter, assistant editor and computer programmer in New York, a master's degree in film (Columbia). Then being a novelist in rural Massachusetts, a stockbroker in Miami, a futures trader in Chicago, a market theorist in San Diego; and a speaker and seminar leader at various times.

He has also authored the book *Nothing*, the recorded talk *Affecting Our Reality* and the novel *The Ripple*. *Handbook* was mostly written in North Carolina. The author currently lives near San Francisco and serves as the house-keeping staff for his cat, Nicky.

Meyer Friedman 582
Suzanne Kobasa 567

Richard Lazarus 560, 567
Karen Matthews 584

Ray Rosenman 582
Hans Selye 556, 561

RECOMMENDED READINGS

For More on All Aspects of Health Psychology:

Friedman, H. S., & DiMatteo, M. R. (1989). *Health psychology.* Englewood Cliffs, NJ: Prentice-Hall.
A comprehensive textbook of health psychology covering stress-related illnesses, health-impairing habits, reactions to illness, and a variety of other topics.

For More on Stress and Illness:

Cousins, N. (1983). *The healing heart: Antidotes to panic and helplessness.* New York: Norton.
An account of how Norman Cousins coped with his heart attack by refusing to succumb to despair and by playing an active role in his rehabilitation program.

Lazarus, R. S., & Folkman, S. (1984). *Stress, appraisal and coping.* New York: Springer.
A discussion of the role of cognitive appraisal in reactions to stress and in coping with stress.

Maslach, C. (1982). *Burnout: The cost of caring.* Englewood Cliffs, NJ: Prentice-Hall.
An account of the causes, prevention, and treatment of a phenomenon that is especially common among human service providers.

For More on Health-Related Behaviors:

Flay, B. R. (1985). Psychosocial approaches to smoking prevention: A review of findings. *Health Psychology, 4,* 449–488.
A review of research findings on a variety of psychosocial approaches to smoking prevention.

Polivy, J., & Herman, C. P. (1983). *Breaking the diet habit: The natural weight alternative.* New York: Basic Books.
A research-based book providing ways to lose weight and maintain weight loss without relying on diets.

For More on Type A Behavior:

Fischman, J. (1987, February). Type A on trial. *Psychology Today,* pp. 42–50.
A popular account of research findings on the relationship between Type A behavior and coronary heart disease, including both positive and negative evidence.

Friedman, M., & Ulmer, D. (1984). *Treating Type A behavior—and your heart.* New York: Knopf.
A book describing the results of a major study on Type A behavior and suggesting ways to reduce one's risk of coronary heart disease.